Fresh Eggs and Dog Beds

Living the Dream in Rural Ireland

By Nick Albert

Dedication

For Austin

Table of Contents

1. The Heart of the Matter 7
2. The Bomb in the Attic 15
3. The End of the Beginning 26
4. Walking and Talking 33
5. An Atlas and a Pin? 41
6. Fifty Shades of Green 47
7. Meeting Mrs Menopause 56
8. The Fire Drill 64
9. The Lottery 71
10. Hunting for Houses 79
11. A Morning with Alan 88
12. Jelly Moulds and Churches 95
13. Unreasonable Demands 104
14. Boulders and Butterflies 112
15. The Last Hope 120
16. Offer Accepted 128
17. The Legal Crisis 137
18. The Banking Crisis 146
19. Heartbreak 155
20. Homeless 165
21. Home at Last 174
22. Explorers 182
23. Stoves and Midgets 192
24. Amber Arrives 202
25. Family Time 210
26. The Chicken Lady 220
27. Visitors and Visiting 231
28. The End of the Tail 239
Acknowledgements 241
About the Author 242
Contact the Author 242
Ant Press Books 243

1. The Heart of the Matter

With a deep sigh, Doctor David Harrison dropped my medical chart back onto his desk, where it threatened to overbalance several piles of papers. My GP looked around his cluttered consulting room and casually ran his fingers through his thick blond hair, momentarily pulling the wavy locks away from his forehead. This simple action suggested he was relaxed and confident in the diagnosis he was about to deliver. It also drew my attention to his clear blue eyes. Their normally humorous twinkle had been replaced by the steady gaze of someone who had something serious to say. Yesterday had been a bad day, my chest still hurt and the bitter taste of bile was burning my throat. Dave had my attention. Nevertheless, I noticed he changed his posture, leaning forward to emphasise his point. He gave me a thin smile, but his voice was serious.

"Nick, if you carry on like this, you *will* be dead in six months – or at best, in a padded cell with nothing but a packet of crayons to keep you entertained."

He made a fist and brought it to his mouth, for a moment I thought he was going to burp, but he leaned forwards and firmly patted my knee with the heel of his fist to emphasise his point. One fist thump for each word.

"Sort – your – life – out, – or – else."

I opened my mouth to respond, but for once words failed me. Dave gave a nod, acknowledging his message had been delivered, then he abruptly stood and strode to the door.

"Now, come outside and see my new car!"

This is where it all started.

For more than ten years, I had been a manager at a multinational pensions and investment firm. When they hired me, it was one of the proudest days of my life. They were a famous and respected brand, with a proud tradition of being one of the best employers in Britain. Now, it seemed like the lunatic accountants had taken over the asylum, constantly changing departments, reassigning responsibilities and outsourcing customer support, IT functions, and the office of spectacular cock-ups to some distant city in India. There the telesales staff have more qualifications than an astronaut, but cost less to keep than an anorexic hamster.

To add to the fun, I was frequently dragged halfway across the country for meetings that did little but add to my workload and frustration. Commuting in England had become a reoccurring nightmare of stress and delay. The traffic is appalling, the trains are expensive and unreliable, and the London underground can be horribly hot and overcrowded. There are few less pleasant ways of not getting around London than standing for two hours on a stationary underground train, with your face jammed into some fat guy's sweaty armpit, whilst wondering how long it's medically safe to hold on to a fart.

In a fast-changing world, staffing levels across our industry were being slashed repeatedly. I had been made redundant eight times in six years, but on each occasion, I had successfully fought for one of the few remaining positions. Sadly, more than 6,000 of my friends and colleagues had been less fortunate, and many of them had been unable to find suitable employment. Now I was one of only six survivors from a staff of several hundred in my division. At times, it seemed like I was the last man standing on the battlefield, just waiting for the sniper's bullet. I could feel that red laser dot itching at the back of my neck, as the accountants identified the next cost saving required to create the illusion of more profits.

The constant fear of forced redundancy, unemployment, and the catastrophe it could bring to our finely-balanced finances, was gnawing away at my sense of humour and undermining my previously robust health. In an effort to replenish our savings, I had begun teaching golf again. That skill was a remnant of a dream that fizzled out in favour of a proper job, not long after I married Lesley and she gave birth to our beautiful daughter, Joanne. Although it was nice to earn a little extra money, suddenly I had no spare time. Life didn't feel like fun anymore; weekends and evenings spent giving lessons at the driving range left me little time for family, no time to play golf, and no place to blow off a little steam. And now the company was entering yet another round of cuts. It was evident that my job would soon cease to exist, probably within months, and I could either fight again for another position, or simply accept redundancy and try to get on with a new life.

The previous week I had openly discussed my options, fears, and opinions with my boss, only to be told that the company felt that I was too valuable to lose. For some reason, this well-meaning vote of confidence only added to my stress. I imagined that somewhere on my boss's desk, my personnel file was marked: Must keep this employee, he will work for peanuts and is reasonably unlikely to screw up. Perhaps sensing I was nearing breaking point, my boss agreed I should take the weekend to consider my position.

On Sunday morning, while I was giving a golf lesson at the driving range, I started to feel unwell. At first I was a little dizzy and flushed, and I noticed I was distracted and unable to concentrate. Thinking I might just be coming down with a head cold, I did my best to carry on working. However, within an hour I was feeling considerably worse, with a sharp pain in my chest and back, cold sweats and a racing heart. Obviously, something was wrong, so I cancelled my remaining lessons and set off for home. Lesley was surprised to see me back from work so early, and she immediately noticed I was looking ashen and unwell. Despite my protests, she called the NHS medical helpline who advised us to go directly to a nearby clinic. Within minutes of arriving, I was on a heart monitor and a nice Indian doctor was checking my blood pressure and shaking his head.

Strangely, I wasn't worried or scared. Perhaps I was subconsciously relieved things had finally come to a head. Despite Lesley's attempt at gallows' humour, asking about my level of life cover and funeral preferences, I could see she was very concerned. Initially, I was quite pragmatic and practical in my thinking – I was, after all, a comparatively young and fit non-smoker, a former karate instructor who enjoyed running most days. I ate a healthy diet and didn't drink much alcohol. My feeling was that if something was wrong with my machine, the doctors would fix it. Although I wasn't happy, I didn't see any need to worry. After about an hour, our GP, Dave Harrison, popped his head around the door.

"Hey, Nick, hi, Lesley," he waved and smiled. "I heard you were here – I thought I'd pop in."

"Thanks, Dave. No need to worry though, I'm feeling a good bit better now. It's all a big fuss over nothing. I only came here because Lesley was worried."

"Well you're not dead yet, I suppose," Dave conceded reluctantly.

"Do you have any idea what's going on?" asked Lesley.

He looked at my chart and nodded. "This tells me nothing, and everything."

"What do you mean?" Lesley asked. "The other doctor said Nick's heart is OK."

"It's like the dog that didn't bark," Dave explained. "The absence of anything definitive can be as telling as a positive result. It looks like he had a bad reaction to all the stress he's been under. I have been warning him about this for months. He's fine for now. I was thinking we might send him home in an hour or so, provided nothing changes."

His blue eyes turned towards me. "Please come and see me at the surgery tomorrow morning." Then, perhaps sensing my reticence, he leaned closer and spoke more sternly, "Nick, we need to talk about this – it's important."

Although Dave was our GP, he was about my age and we had been friends since we met five years earlier. His quiet intelligence and polite, unassuming manner is the antithesis of my energetic humour and flamboyant laughter. He is tall and blond and self-consciously gangly, I'm of average height, a keen sportsman, and the little hair I have left is mostly dark. Nevertheless, our first conversation quickly revealed a shared interest in the wry humour of Gary Larson's Far Side cartoons, Star Trek, and the old Kung Fu TV show. Such an eclectic collision of minds could only lead to friendship. He was also a fine doctor. So, as instructed, bright and early the following morning I presented myself at the surgery.

After completing another round of medical tests and studying my charts, Dave leaned back in his chair, put his hands behind his head and crossed his long legs.

"How long have we been friends?" he asked.

I looked to the ceiling for inspiration. "Summer of 1999 – I think. Charity cricket match, here in the village."

"Ah yes, another triumphant performance!"

"Hardly! You were out for a duck, first ball of the day. We sat together in the beer tent and chatted all day," I said.

"Really? I don't remember that."

"The cricket or the chat?"

"Oh, the cricket of course. I remember us chatting about Star Trek. You said something about space aliens landing on the cricket pitch, and that got us talking about Douglas Adams, then we had another beer..." He pursed his lips and frowned, little creases disturbed the smooth skin of his forehead. "I can't remember much else."

"That's hardly surprising," I said. "By the afternoon, you were too drunk to take to the field. That was probably a bonus, the village team won the match by about 20 runs."

Dave smiled, stretching his arms wide, palms skywards. "There, you see, my selfless sacrifice saved the day. And now I'm going to save your day."

I tipped my head in quiet acknowledgement. After a moment of silence, Dave sat forward and tapped my chart with his finger, indicating the subject of conversation was about to change. He didn't speak, but his finger continued its inconsistent drumming. After a full minute, he gently laid his palm onto my medical records.

"Listen, Nick, the human body is a wondrous machine. It can absorb all manner of punishment and yet heal itself. With poisons and toxins it can even build up a resistance, like with alcohol. When you first drink, you're under the table after a couple of glasses. But if you continue drinking regularly, you discover you can drink all night and hardly feel the effects."

"So, you didn't waste your time at medical school then?" I quipped.

"Not at all, it was all serious research. Lots of hangovers, but it had to be done."

"What's all this got to do with me?"

"Well – here's the thing. Stress is different. It seems like the body and mind can absorb almost any amount of stress without any negative side effects. In fact, some people, like you, almost seem to thrive on it. Then one day – bang! You can't take any more. Worse than that, you suddenly can't take any stress at all. That's what I think has happened to you." His palm patted my chart again. "In the absence of an alternative explanation, it's the only diagnosis that makes sense."

I sat quietly for a moment before asking, "What does all this mean, how do I get better?"

"Well, you need to get away from all this stress. Your body can't take it any longer. There are some drugs we could try temporarily, but that would merely be postponing the inevitable. Yesterday you had a big warning, next time it could be a lot worse."

I put my head in my hands and we fell silent for a while. Dave was being very clever, he wanted me to think seriously about what had happened. I wasn't frightened, but I was angry. Angry with my employer for exposing me and my colleagues to such unnecessary stress. Angry with myself for allowing it to happen, for being too weak and selfish to stand up and say "Enough!" and angry with my body for failing me. It had always seemed to me that, provided I looked after my body, it would look after me. If I had a good diet, didn't drink excessively and kept fit, it was reasonable to expect that I would stay fairly healthy. That was the deal. In my limited experience of ill health, most things that broke could be fixed, with the application of a little medicine and time.

I had never considered my body would let me down. Breaking a leg, getting cancer, or catching some virus were all acceptable medical problems for a guy, but I saw nothing macho about being a victim of stress. I knew I wasn't a coward, I didn't earn my karate black belt without learning how to face up to my fears. But now suddenly I was being told I couldn't handle stress anymore. Did that somehow make me less manly, a less dependable husband?

Feeling like a heavyweight boxer who had just been told the next punch would be fatal, I turned to Dave for advice.

"Okay. What do you suggest I do?"

"Well, that's up to you my friend, but I think you've got some important decisions to make. And in my opinion you should make them quickly."

After this stern warning, we moved outside to the carpark, where we could sit on a low wall, enjoy a little fresh air in the winter sunshine and admire Dave's new car. Away from the office, the conversation took on a lighter tone as we searched for a solution to my problem.

"Honestly, Nick, there's no point working so hard and putting up with all that shit if it means you're going to drop dead before you're 40."

"But I'm already 45."

"Are you? Christ! You look well for a dead man! What's the point of having all that money, if you're dead anyway?"

"But I don't have any money, Dave, it's no more than a house of cards. I feel like I'm in debt up to my flipping eyeballs. I seem to be running all the time just to keep up. I can't even afford a day off."

"Me neither, mate. This car cost me a ruddy fortune and I'm always running around seeing patients at all hours. I never seem to get time off." He pulled a handkerchief out of his jacket pocket and wiped an invisible speck from his windscreen. "Still, I get over 40 mpg, and it goes like stink!"

"You need a break, Dave," I joked. "All that work is bad for you."

"Don't start! Anyway, we're talking about you here. What are you going to do about it?"

"I'm not sure yet. I've been talking about change recently with Lesley. We think that, provided we can sell the house for a decent price, I could jack my job in and accept the redundancy package. Then we might be able to buy a place somewhere for cash and start a new life. Simple living, without any debts or credit cards."

"Where would you go?" he asked.

"We were considering Scotland, perhaps Skye, or Portugal, or maybe Spain. We even looked at France – prices look pretty attractive there at the moment. If we can sell the house, we might afford a small holding with a few acres. Maybe we could get some goats."

My doctor leaned back on the wall, ran his fingers through his unruly hair and gave a big sigh. "It sounds idyllic. Can I come?"

"Nah! You've got all those people in the waiting room to see to. Get back to work, this car won't pay for itself you know."

"Piss off," he said. "Anyway, they're all a bunch of old farts with piles and boils. Such a waste of my enormous talent!" He stood. With a smile he said, "Good luck, I hope it goes well for you. If it helps, tell your boss that if he doesn't let you go, you'll probably go nuts within six months."

"Thanks, mate. I think!" I shook his hand and turned for home.

"Hey!" he shouted, making me look over my shoulder. "Don't forget. It's never too late to be who you could have been." He crossed his eyes and gave me a Vulcan salute. "Live long and prosper!"

We went our separate ways. He walked reluctantly back to his waiting room full of coughs and sneezes, and I strode towards the prospect of starting a new life. Although it was a cold and frosty morning, the winter sun had warmed our backs while we chatted. I was grateful Dave had taken the time and trouble to help me get my life back in balance. As I walked the short distance home, there was a tentative spring in my step and an air of positivity engulfed me like a warm blanket. I knew everything was going to be alright.

While Lesley and I ate a late breakfast together, fed the chickens, and walked our two dogs, I told her everything Dave had said, from his dire warnings to his suggested cure. I think we both accepted something had to change, for both our sakes. Each time I had been thrust into the vicious merry-go-round of redundancy and redeployment, Lesley and I had spent hours discussing our options. I would scratch my head and make my lists, citing the positives and negatives, and calculating the finances. She would share her ideas and suggestions, some of them good, others more like verbal hand grenades casually thrown into the discussion. Where my planning is always practical and cautious, Lesley's is more emotional and impulsive. Because of that balance, we make a good team. Ultimately, we both yearned for a better life, but the path forwards seldom seemed so obvious. This time there was another factor. With my health to consider, our decision was a no-brainer.

At lunchtime on Monday I called my boss and told him I wanted out. Two hours later, he called me back and my wish was granted. I was to be made redundant. At that moment, I felt as if a great weight was lifted from my shoulders. At the same time a cold hand seemed to grip my bowel. I thought, "That's it. No going back now."

2. The Bomb in the Attic

A lot of things had happened during the previous few years to bring Lesley and me to this place in our lives. Our daughter, Joanne, was all grown up and buying her own house, as she rocketed towards spectacular success in her career. My father had died recently, after a slow decline into dementia followed by a massive stroke. He was always a big influence in my life and, like many sons, I would subconsciously seek his approval for everything I did. His passing, along with another tragedy and the recent news that a close friend had been diagnosed with brain and bowel cancer, left me feeling I should be doing more (or perhaps less) with my life. On the upside, Lesley had given up work recently and was now enjoying being what she liked to refer to as 'a lady of leisure'.

Retrospectively, in some ways we had become emotional nomads, travelling from challenge to challenge as if they were waterholes in the desert. We were at our most comfortable when fully engaged in a task that had a clear path to an obvious conclusion. Lesley is notorious for suddenly deciding that life would be decidedly better if only we lived somewhere else, or had different jobs, or if the planet was just moved a bit to the left. Usually, these periods of situational agitation can be defused by launching into some sort of endeavour, like decorating the house, or taking evening classes.

Sometimes, even the seemingly pointless exercise of doing jigsaw puzzles could help to fill the void between projects. A puzzle, after all, is a simple challenge with a clear goal that can be achieved with obvious steps. If the challenge seems too large, you can break it down by first finding the corners and connecting the edges and so on, until the picture is completed. We may have felt some small sense of achievement once the project was finished, but this would always be followed by a feeling of emptiness – until we began our next scheme, or another jigsaw puzzle.

As young parents, the normal demands of everyday life provided some measure of simplicity to our lives. Each day was planned around our daughter, the need to put food on the table and to pay the bills. Once Joanne was old enough to be more independent, Lesley and I instinctively started to look for new challenges, changing jobs, learning new skills, and overseeing the addition of an extension to our Victorian terraced house.

A few years later, when the building work was complete and around the time when Joanne was getting old enough to move out, we got into the habit of window shopping for houses during the weekends. I don't think we had any serious intention of moving, but I had recently been promoted again and the housing markets were buoyant, so we were curious to see what was available. One day we spotted an enchanting but derelict cottage, in a pretty village just outside Colchester, in Essex, England. It contained one elderly resident, a friend of the recently-deceased original owner. The family who had inherited the cottage wanted to sell as quickly as possible, but there was a problem. Because the current and previous residents were so old and frail, the entire property had remained untouched, without maintenance or repair, for almost 30 years. With everything but the roof and walls needing replacing or restoring, it was going to be a major renovation project. The state of the cottage would have put a lot of people off. Our talents on that front were limited to decorating, putting up shelves, and replacing a broken light fitting. Nonetheless, we fell instantly in love with the property and committed to becoming the new owners. With Joanne's enthusiastic support, and a huge bridging loan from my bank, three months later we moved in.

Almost immediately things seemed to go wrong. A couple of days after moving in, the sale of our original property fell through. We were the owners of two houses, and with a hungry mortgage and a huge bridging loan to feed, there was no money available to hire a builder. The renovations were put on hold. We were fortunate that it only took four months before we sold our first house, but it was still a considerable strain on our nerves and finances. Not to be left out, my employer joined in the fun by announcing a massive cut in staff nationwide. I survived the cull, but acquired a new project requiring trips to every corner of the country and hundreds of nights away. Undaunted and happy to still have an income, Lesley and I got our heads down and started the process of creating a new home.

As this was our first major renovation project, we used professional builders, plumbers, and electricians to do the skilled work. To save on costs, most of the clearing away, clearing up, and decorating would be down to us. I was the self-appointed project manager, so it fell to me to draw up the plans, hire the builders, manage the order of work, and make sure the money was in the bank when we needed it.

The house had no central heating, all the electrics were from the 1930s, there was significant woodworm damage in the floors, and all the windows were rotten. The kitchen was unbelievably filthy and caked in grease, but not nearly as foul as the toilet, which showed significant signs of impatience and inaccuracy from the elderly male residents. Curiously, the bathroom had a top-quality corner bath, but it was fitted with mismatched second-hand taps. There was a swanky new double garage with remote-controlled doors, but no sign of there ever having been a car.

The first order of business was to replace all the rotten windows with the latest energy retaining UPVC double-glazed units. With meticulous planning, I arranged for the messy job of installation to take place while Lesley was away visiting friends. On the agreed day, the window fitters arrived bright and early – four hours late and just in time for lunch. When they returned from the pub, I politely accosted the foreman.

"You guys seem to be a long way behind," I said. "Are you going to have enough time to get the job done today?"

He gripped my shoulder firmly and then applied a little extra pressure. This gesture was either meant to comfort my fears, or warn me to mind my own business.

"Don't worry, Nick." He waved his arm expansively and breathed beery fumes and bits of cheese and onion crisps into my face. "My lads will have this lot sorted before you know it!"

Like a swarm of ants, they attacked the house with hammers and crowbars. Stage one of our renovations were underway. It was fascinating to watch the lads ripping and smashing and humping and dumping – and all with such violence and enthusiasm. In just four hours, all the windows were out and the skip I'd just rented was full to the brim. With the windows removed, the chill November wind was blowing uninterrupted straight through the house, flapping the cobwebs, swirling the woodworm dust, and slamming any unattended doors. There was also an exponential increase in the amount of traffic noise, something we hadn't noticed as a problem when we viewed the house.

17

I had supposed the double-glazing company would dispose of the old windows as a part of the cost, rather than wasting my skip, and as I was already wearing two jumpers, a coat, and a woolly hat, I decided to mention this to the foreman. As I approached his van, I couldn't help but notice the lads appeared to be packing up for the day.

"Excuse me," I said, "but where are you going?"

"It's four o'clock. Knocking-off time," the foreman said, tapping his watch to emphasise his point.

"But what about my windows?"

"They're in the skip," he said, pointing at my skip.

"I know that, I can see that. I meant what about my new windows?"

"Don't worry, Nick, they'll be fitted tomorrow."

"Tomorrow?! But what about tonight, I'll probably freeze to death."

The foreman stepped back as if he had been slapped. As he peered into our front room, through the cavity that was once a window but was now no more than a wind-hole, I saw his eyes take in the rotting floorboards, the peeling wallpaper, the dust sheeted furniture, and the soot-stained walls. He turned to me and spoke in a horror-struck voice.

"Good God, you're not actually living here are you?"

"Yes. Since last week," I said.

The foreman gave a shudder. "Well, I'm sorry. The work order is for us to remove the windows today and fit the new ones tomorrow. The office must have thought you were living out or something. You'll have to get a hotel."

"I can't do that, all our stuff is in there. Someone will steal it."

"I suppose they will." He frowned, then added, "Well, I guess you'd better wrap up warm, it's going to be a cold night."

I shook my head firmly. "No! That won't do at all. You'll have to fit the windows today."

"Sorry," he shrugged noncommittally and tapped his watch again. "It's long past knocking off time. Anyway, it's Guy Fawkes tonight, I'm taking my kids to a big fireworks display."

My heart sank as I realised what lay ahead. No windows and a long, cold night of traffic noise and comforting two dogs terrified of fireworks.

"I guess I'll see you in the morning," I said morbidly.

"That's the spirit!" He gave me a comforting pat on the back. As he walked away, he looked over his shoulder and added insult to injury. "Oh, and thanks for letting us use your skip."

To be fair, the lads returned the following day, as promised, and made a cracking job of installing our new windows. Even without central heating, the house was considerably warmer, and the road noise from the passing traffic became almost tolerable. That experience gave me a small insight into how project management can be fraught with problems, but greater revelations were soon to follow.

Once our woodworm problem had been chemically eradicated, using a local firm that gave me a ten-year guarantee and went bankrupt the following week, the next tasks on our wish list were installing central heating, upgrading the electrics, replacing rotten floorboards, adding an office and a second toilet, and fitting the new kitchen. Many of these jobs had to happen in parallel. For example: the central heating needed the new electrics, but the wiring could not be laid until the boiler was fitted, and, the floorboards could only be replaced after each section of wiring and pipework was installed. The office and toilet couldn't be built until the plumbing was fitted, but the plumbing could only be fitted after the frame for the office walls were... well, you get the picture. Each workman's ability to do his job relied on at least two others, and their ability and reliability. Throw into the mix the problem of missing or incorrect parts, and the joys of ripping up our lovely new floorboards to rescue our overly inquisitive cats, and the entire project risked quickly disintegrating into a farce. Lesley and I were living in this filthy, rubble-strewn building site, and I was travelling to business meetings as far afield as Glasgow, Jersey, and Madrid. Notwithstanding Lesley's hard work and rugged determination, our saviour during this difficult time was Wally Sidebottom.

The renovations at our previous property had gone so well, that we asked the same builder to do the honours at our new home. Despite his arthritic knees, bad back, and the prospect of a 70 mile daily commute, Wally agreed to come out of retirement for one last job, before moving to Spain. We were thankful that he did. Men of his skill, talent, honesty, and dependability are worth their

19

weight in bacon butties. Wally and his guys were at the house and working by 7.30 am every morning, and unless we interrupted with tea, sandwiches and cake, they didn't stop until 4 pm. God bless them all! Unfortunately, such praise couldn't apply to everyone we employed.

To the unsuspecting homeowner, tradesmen can be a real lifesaver. But like parachutes, you only realise yours doesn't work properly when it's too late. That was certainly the case with Ploddy the Plumber. He was the only member of the renovation team that didn't work for Wally or come with his personal endorsement. Unfortunately, the guy Wally recommended was unavailable, so I had to shop around. In retrospect, the fact that Ploddy the Plumber was immediately available, even though his quote was half that of any others, should have rung some alarm bells. But he was an affable and polite guy who spoke with great confidence about his ability. He was particularly effervescent about his experience of marrying pumped heating systems with old gravity flow back boilers – coincidentally, a skill we required.

Although Wally and the other guys were too professional to say anything impolite about Ploddy, their cold stares and long silences in his presence should have also rung some alarm bells with us. However, Lesley is too sweet to think badly of someone without direct intervention, and I was away for a week, enduring white-knuckle daily commuter flights between Guernsey and Jersey. So it was only when the hot water tank in the loft began bellowing like a steam whistle, that we realised Ploddy was not quite the expert he claimed to be. Unfortunately, by then Ploddy had cashed my cheque and changed his phone number, never to be seen again.

But all was not lost, as Wally's first pick, Peter-the-Particularly-Proficient-Plumber, came to the rescue. Among much tooth sucking and head shaking, he inspected Ploddy's work and pulled out his camera.

"I've got to get a picture of this lot," he said, "in all my years, I've never seen the like!"

"Is it that bad?" I asked, suspecting I already knew the answer.

Peter removed his tweed flat cap, scratched his head and squinted at the muddle of intertwined pipes and valves that now adorned my loft.

"Frankly, Nick, I don't know. I've never seen anything like it, and I'm struggling to figure out what most of these pipes are expected to do. This lot may have been appropriate for one of them new-killer power stations, but it's just overkill for a domestic heating system." He pointed to the big green drum that lay in the centre of the jumbled pipework. "That cylinder definitely shouldn't have been installed on its side. This bit's gravity flow from your back boiler. It'll trap the heat and build up pressure like a bomb."

With perfect timing, there was a deep gurgling rumble, followed by a second more threatening reverberation.

"What the hell was that?" Peter asked, his eyes wide.

I held up a finger. "Wait for it!"

There was a second and a third rumble, trembling the rafters under our feet like distant thunder followed by a high-pitched scream from outside.

"That's the sound of a ten-foot plume of steam escaping from the overflow pipe outside," I shouted, "it happens as regular as clockwork."

"Good job it does, otherwise the cylinder would have exploded and your roof would be across the street."

"Good to know," I said with a grim smile. "Can it be fixed?"

Peter blew out a long breath and scratched his head. Realising his flat cap was in the way, he took it off and scratched thoughtfully before answering.

"Well, the tank needs replacing, this one's too tall to fit under the roof. That's probably why that muppet lay it on its side. Then the pipework's wrong, them valves and that, he's tried to build a pressurised system, that's wrong as well." He put his hat on again and shrugged. "Look, it's probably better to rip the lot out and start again. It'll cost a bit, but it's the best way."

"OK, if that's the best solution. When can you start?"

Peter poked a valve with his finger and it fell off with a clatter. He gave me a wink. "It looks like I already have!"

Peter did a fantastic job, and at a decidedly reasonable price. Once the professionals had finished their work, it was time for the amateurs to get grafting. Before we could consider any landscaping, there was a considerable amount of clearing to do. Our three-quarter acre garden had once been a charming orchard, and part of the same land that Beth Chatto bought to craft the famous garden just 100 yards away from our front door. Unlike her beautiful creation, our land was untouched for 30 years and had become a wall of impenetrable bramble, which would take several months to clear.

A search of the outbuildings and accessible parts of the garden revealed 30 years of collected junk, including several hundred sheets of glass and piles of asbestos sheeting. At the rear of the house was a huge greenhouse constructed from many dozens of old window frames, presumably taken from skips and building sites around the village. Disposing of the rubbish would eventually fill 12 large skips, costing us thousands of pounds in the process, and substantially denting our budget. Doing the heavy lifting and dismantling the greenhouse was a two-man job, so with some begging and the offer of a barbecue, I enlisted the help of my best friend, Ray, his wife, Jeannine, and their two boys.

It was a memorable and warm, sunny Sunday afternoon. While the boys chased butterflies and played hide and seek, Lesley and Jeannine chatted and drank wine, as happy as if they were sisters. The business of clearing the rubbish went better than expected, particularly once the greenhouse collapsed after one hearty shove. We only needed to carefully collect the bits and cart them off to the skip. It was like an Amish barn raising in reverse. Whilst Ray was happy for Jeannine to be a full-time mother and housewife, he was very clear that outdoors cooking over charcoal was man's work. As he gently cremated our food, we chatted and drank beer. I stretched out, as far as the rickety garden chair would allow.

"This is nice, we must do this more often," I said.

"I think you're running out of rubbish." He waved his beer towards the concrete plinth that had once housed the greenhouse.

"I mean getting together – and the golf. We've hardly seen each other for months," I said.

"I guess we've both been busy. I've been on night shifts a lot recently. The money's good, but it plays havoc with my social life."

"I can imagine. Anyway, thanks again for your help today, mate." I raised my beer can in a mock toast.

"You're welcome. Anyways, I owe you for all the golf lessons you've given me," he quipped.

"Think nothing of it. I always thought giving you free lessons was the only way to buy your friendship."

"Damn right! I couldn't abide being around a posh twat like you otherwise!" Although his mirrored sunglasses hid the humour in his eyes, after ten years, I knew when he was joking.

"Well, it's a good thing that I'm better at coaching golf than you are at cooking burgers, or you'd still be a 24 handicapper." I pointed at something that may once have been a meat patty, "That one's officially on fire."

"Oh! Crap!" He casually doused the flames with a splash of beer. "No harm done."

I looked across the lumpy lawn to where Lesley was showing Jeannine some flowers that had magically sprouted once we chopped back the bramble.

"How are you two getting on now you've moved back into the house?" I asked quietly.

"It's better than living in a caravan on the driveway." Ray pulled a sour face. "But I'm still sleeping on the couch, if that's what you mean."

"Give it time, she'll come around. How are the boys now?" I asked.

"A bit better. We tried to hide the fact that we were having problems, I wouldn't go out to the caravan until they were in bed, and I'd be back indoors before they got up, but we've nosey neighbours so I guess it was inevitable they'd find out."

For a moment, I watched the boys as they chased each other, dodging between our wives. "I think they'll be OK, they're strong lads."

He nodded. "Jeannine and I are going to make a go of it, not just for the boys. We really want to make it work."

"That's good." I smiled. "I'm glad for you both, you deserve a long and happy life, which is more than I can say for those sausages!"

Almost four years later, all the renovations were complete and the house looked superb, beautifully presented with real curb appeal. Lesley's mighty efforts had produced a magnificent garden that was the envy of many visitors, especially during the recent Open Gardens Day in the village. After so much hard work, renovating the house and gardens while I was still working full time and Lesley was completing her Open University course, we had a real sense of achievement. But at the same time, we were getting restless, perhaps subconsciously feeling the need to get into the next project.

With so much turmoil at work, money, or the lack of it, was a constant worry for me, even though we were not spending wildly, nor living the high life beyond our means. In common with most middle-class families at that time, our only debts were a reasonable mortgage, a small bank loan and a few credit cards. Although we could meet the repayments and even add a little to our savings account each month, I was acutely aware of how tenuous the situation was. If I were to suffer even a small drop in pay, or worse, lose my job, we were only a few weeks away from financial disaster. Just 18 months after we were married, a cruel twist of fate during an overseas contract left Lesley and me out of step with our financial commitments and potentially facing homelessness. It was shocking how quickly the reversal of fortune had occurred, with seemingly insignificant events turning into major stumbling blocks. In the end, we worked our way out of the mess, and the experience made us stronger, but the memory of that time is like an icicle driving into my heart.

With redundancy a daily talking point at work, the fear of a repetition now weighed heavily on my mind. I had recently started having premonitions of disaster, waking in the night, panting, with the sheets soaked in sweat. Even though the post brought daily offers of new credit cards and cheaper bank loans, I felt strongly motivated to find a way out from under this burden of debt. In another life, I might have been diagnosed with a mid-life crisis and given a prescription for a motorbike and an illicit affair with a 19-year-old blonde Latvian girl. One cure would have been fun, the other would surely have killed me – you may decide which. In any event, money was tight and neither stress treatment was available on the National Health Service in England.

Time spent with friends and family is always a valuable distraction from such stress, but despite our promise to meet more often, my crazy schedule meant that my golf days with Ray were sporadic at best. We managed a few games at weekends when our diaries aligned, a week in Portugal to celebrate Ray's 40th birthday, and a couple of beers after my father died, but otherwise our contacts were irregular. The last time we all got together was at my daughter's birthday party in Braintree. The boys were both a couple of feet taller and fine young men. Ray and Jeannine were like young lovers, dancing together and holding hands a lot. They showed us they had wedding rings tattooed on their ring fingers. Lesley and I were delighted to see them so happy. At the end of the night we agreed to meet soon for another barbecue.

A couple of weeks later, I arrived home after another long day of commuting and train delays. As I came through the door, Lesley was waiting in the hall. I gave her a kiss on the cheek, she looked a little stern and I mentally checked my diary in case I had forgotten an anniversary. Nothing came to mind, so I decided it was safe to follow her into the sitting room.

"Jeannine just phoned," Lesley said, "you'd better sit down."

"Oh crap!" I groaned. "Don't tell me they've split up again."

"Sit down, it's not that." Lesley pointed at the couch. I remained standing, ready for a quick exit in case it transpired I had indeed forgotten something.

"I'll stand. What have I done?" I asked. "Are they coming over?"

"Sit down."

I rolled my eyes. "Whaaat?"

"There was a car crash. Ray's dead," she said.

I sat down.

3. The End of the Beginning

Despite the heroic efforts of the Essex Air Ambulance and the doctors, Ray died at the ridiculously young age of 41, from injuries sustained in the car accident. He was the nicest and most genuine person I had ever known. The funeral was a suitably sombre affair. There was a huge turnout, with dozens of friends and family, people from his work, and a large group from the golf club. We all wanted to say the same thing: "I'm so sorry, what a waste, he was so young."

Jeannine was inconsolable, the boys were numb with shock, unable to process what had happened. I'm not very good at funerals, but then who is? Perhaps I'm too empathetic, but I find myself trying to ease the pain. I'm inclined to crack jokes and use dark humour. Not everybody gets that, but I know Ray would have. That's why I miss him.

***

In quick succession, I had lost my father and my best friend, discovered another friend was fighting bowel and brain cancer, and yet again my job was under threat. With hindsight, it was obvious the stress was building, as was my dissatisfaction with our lifestyle. Although my decision to take redundancy brought some temporary relief, it didn't solve the problems we were facing.

As soon as my boss told me I was going to be made redundant, my status changed from valued employee to toxic brand. My job gave me access to sensitive financial information and client data for judges and politicians, so I understood the why and the wherefore, but it still hurt. I had to report to our London office the next day. My security pass no longer worked, so I had trouble getting inside the building. Eventually my boss came down to reception and walked me up to his office. I thought he looked tired and a little embarrassed. After my official termination interview, he told me I was being placed on gardening leave until my termination date some five months away. It was an extraordinarily generous gesture, for which I was most grateful.

We shook hands and he wished me well. Under the careful supervision of a secretary, I was required to hand over my security pass, car keys, laptop, mobile phone, and any notes I had relating to current projects. I spent the afternoon briefing the colleague who was taking over my portfolio. He seemed irritated and distracted, I guess he was unhappy his workload had just doubled, or perhaps he'd heard I was cracking up. In any event, we got through the meeting as best we could. Finally, as if I was a prisoner cleared for release, he escorted me down to reception and out the door.

I was unemployed, standing on the pavement and clutching my wretched little cardboard box, filled with my sad collection of personal items. Ten years of sweat, toil, joy, and laughter were over in an instant. As I crossed the street, I turned for a moment to look up at that famous redbrick building with its gothic arches, statues, and gargoyles. I knew I was going to miss the companionship, the challenge, and the pride. But that life was over, so I stood tall and confidently strode towards the tube station and the journey home.

When my train stopped at Chelmsford, I spotted a young man disembarking. He was wearing a business suit and carrying a cardboard box similar to mine. For an instant we shared a look that said, "You too?" Quickly he looked away. A sudden flash of doubt flooded my blood with adrenalin and set my heart racing. I had an impulsive urge to run back towards the security of employment and the comfort of a regular salary and a good pension scheme. A brief vision flashed in my mind, of me pounding on the doors and shouting that I'd changed my mind, of being invited back into the fold, of being part of the team again, enjoying the sense of pride and success, the long lunches, expensive wine, and first class travel. But the vision faded, replaced with the prospect of a new life and other exciting things.

Lesley was waiting for me at Manningtree station. We kissed as I climbed into the car.

"All done?" she asked.

"All done," I confirmed. "Five months' garden leave on full pay, and I still qualify for my bonus."

"Good job too," she smiled. "We've a lot to do…"

"…and no idea where to start," I added.

I like things to be predictable and orderly, happening in exactly the sequence I prophesy on one of my many lists. If I can't have

27

every one of my toy boats lined up, at a minimum, they should all be in the same pond. Although she is perfectly capable of navigating and steering our lives, my darling wife is happier to sail through life at the whim of the wind, trusting I have my hand on the tiller and an eye on the compass. At that moment, we were rudderless in a storm, and our ship was in grave danger of sinking. We needed a proper plan.

Lesley and I were agreed we wanted to start a new life. We both wanted something simpler that gave us more space and less stress. But beyond that basic concept, the picture became somewhat fuzzy. Up until then, our thinking had been purely hypothetical and decidedly vague. After selling our house, we would move to a different county, or another country. There I would probably try to find some work. In the unlikely event that we couldn't sell the house quickly, I would be forced to try and find work locally at a similar, or better salary. However, this option seemed doubtful, at age 45, and in a changing and competitive job market. Now my redundancy was forcing our hand, we had to make choices, decisions, and real plans. It was a tricky conundrum, and one we could only solve by talking together whilst taking long walks with our dogs.

***

At that time, we had two dogs, Brandy and Romany. Brandy was a pedigree Lhasa Apso bitch, one of a pair we had purchased from a local breeder some ten years previously. Her sister, Tammy, had sadly died after a long illness aged just seven. Brandy had a thick coat the colour of warm honey and 'love me' eyes, which were like looking into her heart and seeing melted chocolate. If you are unfamiliar with the breed, the Lhasa Apso originates from Tibet where the name means 'Barking Lion' or 'Little Lion', depending on which book you read. They are loyal, intelligent, playful and inquisitive dogs with a warning bark twice their diminutive size.

I first encountered the breed quite by accident, when I happened to bump into Sally, a work colleague on her day off. I had just finished a meeting and was heading to my car, and she was walking towards the park with two of the most adorable dogs I had ever seen. We got chatting and it soon transpired that Sally had kept Lhasa Apsos for several years, and the pair she was walking had recently been mated. The bitch was due to give birth in a month, with the puppies being available for purchase about ten weeks later. This sparked an understandable desire in me to own a dog again, and I was already starting to suspect which breed I would like.

I couldn't wait to get home and tell Lesley what I'd seen. She was equally interested and after a visit to Sally's home to meet the dogs, and several more to see the puppies, we were in love with the breed. Owning a dog is not a decision to be taken lightly, we wanted to be sure we were doing the right thing.

"It would be good for Joanne to have some responsibility," I said to Lesley, as we drove home.

"Absolutely," Lesley said. "It would be great for her, and such a surprise."

"She still doesn't suspect anything?"

"Not a thing!" Lesley smiled. "I can't wait to see her face."

"It's going to be fun, presenting her with her first puppy."

"Or two," Lesley mumbled.

"Excuse me?" I said.

"Two puppies," she said, her eyes bright. "Two would be better."

"They would?" I asked.

"Sure. They could keep each other company," she explained.

"Won't that be Joanne's job?"

"Well yes, but not all the time. She has to go to school, you have to go to work, and so do I. One puppy would get lonely. We should get two." Lesley nodded, confirming the validity of her argument.

"They are *rather* expensive," I pointed out.

"If we get two bitches, then perhaps later we could breed them ourselves. Just the once. The money could be handy."

We fell into silence and I concentrated on driving. I thought for a while and weighed up the options. By the time we arrived home, I had made up my mind. We had a large Victorian house, with a big, well-fenced garden. Two small puppies would take up only slightly more room than one average sized dog. And they were the cutest creatures I'd ever seen.

"Okay, we'll get two dogs," I said. "I'll call Sally and let her know."

Lesley gave me a huge hug and a kiss. I took this rare public display of affection as a sign we were in agreement.

"But not a word to Joanne," I warned. "We mustn't spoil the surprise."

Lesley and I made one more trip to Sally's house to pick our two puppies. We chose a bitch from each litter. One was white and the other brown. We had to wait another month before the puppies were ready and it was hard to hide our excitement from our daughter. I didn't want to spoil the surprise, or lead her into thinking that she was getting a pony.

The big day arrived. I had arranged to collect our puppies from Sally on my journey home from work. Everything went to plan, and at 6 pm I stepped into our sitting room clutching a small cardboard box and a sizable stack of paperwork from my office. Joanne was sitting on the couch with her legs drawn up, watching television. Still a young girl, she was as pretty as her mother, tall for her age and athletically slim, with short brown hair, sparkling blue eyes, and a cheeky smile displaying the silver braces on her teeth. Although normally a diligent student, she had recently started secondary school and on this day, she was keen to avoid her homework by reprimanding me for my own.

"Aw, Dad!" she groaned. "Have you brought loads of work home again? It's Friday, I thought we were going to the cinema. You promised."

"This isn't my work, it's something for you to do," I countered, dropping the box onto her lap.

She was quick to respond. "I can't help you, I've got loads of homework to do, I've just remembered."

"Tuff luck," I said, with mock sternness. "You'll have to help."

Lesley was in on the gag. "You should do as your father says," she said from the doorway, where she stood in full-on mother pose, with her arms folded.

Joanne knew when she was beaten, but she wasn't going to go down without a fight. She fixed a full teenage pout onto her face and was about to launch into another objection, when the box on her lap started to move and whimper. Open mouthed with suspicion and surprise, our daughter looked at our beaming smiles and cautiously opened the box. Peering inside she gave a yelp of delight. Looking up at her were two squiggly little balls of fur, both desperately scrabbling for her attention. Carefully, she lifted them out. Like miniature overstuffed caricatures of the perfect puppy, covered in velvety soft fur and equipped with beautiful deep brown eyes, each was no larger than her hand.

"Oh my God!" she sighed. "I can't believe this. They're so cute!"

"We've only got them for an hour, then they're going to the pound," I joked.

"WHAT?" Joanne looked at me in shock, just in time to witness my wife giving me a hearty thump on the arm.

"Don't be so cruel," she chided me. "They're our dogs and they are here to stay."

"What are they?"

"They're Lhasa Apsos," Lesley said.

"I've never heard of them. They're gorgeous," Joanne said, burying her face into puppy heaven.

"According to the *Complete Book of Lhasa Apsos*, they are lively, playful, spirited, devoted, alert, steady, obedient, energetic, friendly, fearless, intelligent and assertive," I said. "A bit like you – except for the obedient bit."

As ever, Joanne was quick to return my serve. "Very funny. How come you can remember all that, but not where you put your car keys?"

"Good question." I conceded defeat with a shrug.

Our banter was interrupted as the puppies decided it was time to explore their new home.

"You'd better take them outside," Lesley suggested. "They must be busting for a wee."

"Are they housetrained?" Joanne asked, as she led the two inquisitive fur-balls towards the back door.

"They're a bit young for that," I answered. "That'll be your first job."

"Actually, that'll be your first job." Lesley pointed to a spreading puddle of liquid on the kitchen tiles.

"Oops!"

The two dogs quickly became our daughter's constant companions. They were happy to lie at her side while she did her homework, or trot along proudly when she took them for long walks in the park. With Joanne's enthusiastic encouragement, Tammy quickly learned to use the slide at the park. To the delight of the other children, the little white dog would patiently wait in line, before climbing the stairs and sliding down the shoot and into Joanne's waiting arms. Brandy was above such childishness, but after much training, she learned how to run after a ball. However, she considered the process of pursuit and retrieval to be somewhat pointless and would usually drop the ball and wander off at the first distraction. As far as she was concerned, if you wanted the ball then you shouldn't have thrown it away in the first place.

After we bred Brandy and Tammy, and mostly at the behest of our daughter, we decided to keep the runt of the two litters, a tiny white puppy who was eventually given the name Romany. She was a wonderful dog, playful and full of beans. Until the day she was old enough to have her first proper walk. Along with her mother and aunt, Romany proudly trotted along with her nose up and her tail held high in the air, like a confident princess in a white fur coat. Once we reached the field and were away from the main road, I let all three dogs off their leads. Brandy and Tammy bounded away along the usual route and Romany trotted along behind, confidently mimicking her mother's every move. When they ran, she ran, when they walked, she walked and when they peed, so did Romany. At the bottom of the hill, the footpath was bisected by a narrow ditch, filled with stagnant water, slime, and the usual litter generated by most fast food eating, beer swilling populations in town centres these days. In line astern, Brandy and Tammy jumped across the three-foot gap with an athletic spring.

Last in line, Romany attempted to replicate their aerial acrobatics, but because she was half the size of her mother, she only covered half the distance. Like a scene from a cartoon, Romany hung in the air for what seemed like several seconds, her legs paddling desperately, before plopping like a fluffy stone into the filthy water below. The poor little thing went in looking like the latest celebrity fashion accessory but emerged looking like an oily rag. With head hung low and her tail tucked between her legs, Romany turned dejectedly for home, her confidence shattered forever, or so we thought.

The following year, we took our caravan to Brean Sands, near Weston-Super-Mare, for a summer camping trip. Close to the funfair, the beach, and several tourist attractions, it was a grand location for a holiday, particularly as we were on a budget and I was trying to entertain a 14-year-old daughter, a wife, and three dogs. As the weather was uncharacteristically hot and sunny, with hardly a breath of wind, we decided to spend a day at the beach.

We set off just after breakfast. Lesley wore light blue shorts, a bikini top and a floppy sun hat. She had pink flip-flops on her feet and carried the large hard-backed book she was planning to read. Joanne wore pink shorts, a white t-shirt and her old trainers. As I was loaded down like a mule in the Himalayas, Joanne also held the dog leads. Brandy and Tammy plodded along stoically, despite having been roused from their morning nap and forced to march for almost ten minutes in the hot sun. Young Romany, finding the sun-baked pavement to be rather too hot for her delicate paws, trotted to one side so she could stay on the cool grass. As usual, Romany walked like she was practising for a dog show, placing each foot with delicate precision, holding her nose high and her white tail waving like a flag. As we passed the shower block, our progress was slowed appreciably while Romany cautiously picked her way through the puddles, careful to keep her paws pristine and white.

It was only a short stroll to the beach, along the paved footpath and then down a track that led through the sand dunes. Even so, carrying two chairs, a beach umbrella, the picnic basket, and a huge bag stuffed with assorted towels, lotions and potions, I was sweating a bit by the time we reached the beach. I very much fancied a cold beer or a nice stroll in a cool breeze.

"Where's the sea gone?" Joanne asked, as we stood on the thin strip of hot, yellow sand and looked out on a wide expanse of flat, grey mud.

"Actually, this isn't the sea," I said, "it's part of the River Severn estuary." I pointed to a low blue smudge on the horizon. "That's the water over there. This estuary has one of the highest tidal ranges in the world, almost 50 feet." I'd been reading the guide book that morning.

"What does that mean?" Joanne enquired cautiously, ever keen to cut my lectures to the minimum.

"It means that in a couple of hours, that water will be here." I pointed to the edge of the sand.

"Can we go for a walk? I'd like to look for sea shells."

I looked to Lesley for permission, but she was already stretched out on a beach towel and reading her book. I took her silence as tacit approval.

"Sure," I said, "but we'll have to watch out for quicksand."

"Cool! Is it dangerous?" Joanne asked, her eyes bright with mischief.

"It can be, and we'll have to keep an eye on the tide. Along here, the water comes in faster than you can run."

"Okay I get it. Come on, let's go."

"Shoes off," Lesley spoke to her book, "take the dogs."

"Ah, Muuum!" Joanne look horrified at the prospect of being separated from her beloved trainers.

"She's right," I said, pulling off my shoes and socks. "This estuary mud is smelly stuff, sticky as well. You won't want that on your trainers."

Grudgingly she complied. I called the dogs and Romany immediately trotted over, keen for an adventure, but Brandy and Tammy were already stretched out in the shade of the beach umbrella. I called them again, but they just snuggled into the warm sand and continued to ignore me.

"Leave them here," Lesley mumbled to her book. "Take Romany."

I looked at Joanne. We shared a shrug before walking down the sloping sand and onto flat mud. After the stifling heat of the bright sand, the damp estuary silt was a cool relief to our feet. The surface was surprisingly firm, much like wet sand, and our feet only sunk in a couple of inches. This was good for Romany and her pristine white fur, as she lifted her feet high, like a prissy teenage prom queen.

The view before us was flat and featureless to the far-off smudge where the waterline blended seamlessly into the hazy blue of the summer sky. A mile or more to the left, a line of horses was trekking along the shoreline, and to my right I could see a small sandy island and a bulbous headland jutting into the water.

Otherwise, the only signs of life were the indecipherable white blobs of distant sea birds, hunting for fish and worms in the countless shallow puddles that dotted the silt. Despite the soft breeze, the air felt thick and humid, muffling the gentle slap of our bare feet like a heavy fog. As the sun beat down on the damp silt, our nostrils filled with the sharp tang of salt, combined with an earthy hint of decay. We walked out for a hundred yards or so, picking up seashells and watching the birds. Romany walked ahead, delicately picking her way through the puddles.

"It's quite beautiful in a sad sort of way, don't you think?" I asked.

"It's all right I guess," Joanne said. "But it smells like poo!"

"Ah yes, well that will be the fragrance of decaying sea life, the molluscs, sea weed – and the poo." I smiled, reassuringly.

"Really?"

"I'd say there's a good bit of sewage discharged into the Severn. There's several cities up river."

"Eew!" my daughter said, looking at her muddy feet and possibly considering an attempt at levitation. She walked to the nearest puddle and kicked at the water until both feet were a bit cleaner. The bright pink of her painted toenails contrasted with the green slime bubbling up around her feet.

"Don't worry. I'm sure it's no more toxic than the swimming pool at the campsite," I said with glee.

"Can we head back?" Joanne asked, perhaps thinking she would prefer to spend some time with her new friends at the leisure park.

"Might as well," I conceded. "Now, where's that silly dog got to?"

"There she is," Joanne pointed to Romany who was a short distance away. She appeared to be stalking a small brown wading bird.

"ROW-MAN-EE!" I shouted, but my call was ignored.

Suddenly the little dog ran ahead, perhaps intending to chase after the bird, but waders are wary of predators and too fast for a pudgy lap dog. Romany did her best, jinking wildly to the right as the bird flew past her nose, but her lack of flexibility caused a loss of traction and our white puppy slid sideways into a shallow puddle. The resulting splash of cooling water seemed to delight her and she immediately jumped up and repeated the slide into the next puddle. We both laughed at her unusual antics, but enough was enough.

"ROW-MAN-EE!" I shouted, but my call was unheeded.

"Let me try," Joanne said. "ROW-MANEEE!" she shouted. Again, no joy. Then she stuck two fingers into her mouth and gave a piercing whistle, which Romany disregarded.

I wiggled a finger in my ear. "Please warn me if you're going to do that again."

The little dog raced about madly, her eyes wide in excitement, leaning over like a bike racer and using her shoulders to surf along the mud. Each 'surf' sprayed water, and stinking estuary mud, several feet into the air and all along each flank of her previously white coat. All the time, she ignored our ever more desperate calls to return. We could do no more than stand back and wait. Joanne reached into her pocket and pulled out a muesli bar.

"You want half?" she asked.

"Oh great," I said, "dinner *and* a show!"

"That dog's gone nuts, it must be the heat getting to her," Joanne said, shaking her head.

"I've never seen anything like it," I agreed.

There was nothing to do but wait, so together we counted the 'mud surfs' and added our own commentary.

"That was a good one," I said. "Easily nine points."

Joanne disagreed. "Not enough shoulder on that one, hardly any spray at all."

After 12 slides, Romany appeared to be slowing, and when the next surfing attempt left her on her back in the centre of the puddle, she'd had enough. With a wiggle and a squirm, she righted herself and pretended to hear our calls for the first time. As she trotted back from this never-to-be-repeated game, there was a huge grin on her mud smeared face. When you combine the modern sophistication of grey with the earthy qualities of beige, you get a colour called greige. In nature, greige is the natural colour of stonework and many types of wildlife. As the stinking mud dried in the baking hot sun, it also became the colour of our previously white puppy. Joanne and I thought the event was hilarious.

"What the hell have you done to Romany?" Lesley wailed, staring at the little dog in outright disbelief.

"We didn't do anything," I pleaded. "Romany went off and began mud surfing. She kept sliding into the puddles."

"We called her back, but she wouldn't come," Joanne added helpfully.

"Don't be ridiculous!" Lesley said. "You must have encouraged her."

"Encouraged her?" I asked, incredulously. "How would I do that? I could hardly give her directions."

Romany didn't help our case. Sensing the rising argument, her tail was down and she was doing a particularly good job of looking pathetic and mistreated.

"I'm sure you two had something to do with it. Look at her!" Lesley tried to pick Romany up, but the smell hit and she thought better of the idea. "Uh! What a stink! You'll have to wash her off. She can't come into the caravan smelling like that."

There was a familiar finality to that instruction. Joanne and I knew better than to argue. So, we collected our stuff together and headed back to the caravan park. Like the distant echo of departing thunder, Lesley added a final instruction.

"And you can wash your feet while you're at it!"

We trudged our way back to the caravan, where we collected a dog towel and some shampoo, and headed back to the wash house to clean our feet and shower the dog. It was warm, so I figured the outside hosepipe would do fine. I expected Romany to disagree, but by then I wasn't feeling particularly sympathetic.

As I was tying the dog lead to the tap, a lady spotted us and came over.

"Oh what a pretty dog," she gushed. "And such an unusual coat. What do you call that colour?"

For a moment, I considered explaining how Romany had just invented the new sport of estuary mud surfing, and how I hoped it may soon become an equal to the dog agility competitions, but I was tired and hungry. So I lied.

"It's called greige," I said. "It's very rare in the breed."

She seemed happy and, with a smile and a nod, went on her way. We gave Romany a good scrubbing, but it took two lots of shampoo and several rinses before the greige dog became white again. Fortunately, the water was quite warm so she didn't complain too much. Once Romany was dried and fluffed up,

Joanne and I washed our feet and we headed back to the caravan, just in time to meet Lesley for lunch. Joanne and I tried again to plead our innocence regarding the mud surfing, but Lesley remained typically sceptical. She still is.

***

Notwithstanding the trials and tribulations of being a dog owner, there is no doubt they are fun to have around, and great therapy. Whenever I'm feeling a little down, or stressed, or happy, or if I am busy working, I know my dogs will always be there, with a wag of the tail and a lick for my hand. And the time we spend walking our dogs is never wasted. Aside from the obvious benefits gained through regular exercise, dog walking is a great time for thinking and talking in a relaxed atmosphere. Something Lesley and I did many times during the early weeks of my garden leave. Our favourite walking route was through Wivenhoe Wood, a short drive from our house.

The wood covers an area of around 40 acres, between Essex University and the town of Wivenhoe, and sits on a hill overlooking the river Colne. I'm no expert, but I understand this well-managed wood has a wide variety of trees and shrubs, including sweet chestnut, oak, ash, sycamore, birch, hawthorn, alder, elder, crack willow, cherry, holly, larch, and Scots pine. There are also large areas of hazel for coppicing. It's well worth a visit, if you are in the area. Despite being so close to several busy roads and the bustling city of Colchester, Wivenhoe Wood, with its well-maintained paths and stunning spring displays of bluebells, is an oasis of calm. It was the one place that I would miss if we moved away, and that possibility was becoming more likely with each conversation.

During the first fortnight of my garden leave, Lesley and I spent hours chewing over the numbers and discussing the options we faced. The autumn weather was mild and dry, so we made the best of our strolls in the wood, sometimes completing the looped walks two or three times, and only stopping when the poor dogs refused to go any further.

As much as we liked our home, it soon became clear we were going to move. We both had a strong desire for change. So we committed to selling our house and finding a new home as quickly as possible. But where should we go?

We were hardly veteran globetrotters. Lesley had only ever lived in Birmingham or Essex, and before we were married, most of my life had been spent in Scotland and Norfolk. Our family holidays were typically British: Skegness, Wales, Norfolk, and Somerset. Apart from business trips, our overseas adventures were limited to a few recent holidays to Egypt, Tunisia, and a couple of off-season late booking gambles that took us to Greece and Spain.

Initially, the best we could do was to draw up a wish list of things we wanted or needed from our new home and, although it wasn't comprehensive, it gave us some rules to work to. Starting with the location, we decided we wanted to be close enough to visit our families in Norfolk and Essex within a day. Travelling by road for six hours, we could consider houses on the south coast of England, as far west as Devon and Wales and north to the Lake District. If we included rail travel, then Cornwall and the Scottish borders came into range, while if we added budget air travel, then Ireland, Scotland, France, Spain and Portugal were also possibilities, providing the house was reasonably near the airport.

The type of property we wanted was always going to be limited by budget and availability, but there were a few things we both agreed on. Our dream property would probably not be a newly-built house; we both preferred homes with some personality, even if it was slightly eccentric. It would have some land, perhaps several acres, giving enough room to grow plenty of vegetables and enough space for our dogs to run free. Ideally the house would be remote enough to provide a sense of freedom and privacy, but close enough to shops and essential services to remain feasible.

It needed to be big enough to accommodate all our oak dining room furniture and several display cabinets, as well as having a large kitchen and at least three bedrooms. We also wanted to be able to add a separate wing or building, should we need to care for our elderly parents, or start a B&B at some point. We were happy to consider a renovation project, even something requiring substantial work, provided there was sufficient budget left over to pay someone else to do the bulk of the work. Lesley declined to describe her dream house any further, saying only that she would 'know it when she saw it'.

With the 'what' decided, we tackled the problem of 'where'.

5. An Atlas and a Pin?

"How much?" my daughter said, her surprise obvious through the crackle of her mobile phone. In the background I could hear the unmistakable sound of a railway station tannoy. I guessed she was probably at Liverpool Street station, on her way home from London.

I told her again what the estate agent had recommended as a selling price for our house.

"Good God! That's way more than you paid for it, isn't it?"

"It's more than three times what we paid," I said. "Even allowing for the renovations we did, it's still a substantial profit. It doesn't make us rich, but along with my redundancy and some savings, it's enough to start afresh."

"That's good," she said. "Did the estate agent think it will sell?"

"It seems that way. We had three different companies do a valuation," I replied. "They seemed very positive, and all the valuations were pretty close. You know how it is though, they want our business and the commission, so they're going to talk up our prospects. But putting that aside, the market seems buoyant, so I guess it's a good time to sell."

"Which agent are you using, or are you going with all of them?"

"We're going to try using one of those posh agents for a month and see how we get on. Apparently, we've turned our little hovel into a very desirable village property," I explained. "They're showing the house as their feature property in their adverts. It's in *House and Home* and *Country Living* magazines. Your mum said it looked so nice, she wanted to buy it."

Joanne laughed. "Have you decided where you want to move to?"

"Not yet. We've done a little speculative window shopping, but nothing serious," I said. "It's a tough decision. Yesterday we tried using an atlas and a pin."

"That sounds like Mummy's idea"

"It was only a bit of fun, but you're right," I admitted.

"How did it go?" Joanne asked.

"Not well," I said. "First she stuck the pin in my thumb."

41

"Accidentally, of course."

"I'm not convinced," I joked. "Then she hit the North Sea and a service station on the M1 motorway."

"Not quite what you had in mind for your dream home?"

"Once Mummy stopped messing around, the game was quite informative," I confessed. "Every place she chose turned out to be unsuitable. At least the list is getting shorter. Now we have a valuation for our house, we've a better idea of the budget we'll have, so our search should have a little more intent."

"Go to Spain," Joanne said. "I can come for free holidays."

"It'd be nice to have you, but I think Spain would be too hot and dry for us. Too hot for me, and too dry for your mum to garden. Essex is bad enough for drought, especially this summer. Much as it's nice for a holiday, I think that the gardener in her would be miserable within a year."

"Really?" my daughter asked. "Surely she'd just grow something else?"

"I'm not so sure," I said. "She likes lush green gardens, and I like lush green golf courses. Anyway, we watched a documentary the other day about how some Brits in Spain lost their homes because of some dodgy planning. It put us right off – at least for the time being."

"I'm sure that was just a one-off problem," she said.

"It probably was, but it made us think," I admitted. "You'd have thought Europe was a pretty safe bet for home buyers, but most countries have peculiar planning rules and local regulations that can catch out the inexperienced. Apparently, France has all these local districts, each with their own officials. It can all be rather confusing. Even Scotland has different rules to England. When my mum bought that land in Skye, she had to employ two solicitors. The whole thing was a nightmare. It took months."

"What about a job?" she asked, always the practical one.

"Well, that's the other thing," I said, "I've–"

"Hang on," Joanne interrupted, "I'm just getting on the train."

I imagined her jostling through the crowd to find a seat. It was a familiar scene, and one I was glad to be away from. I waited until she was seated before resuming the conversation.

"Right, I've got a seat," she said. "I'll probably lose the signal once the train pulls out."

"I don't miss that daily torture," I said. "I don't want to go back to commuting again, that's for sure."

"I don't blame you. I wish I didn't have to commute." Her voice sounded tired. "Anyway, what will you do for work?"

"I've no idea," I remarked. "Work isn't very high on my list of priorities just now."

"Really? That doesn't sound like you at all. You're usually so organised."

"Truth be told, until we've sold this place and bought another, I can't begin looking for work. I don't even know which country we'll be in, or how much money we're going to need."

"That must be nice. Most people have to find a job first, and then figure how to commute or buy a house nearby."

"It is, but only if things work out," I admitted. "If we stay in the British Isles, at least I won't have to learn a language before I can find another job."

"*Parlez vous francais?*" she joked.

"Not much. Anyway, that's not why I called. As this is going to be our last Christmas in Essex, we thought it would be nice to have you and Muriel over for Christmas dinner. What do you think?"

"Sure, that'll be lovely," Joanne said. "How does Muriel feel about the possibility of her daughter moving overseas?"

"She's been really supportive," I said. "Perhaps she's hoping for free holidays in the sun as well."

"If she is, you'd better move somewhere warm, that's for sure!"

"No problem. Where would you prefer? Barbados, Australia, or should we just buy a yacht?" I joked.

"Ooh! A yacht would be nice, we could–"

I'm sure she had more to say, but the connection was lost. I went back to the computer and continued my internet search for our new house.

***

When my wife says "I've been thinking" it sends chills down my spine, as it's generally followed with a request to relocate the newly erected greenhouse, knock down a wall, build a taller house, or paint the planet a different colour. I usually counter humorously.

"Now, dear, I thought we discussed this and decided you were going to stop thinking for a while."

To which she traditionally responds by delivering a loving punch to my arm, worthy of a heavyweight boxer. It's all part of the give-and-take present in a healthy marriage.

One evening, about a week into the house hunting process, Lesley sidled up to me in the small room I used as my office.

"Nick?" she said as sweetly as a little girl about to ask her father for a pony. "I've been thinking."

I glanced away from the computer and eyed my wife suspiciously over the top of my reading glasses. In the weeks leading up to my stress event, she had become equally gloomy and tired, almost bordering on depression. Now as I looked into her pretty blue eyes, I could see a new sparkle of enthusiasm and hope. Her long brown hair was tied up with a frilly band, exposing the soft curve of her neck and she was wearing a white blouse and beige hipsters that accentuated her trim figure.

Moments earlier Lesley had returned from a trip to town to get some shopping, and now she was holding a copy of *Smallholder* magazine. I noticed Brandy and Romany were happily dancing around my wife's heels, perhaps sensing her excitement. Suspecting something big was coming my way, I turned and gave her my full attention. Lesley drew herself up to her full height, took a deep breath and with a huge smile, delivered the punch line.

"I-R-E-L-A-N-D!"

"Ireland?" I asked. "What about Ireland?"

"We could move to Ireland!"

"We could?"

"Yes!" she said, triumphantly.

"Really?" I asked sceptically.

"Yes!" she replied with exasperation.

"But why Ireland, doesn't it always rain there?"

"Not all the time – silly! Anyway, I wouldn't mind."

Remembering how she had "felt a bit cold" in the fifty-degree midday heat during a recent trip to Egypt, I raised my eyebrows until they got to within a few inches of my receding hairline.

"Are you sure?"

She gave a big sigh. "Look, forget that for a minute. It's a good idea. I've been looking at houses in this," she waved the magazine at me, "and Ireland is the best. It's cheaper than France, closer than Scotland, and the economy is doing well. They call it the Celtic Tiger." Her enthusiasm was infectious.

I nodded at the magazine. "Go on then, I'll bite."

She gave me another beaming smile and, leaning over, pointed to an advertisement in the magazine. It showed a small cottage without a roof, overlooking a beautiful valley. The text read, "Pile of stones on two acres with optional donkey, outline planning permission for a four-bedroom house – €58,000." The honesty and humour of the advertisement was immediately very attractive. There was a website, a name, and a phone number. I felt compelled to investigate further.

With a little internet research, it didn't take long to discover the estate agent who placed the advertisement was based in County Clare, in the west of Ireland. Alan Sykes is a quirky English fellow and by all accounts the go-to guy for the type of property we wanted. He has won awards for his honesty as an estate agent although presumably not from his competitors, some of whom might view such dubious values as a breach of a secret code. To the naïve house buyer, it can sometimes seem that an honest estate agent is as rare as a delivery arriving on time, or a celebrity admitting to an affair, or a computer security patch actually patching your security. In any event, we were intrigued enough to look at his website. I pulled up a second chair so Lesley could see.

There appeared to be hundreds of properties on offer, from small plots of soggy earth with little prospect of ever being anything but small plots of soggy earth, to huge mansions with swimming pools and helicopter landing pads. The website was conveniently arranged by price, so it was easy to review every property within our budget. It quickly became clear Lesley was correct. Compared to the other countries we'd looked at, there were considerably more properties available in Ireland of the style we were looking for, and many were well within our price range. Neither of us had visited Ireland, but I had lived in Scotland for a few years as a child, and later holidayed there with Lesley. Although not quite the same, Ireland at least offered the prospect of being reasonably similar and therefore potentially familiar. The

CIA website (an excellent resource of information) revealed that since the signing of the Good Friday Agreement, and the ending of The Troubles, Ireland had developed a healthy and expanding economy. It also boasted a very low crime rate and slightly better weather than some of the alternatives like Wales and Scotland.

"What do you think?" Lesley asked, leaning into my shoulder as she peered at the computer screen. Her hair smelled like apples and vanilla.

"I think you might be onto something," I said. "It hadn't occurred to me to look west. Ireland is a safe and friendly country, with a healthy economy and lots of delightful houses for sale."

"Bit of a hidden gem then?" Lesley smiled.

"It certainly looks that way," I admitted. "Also, Ireland is very much a part of Europe and the free travel area. That means we could live there without any visas or permits. It would be the same as moving to Scotland, or Norfolk!"

Lesley was positively beaming.

"And there's something else," I added. "They use the Euro, and right now the Sterling exchange rate is excellent, making these houses about 25 per cent cheaper. In my book, that changes possible to plausible."

"I think we need a holiday." My lovely wife was almost fizzing with excitement. "We should plan a trip to Ireland. If we like it, perhaps we can do a little house hunting while we're there."

"I agree." I nodded and pointed at the advert. "Let's give this guy a call."

6. Fifty Shades of Green

On a map, the outline of the island of Ireland looks a little like the craggy face of an old man, facing to the left. Dublin sits at the back of the head and the unruly mop of hair at the top is the northern counties, from Dundalk in the east to Strabane in the north. The eyes are below Donegal, and to the south is a bulbous nose running from Sligo to Galway. The Loop Head peninsula is the top lip, the mighty River Shannon the mouth, and the Dingle peninsula the chin and beard. Because Shannon Airport was a one hour flight from Stansted, our local airport, I decided to focus our house hunting on the 50-mile swathe of land along the north side of the River Shannon, from Loop Head, past Kilrush, Ennis, Shannon Airport, Limerick, and inland to the spectacular scenery around Lough Derg.

As Mr Sykes' phone seemed to be permanently engaged, Lesley went outside to feed our three chickens and the aviary birds. While I waited for her to return, I looked for some information about County Clare and periodically stabbed the redial button on the telephone. What I found certainly piqued my interest.

Although County Clare and Essex were very similar in size, Clare had a population of just 109,000, whereas Essex was almost bursting at the seams with 1.78 million inhabitants. I love quiet open spaces, so I was intrigued to discover there were less people in County Clare than there were in Colchester, the county town of Essex. The pictures I saw clearly showed 'The Banner County' to be a beautiful place, from the many picturesque lakes feeding the wide, slow-flowing waters of the River Shannon, through the bare limestone and desolate magnificence of the Burren, to the wild Atlantic Ocean, crashing its waves onto the rugged Cliffs of Moher.

The countryside appeared to be comprised of rolling hills and large flat valleys, dotted with tiny fields enclosed by dry stone walls – a landscape perfect for livestock farming and tourists, but little else. However, County Clare boasted several excellent golf courses, including those at Dromoland Castle and Lahinch, which is ranked as one of the best golf courses in the world. The County town of Ennis seemed unspoilt by the march of time, with the pictures showing no signs of obscene modern retail structures or high-rise apartment blocks. Quite the opposite, the narrow streets were lined with small, family owned shops and bustling with happy people. Although it looked much like England in the 1960s, the pictures had only been taken the previous summer during the Ennis street festival.

Despite Lesley's assertion that she wouldn't mind a bit of rain, I still visited the website of Met Éireann, the Irish National Meteorological Service, and checked out the local climate. With its exposure to the Atlantic Ocean, County Clare certainly seemed to get its share of wind and rain, almost double that of Essex. We probably wouldn't see many hosepipe bans in Ireland – a nice change from the regular droughts we experienced in East Anglia. The warm waters of the Gulf Stream gave County Clare a more moderate climate than Essex, with slightly cooler summers and generally warmer winters. To my mind, it was a good trade-off, something I was sharing enthusiastically with Lesley when I heard a distant tinny voice. It took a moment for me to realise that my constant stabbing of the redial button had been successful.

"Hello?" I said, grabbing at the phone. "Is this the estate agent?"

"Yes. Alan speaking. But we're called auctioneers in Ireland." The accent was British and a little clipped. I guessed Mr Sykes was having a busy day, so I got straight down to business.

"Hi. I'm Nick Albert. My wife and I live in England and we're thinking of coming to Ireland to look at some houses."

"Aha..." Caution and a little disinterest conveyed with a single grunt. I pressed on.

"We saw your advert in *Smallholder* magazine. The one about the pile of stones and the optional donkey. It's very good," I added.

"That's sold," he said, unapologetically. "But the donkey's still for sale."

"Err, no thanks. We were looking at your website. There's several properties we like," I said, trying hard to convey my enthusiasm.

"Very good," he replied, but his voice suggested otherwise.

"Ask him about this one," Lesley hissed, her finger stabbing at one of the property papers I had printed earlier.

48

"We are quite interested in the house with outbuildings on five acres. It's near Scariff, a place called Toba-naught."

"Oh, you mean Tobernagat." He corrected my pronunciation and confirmed the price.

"Yes," I said, "that's the one!"

"It's sold," he replied.

"Oh dear," I said.

Lesley helpfully stabbed at another paper and nudged me hard with her elbow. "What about…"

"Hang on a sec…"

I could hear voices in the background, and then snippets of a conversation. I waited.

"What's he saying?" Lesley asked.

"He's talking to someone else," I whispered.

"Right!" A voice boomed in my ear. I moved the telephone away to protect my eardrums from further damage. "You have my undivided attention."

I tried again. "My wife and I–"

"Hang on," he interrupted again, "the other phone's ringing. I've been waiting for a call."

Without another word, he put me on hold. Muzak assaulted my ear, proving I hadn't been cut-off. I stabbed the speakerphone button, allowing Lesley to share the entertainment. It wasn't a pleasant and soothing Irish tune, cleverly chosen to help pass the time and sooth our stress while we waited. This was a bastardised electronic version of Danny Boy, played a little too quickly and rather loud.

"Doesn't he know were calling from overseas?" Lesley asked.

"I did say." I gave her an apologetic shrug.

"Hello?" The voice blasted from the speakerphone, making us both jump. "Look, I'm sorry about that. It was a call from America. You really do have my attention now. I promise, OK?"

It wasn't OK, but I said it was. I introduced myself and explained again that Lesley and I were interested in looking at rural properties with a few acres of land, and we were considering relocating to Ireland.

"New or second-hand?" he snapped.

It was a distinction I had never encountered when shopping for houses. In my head, I applied the motor vehicle analogy.

"We'd prefer a second-hand house – with some land. Something with some character," I explained.

"When are you coming over?" he asked.

"We haven't booked our flights yet," I admitted, "but probably next week. It'll be our first visit. We'd like to arrange several viewings."

"Not a problem. When you have your flights booked, just send me an email with the details of the properties you want to see and I'll fix it up."

"Alright, that'll be great," I said.

Lesley waved another set of property details at me.

"Before I go, can you tell me about another property?"

"No point," he said, his voice was bafflingly cheerful.

"Excuse me?" I was confused.

"The thing is, because the economy is doing so well, the Irish buyers are only interested in driving a black Mercedes and buying new-build houses. They're popping up all over the place, identical houses on ¾ acre plots. Bloody eyesores if you ask me," he snapped, "they're like concrete jelly moulds. Anyway, as a result, many second-hand things, principally cars and houses, are more difficult to sell."

"So that's good for us?" I suggested.

"Yes and no," he said. "Second-hand house prices here are low, but they're selling like hotcakes, mostly to overseas buyers from England, Germany, and America. Many of the properties are never occupied, they're just being banked for future sale when the prices rise. Some investors are even buying directly from my website. That call I just took was from an American millionaire, he's bought five properties this month alone."

"Good grief," I said.

"Anyway, there's no point discussing any properties until you're here. Otherwise you'll just be disappointed." His voice softened a little. "But don't worry, there are loads to choose from. Plenty of old farmhouses with lots of character. Book your flights, and we'll talk."

"OK, I'll send you an email." Before ending the call, I had one more question. "Do you like it there?"

"It's a bit cold and wet sometimes, and the Irish are all mad," he joked, "but it's a wonderful country. I love it – and so will you!"

"I think we just might," I replied.

**

When we started married life 22 years before, Lesley and I had a Victorian terraced house with 120 feet of garden. Later we progressed to a two-bedroom cottage with three quarters of an acre. So, the prospect of owning a smallholding of up to five acres, even if it was a bit of a renovation project, was extremely attractive. Furthermore, we were encouraged to discover Ryanair had three daily return flights from London Stansted directly to Shannon Airport, which was just a short drive from Ennis. As our daughter and Lesley's mother both lived close to Stansted, with a flight time of around an hour, we could visit door to door far more quickly than we could have driven from Wales, Scotland or Cornwall. It was time to begin the tricky business of house hunting.

In quick succession we booked flights, reserved a hire car, and arranged accommodation at a B&B a little way north of Ennis. As instructed, we created a primary list of 'must-see' properties and emailed it to Alan, along with our travel arrangements. All the properties had at least an acre of land and all but one were second-hand houses. After adding a couple more houses from other, more traditional-looking, auctioneers in Ennis, I had a nice tidy list detailing our itinerary for the five-day trip. We also kept a back-up list of some other houses that appeared to be less attractive, but might still be worth a visit. The week we had to wait before our flight to Ireland dragged by like dreams in treacle. As excited as children waiting for Christmas, we kept re-reading the property details for each house and checking the internet to see if our favourites were still available, or whether anything interesting had been added. Finally, the great day arrived.

It was a cold and frosty morning near the end of 2003. We'd booked our dogs into the kennels, arranged for a friend to tend our chickens, and were just loading our bags into the car before setting off for the airport, when our new neighbour, Richard, walked by.

He was a merchant banker. A tall and elegant man, who always seemed to wear a fine quality suit, a silk tie, and the best brogues. I noticed he walked with long, purposeful steps, not quite a march, but suggestive of a military background. We only knew him and his wife, Ruth, to smile, wave and chat with. He seemed like a nice chap, but as they'd moved in recently, and both he and I worked odd hours, we hadn't had much social contact.

I was aware that all his family were members of the Plymouth Brethren, a religious sect, most obviously because the wives all wore headscarves and walked two paces behind their husbands. I also knew several members of his extended family had recently bought houses in the village. After we shared the usual morning greetings, he pointed to our suitcases.

"Are you off on holiday?" he asked politely.

"Yes," I replied, "we're off to Ireland."

"Oh, how lovely." He seemed genuinely impressed. "Which part?"

"County Clare," Lesley interjected, as excited as a little girl on her way to collect her first pony. "We're looking at houses."

"That's a beautiful part of the country," Richard said. "Are you buying a holiday home?"

"We're thinking of moving there," I admitted. "We've just put this house on the market. The for-sale sign should be going up tomorrow."

As I expanded on our desire to move to a smallholding somewhere out west, his cool grey eyes looked over my shoulder towards our house. I swear I could see the cogs turning in his brain as he calculated and assessed the possibilities. Richard politely waited until I paused my enthusiastic ramble to take a breath.

"How much are you asking?" he said, nodding towards our home.

"Why do you ask, Richard?" I questioned jokingly. "Do you want to buy it?"

"Well, you never know," he said with a very serious face. "I'd like to buy a house for my parents, something closer to our home, and you can't get much closer than this."

Realising he was serious, I told him our asking price. Richard didn't flinch or blink, he just nodded.

Lesley was smiling. "Well, if you want to look around, just let us know."

"Yes, I'd like that," Richard said. "When are you returning from your trip?"

"We'll be back on Friday night," she said.

"Actually," I looked at my watch, "we have a little time before our flight."

"That would be splendid!" He gave me a curt nod. "I'll just summon my wife."

I was pleased we'd spruced the place up ready for the estate agent's photographs, as Richard and Ruth toured the house for about 30 minutes. Although Lesley and I stood back respectfully, we could still hear them making all the right noises about knocking down walls and adding toilets and chairlifts. After viewing the house, they had a quick look at our garage before we took a turn around the garden.

"Ooh, you have chickens!" Ruth exclaimed. "We love chickens. It would be so nice to have fresh eggs every day."

Lesley and I shared a knowing look.

As rescued battery hens, transported from that miserable existence into the luxury and comfort of retirement in rural Essex, we'd expected our chickens to be happy and grateful. It was not to be. Despite being showered with love, kindness and the best free-range chicken food, they remained stubbornly vicious, spiteful, and thoroughly deserving of their names: Hitler, Stalin, and Khan. Regardless of our best intentions, the chickens would attack anyone collecting eggs, or cleaning the coop. Such tasks required alacrity, a steely nerve, and the wearing of the face and hand protection otherwise reserved for commercial chainsaw users. Even so, any area of exposed flesh would instantly receive several fast pecks or, worse, Stalin's trademark bite and twist, delivered with sufficient force to remove a chunk of skin. Such ingratitude should have been rewarded with a swift neck wringing, but being a couple of old softies, we just cared for our mentally damaged charges as best we could and soldiered on.

"If you buy our house, you can keep the chickens," I said graciously.

"That would be just splendid!" Ruth clapped her hands in joy. "Wouldn't it be splendid, Richard? Just imagine, fresh eggs every day."

There was a momentary lull in the conversation where I should have mentioned our disappointment at the dwindling crop of eggs from our aging chickens, or their almost legendary violence towards all trespassers in their pen, but I didn't. Poor Ruth looked so happy, it would have been a shame to ruin her day.

At the end of our tour, Richard thanked us for our time and wished us well on our trip. In a perfect world, they would have bought the house right then, but it wasn't to be. Still, at worst we had wasted 30 minutes and gained a little confidence about the chances of selling our house.

***

Aside from the rush-hour traffic, the short drive to Stansted was uneventful, and after parking our car and riding the transfer bus, we joined the milling, multi-cultural confusion of people in the airport concourse. Despite the immense crowds, we soon found our check-in desk and were greeted with a smile worthy of long lost friends returning to the homeland. The assistant efficiently processed our baggage and presented us with our boarding cards. She was a very pretty Irish girl, with a charming, soft, lilting accent. When she said, "Enjoy your visit," I believe she meant every word.

Standing in the long queue of frustrated, anxious and sweating travellers as we waited to pass through security was a much less pleasant experience. Whenever I exit the metal detector doorway without setting off the alarm, I always feel like raising my arms aloft, shouting, "YES!" and doing a little dance. Given my rising enthusiasm, I was tempted, but I wisely resisted the urge. The crowds airside were even worse than we had expected, so it was all we could do to score a cup of tea and visit the loo before it was time to board our plane.

Despite the reputation of budget airlines, I have always found Ryanair to be quick and efficient. The flight to Ireland was timely, smooth, and enjoyably uneventful. I love flying, but I am rather prone to airsickness, so I spent most of the flight looking out the window. Through breaks in the cloud I could see the ferries below, looking like toy boats, sailing between Holyhead and Dublin. I wondered if we would be making the same trip soon, with our furniture and dogs. The sky started to clear as we passed over the Irish coastline, and almost immediately the pilot set the aircraft on a gradual descent towards Shannon airport.

I was struck by how lush and beautiful the land looked, and by how much space there appeared to be between each village and town. We flew over forests and endless fields, tiny plots of land, each separated from the next by dry stone walls. Johnny Cash sang about Ireland's 40 shades of green, but I swear I could easily have counted 50. In no time, we were passing the spectacular Slieve Bloom Mountains and then Lough Derg at the base of the River Shannon. As we flew over traffic-free roads and a castle, I could see Limerick to our left along with some houses and an industrial estate.

The plane flew lower, and just as it seemed we were going to land in a field, the runway appeared beneath us, and we were down. Instantly the spoilers deployed, the engines roared in full reverse thrust and the brakes groaned as the pilot attempted to leave the runway at the first available exit. My seatbelt dug into my lap for a moment as we were thrown forward, and I heard a few people give a yelp of surprise at our seemingly harsh treatment. But seconds later the pressure ceased, only to be replaced by the ear-splitting trumpets of Ryanair celebrating another on-time landing.

The stewardess welcomed us all to Ireland and asked that we remain in our seats until the plane had stopped and the captain had switched off the fasten seatbelts sign, an instruction that was completely ignored by almost every passenger. After breezing through immigration, where the official merely glanced at our passports before casually waving us forward, we passed through the delightfully quiet arrivals hall, retrieved our bags, and walked a negligible distance to collect our hire car. After the stress of leaving England, arriving in Ireland was a revelation. Within 20 minutes of touching down at Shannon Airport, we had driven out of the gates and were enjoying our first view of Ireland.

I soon got the hang of our hire car and, with only one wrong turn and two additional orbits of a roundabout, we navigated our way to the dual carriageway leading north towards Ennis and our B&B. Although it was already late afternoon, as we were 500 miles further west, there was a good chance it would still be light when we reached our destination. The road signage in Ireland is similar to that of most European countries and easy enough to follow, but the traffic lights differ by not giving the amber 'get ready' warning before changing to 'go'. Fortunately, unlike England, nobody seemed to care if I was a little tardy pulling away.

My initial impression of Ireland during the drive to Ennis was that it was green, clean and wonderfully quiet.

"This is lovely. Everything's so lush and green," Lesley commented once we were safely underway.

"Yes, it is," I replied. "And what don't you see?"

Lesley gave me a frown and a shrug.

"Look at that bridge," I pointed, "and the hedgerow."

"I don't see people, or any cars, if that's what you mean. It's as if the world ended while we were loading the car."

"True," I admitted, "but I was referring to the lack of rubbish and graffiti."

"Oh yes! I guess you don't always notice what isn't there," Lesley commented.

"It is lovely though."

"Look!" It was Lesley's turn to point. "It's a castle."

"It looks big," I said. "We must visit, if there's time. What's it called?"

"Bun something..." She leaned forward and squinted at the sign. "Bunratty castle and Folk Park. It sounds like a fun day out."

"It does," I admitted. Although I smiled, suddenly I wasn't so happy. I looked in my mirror for the third time in as many minutes. "Now what's going on here?"

"What's wrong?"

"We're on a completely empty motorway, but this car behind is tailgating me." Glancing over my shoulder, I could clearly see the lady driver's impassive face. I could see her blue eyes, the rings on her fingers, but I couldn't see the car bonnet or number plate. "She can't be more than a couple of feet away. What the hell is she playing at?"

"Did you cut her up?" Lesley asked, somewhat unhelpfully.

"No!" I insisted. "We haven't seen a car for ten miles. She just caught up and started tailgating."

"Try slowing down a bit, she might pass."

"I did. Look, I'm down to 40," I said, pointing at the speedometer. Although Ireland had just converted to kilometres, most road signs and cars were still showing miles.

"Try speeding up," my wife instructed. "She'll probably drop back."

I did, all the way to 90 miles an hour, but our new friend stuck to my bumper like a limpet.

"This is starting to feel like one of those movies that ends with, 'and then he turned the gun on himself', except it's a woman driving." At that moment, I noticed something telling. "Oh, look!"

I pointed at the other carriageway, which was completely empty, save for one car being tailgated by two others. It seemed we had stumbled upon a dangerous driving habit that was somewhat of a custom in Ireland. Apparently unaware of her transgression, our determined bumper sticker stuck with us for another mile, before turning off at the next junction. We gave her a friendly wave, which was returned, along with a happy smile.

"How different to home," Lesley commented.

I had to agree. Tailgating of this sort, in most other countries, would quickly lead to fist waving, shouting and physical violence. But in Ireland it was completely ignored, or treated as a local tradition. Perhaps there is an exception in their highway code. I did wonder if the same rules applied when standing in a bank or shop. If I found myself in a queue behind the lady who had just tailgated my car for the last ten miles, was I expected to stand one inch from her bottom? And if I did, would she comment? Would my wife? Either way, we had learned an early lesson about Ireland.

"Perhaps not everything here is as it seems…"

The motorway ended abruptly and a series of skid marks led to a roundabout. We followed the signposts towards Ennis and found ourselves driving along a quiet country road. To the sides, the unspoilt countryside stretched into the distance. The rich green fields were divided with drystone walls and dotted with bushes and trees. In places, we saw small stone enclosures with rusty corrugated iron roofs, presumably built to provide livestock with some measure of protection from the elements.

Ahead, the road was narrower than a modern British highway, and lacking any road markings. The embankments at the roadside rose to block our view of the countryside, the feeling of enclosure was further enhanced by the trees that arched overhead like interlocked arms. Travelling towards us from this green tunnel, was a vintage Morris Traveller – clearly not a restoration, but a car in everyday use. Instantly I was transported back to the England of my youth. Recalling memories of riding with my father in his black 1959 Ford Popular, with its little engine purring gently and the sweet smell of the leather seats. I thought of the long careless summers I had spent hunting for grasshoppers and playing hide-and-seek in the woods. The memories were so vivid, I could almost pluck them from the air with my hand. A lump of nostalgia gripped my chest and I felt my eyes water.

"This is nice," I commented, my voice thick with emotion. "I feel as if we've driven back to the 1960s"

"Perhaps we have," Lesley smiled. "It's certainly unspoilt."

Our route to the B&B took us through the village of Clarecastle. To our right was the blocky remains of the namesake castle and an antiques centre, and off to the left we could see the imposing bulk of the Roche pharmaceutical plant sitting high above the banks of the river Fergus. Even though this huge factory seemed out of place in such a pretty landscape, I imagined it would be welcome as a major employer for the area.

We soon reached the town of Ennis, and although we only passed through along the main road, by catching every set of traffic lights, we had a few moments to glance around. My first impression was that there seemed to be a lot of large, stern, grey buildings, reminiscent of Edinburgh in Scotland. To our left was the imposing bulk of St. Flannan's College, which looked suspiciously like a Victorian prison or a military barracks, and would not have been out of place as a school for trainee wizards. To our right lay the bulk of the town, where the skyline of low buildings was interrupted by the towering spire of the cathedral and a nearby clock tower. Lesley pointed to a sign for a golf course, and two miles further she spotted a second. Although I knew Ireland had more golf courses per capita than anywhere in Europe, it was reassuring to see there were two so near to Ennis.

There was more traffic now, and we were keen to reach our destination, so we stopped sightseeing and drove on. After passing the general hospital, which outwardly appeared unchanged since the 1950s, we headed north to where we spotted the first major sign of industrialisation since entering the outskirts of the town. Using the business park as our landmark, we travelled another mile up the Gort road and there we easily found our holiday accommodation. Our first Irish navigation was a resounding success.

The B&B was a large and grand-looking modern house, set well back from the road. It was painted predominately sky blue, with a little white on the pillars and window sills. In the failing light of dusk, I could see a large lake, or perhaps a flooded river, to the rear of the property, and beyond that hills and a few groups of trees. At some point, much of the front lawn had been converted to parking, but there was only one other vehicle, a black Mercedes, covered in a thick layer of frost. As I lugged our bags towards the house, the front door opened and we were greeted by a portly, middle-aged, blonde-haired woman. She smiled and threw her arms wide in greeting.

"Hello!" she boomed. "You must be Lesley and Mick."

"Nick," I corrected. "Yes, we are."

"I'm Mary. Please come in." She smiled warmly.

We shuffled through the door and stood in the hallway while Mary pointed out the guest sitting room and the dining area. The inside of the house felt colder than the outside.

"Breakfast's from nine to ten," she said. "There's no meals, but there's plenty of places in Ennis you can eat."

"Did you say breakfast is at nine?" I asked.

"That's right, Mick. Not too early for you, is it?"

"Hardly," I replied, "It's Nick. We're normally up at seven."

"Early to bed and early to rise," Lesley added.

I noticed a dragon's breath of vapour as she spoke. It was freezing in this house.

"How are you enjoying your holidays, Mick?" Mary asked.

"It's Nick," I said again. "We've just arrived today."

"Oh, you must be tired," she said. "I'll show you to your room. This way."

We followed up the wide staircase. Mary was flapping her hands at her face.

"Goodness! Isn't it warm today?" she asked.

Lesley and I shared a look.

"It's frosty outside," I pointed out.

"Here's your room. I've put you at the front."

Mary threw open the door and stepped aside.

"Here's your keys," she gave them to me, along with another warm smile. "I'll leave you to it, Mick."

"Nick…" I said to her retreating back.

It was a standard double bedroom, not much larger than the standard double bed that almost filled it. The carpet was a dark two-tone red and the beige wallpaper had a darker brown swirly pattern, reminiscent of something that was discontinued in 1972. This oppressive colour scheme was enhanced by several large pictures of Jesus which adorned the walls. His suspicious eyes followed me as I entered the room. High on the wall at the head of the bed, there was a huge wooden crucifix, which threatened the risk of crush injuries, or death, should the headboard move too enthusiastically in the night. I shrugged, at least we had carpets, a nice view of the road, and an ensuite bathroom with a toilet, a sink, and a mouldy shower. Lesley strode across the room and shut the windows.

"It's freezing in here," she said.

I felt the radiator, but whipped my hand away for fear of frostbite. "What's the matter with that woman, can't she feel the cold?"

"It's not her fault. I expect she's going through the *change*," Lesley whispered the last word.

"Oh wonderful," I said. "I'll call her Mrs Menopause."

"Don't you dare!" She gave me a thump.

I dumped our bag onto the bed and watched in horror as the huge crucifix wobbled alarmingly.

"Well, we're not going to get creatively warm in that bed!" I complained. "Come on, let's go to town. I'm starving."

We didn't get very far. Mrs Menopause was waiting for us at the bottom of the stairs.

"Hello, my dears," she said. "Are you going out already?"

"Yes," Lesley replied, "were heading into Ennis to have a meal."

"We've been travelling all day and we're starving," I added, hoping we wouldn't be delayed further.

"I've got you a few leaflets, Mick," Mary said, obviously deaf to my growling stomach. She held out a fistful of brochures. "There's lots of interesting places to visit in Clare."

"Thank you. It's Nick," I said, taking the proffered papers. Despite my impending malnutrition, I appreciated her kindness. "We'll have a look at these over dinner, but we may not have much time for sightseeing, we're looking at houses."

"House hunting, are you?" she exclaimed. "Are you moving to Ireland?"

"We're thinking about it," Lesley said.

"Do you have family here then?"

"No," I admitted, "this is our first trip."

"Oh! Well you're most welcome," Mary said, and I believe she meant it too.

"Thank you," Lesley and I said, in perfect unison.

"Whatever made you choose Ireland, Mick?"

"It's..." I gave up. "There seem to be a lot of nice old houses for sale here."

"We're looking for a smallholding," my wife added.

Mary look shocked. She rocked backwards as if she'd been slapped.

"Why on earth would you want to buy a *second-hand* house?"

"We like old places," Lesley explained. "We want something with character."

"You'll certainly find that in Clare!" she laughed. "Are you sure you wouldn't prefer a nice new-build place? My brother's a builder. He could easily fix you up."

"No, thanks. We've set our heart on a small farm, or an old house with a bit of land."

"On your own heads!" Mary smiled. "I hope you've brought your wellies."

"Aaah!" I exclaimed, slapping my forehead.

Mary kindly offered to lend us two pairs of wellington boots for the week. This was a horrific packing oversight on our part, particularly when house-hunting in rural Ireland in the winter. It gave me some pause for thought. If we were that naïve about footwear, what else were we going to get wrong?

I started the car and turned the heater to full. While we waited for the frost to clear from the windscreen, I gave Alan Sykes a call. We'd arranged to meet him at his office at ten the next morning, but my carefully calculated itinerary had not allowed for breakfast being served at 9 am. I can't abide being late for meetings.

For once Alan answered his phone immediately.

"Hi Alan. It's Nick Albert."

"Who?" he asked.

"Nick and Lesley Albert, from England," I said. "We spoke on the phone and I've sent you emails. We're coming to see you tomorrow."

"You are?"

"Yes!" I said, rather too firmly. "We're here for a week to see a load of properties. You agreed we would meet tomorrow."

"Did I reply to your email?" he asked.

Our house-hunting expedition was not getting off to a good start.

"Yes," I replied. "We arranged to meet at ten at your office." My fingers tapped an angry rhythm on the steering wheel.

"Oh yes. I think I remember," he said, the vagueness in his voice suggested he felt otherwise.

"Actually, we won't be there until around 11. Sorry!"

"That's grand!" he said. "There's no rush. Go into Ennis in the morning and buy some maps."

"We already have a map of Ireland."

"Ordinance Survey?" he asked.

"RAC," I replied.

"No good." His voice held no hint of sympathy for my wasted £3.99. "House hunting here is like hunting for houses. Most of the roads and townlands don't appear on regular maps. You'll need OS maps, or you'll never find any of them. You won't even find my place without a map. Get numbers 52, 57 and 58. That'll do for starters."

"OK. Thanks." I was intrigued and confused but left it at that. There would be time for questions later.

"Call me tomorrow when you have the maps, and I'll give you directions." And with a click he was gone.

I looked at my wife and shrugged. "Alan said we have to buy maps."

8. The Fire Drill

We drove into town without any real idea of where we were headed. Despite going slowly and peering out of the windows as we searched for parking, the short trip was pleasant and uneventful. The other drivers were courteous, patient and understanding. They happily paused to allow us to pull out from side roads, and forgave our lane infractions with a smile and a friendly wave. Compared to driving in London, this was motoring heaven. We found a convenient parking spot directly in front of the grey and glowering bulk of Ennis cathedral, and began walking towards what appeared to be the town centre.

"Do you want to get one of those lottery scratch cards?" I asked, pointing to a man standing outside a newsagent. He was busily scratching away at his card with a coin.

"Do you?" Lesley asked.

As I watched, the man leaned into his car and tossed the scratch card onto the dashboard before striding away. I noticed there were several other used lottery tickets already on the dashboard. No luck again.

"No. The prize would be in euros, so we'd have to buy another suitcase," I joked. "Perhaps later."

Lesley smiled. It made me feel good. It always does.

After living in south east England for so many years, we found walking around Ennis at night to be refreshingly different. Late at night in many British towns and cities, I would be aware of a heavy police presence, public drunkenness, and the constant anticipation of sudden violence. Daylight would reveal streets littered with discarded takeaway containers, broken glass, vomit, and the signs of pointless vandalism. In Ennis, the streets were safe, clean and entirely devoid of any signs of rubbish or graffiti. It felt as if everyone we passed made eye contact, and smiled, and they were willing to stop and chat at the slightest provocation. Initially, we were convinced we were being mistaken for someone else (perhaps someone famous, richer and better looking), but it was soon clear that people were just more open and sociable than we were accustomed to.

One of the attractions of Ireland is how people still have the inclination, and time, to stop and talk to passing friends and strangers. In most British cities, in my experience, if I deliberately made eye contact with random strangers, I would be treated like an escaped mental patient, or end up having a conversation with one. Perhaps, along with the natural affability of the Irish, this tendency to acknowledge the presence of other people comes from the proportionally smaller population. That being said, there were a lot of people walking around Ennis that night, and our random conversations had drawn a small crowd, and were threatening to derail our progress towards hot food and cold beer.

As we stepped away from our sixth chat in as many yards, I could see two other couples eyeing us up, presumably eager to engage in dialogue. I was keen to remain polite, but we were unfed since breakfast, so with a deft sidestep, I pulled Lesley into the first open doorway. We found ourselves in an impossibly busy eatery, called Poets Corner. It was actually a bar and restaurant attached to a corner of the Old Ground Hotel. The room was stunning to behold – like a gentleman's club overrun by twenty families of farmers. It was in two parts, like a bent elbow, with doors to the kitchen at one end and the toilets at the other. The L-shaped bar was constructed from exquisite oak, with a deep polished lustre the colour of old horse chestnut seeds. The matching benches were covered in luxurious green leather, and the walls were lined in oak panels and dotted with pictures of famous poets.

Standing in the doorway at the point of the elbow, we were almost overwhelmed by a wall of noise. It looked as if every available flat surface was being used to balance a plate of food. There must have been a hundred people eating, and everyone was either laughing or talking or both. My first instinct was to do an about turn and seek somewhere quieter to eat, but my olfactory senses were working overtime detecting garlic, fresh herbs, soup, and the rich aroma of perfectly cooked chips. I glanced at a few tables and noticed the plates were piled high with wholesome food, and those that weren't were empty – a sure sign of happy customers. No wonder this place was packed out. My stomach growled so loudly I expected people to turn and stare. Lesley noticed a couple, far to our right who were standing to leave. She nudged me and pointed.

"I'll grab that table, and you get the drinks," she said. "I'll have a coffee."

Acquiring the coffee was easy, but buying my first ever pint of Guinness was a slightly embarrassing affair. As I was reasonably familiar with the British system, where one attracts the attention of the barperson by waving money, and maintains continued 'ownership' through eye contact or conversation until the transaction is complete, I was flummoxed when I ordered my pint and the barman left the job half done and walked away. In my inexperience, I was unaware there is a special technique to pouring the perfect pint of Guinness. It involves half-filling the glass and leaving it to settle, before returning to finish the job a few minutes later.

In between these two stages, the barkeep will usually continue serving several other customers whilst apparently ignoring the person who ordered the Guinness. My British accent, cash waving and protests exposed my inexperience, but a potentially disastrous start to our holiday was avoided when the charmingly patient barkeeper kindly explained the process, before delivering my drink with a smile. There was a perfect shamrock drawn in the foam head.

At our table, I excitedly shared my experience with Lesley before tasting my drink with great formality and care. My pint of Guinness was delicious, well worth the wait, and every bit as nice as the meal that followed. We started with deep bowls of thick and creamy vegetable soup, accompanied by a divine selection of freshly baked breads. For the main course, Lesley had beef wellington with roasted vegetables, and I ordered penne pasta with leeks and mushrooms. Once we had cleaned our soup bowls and eaten the last of our bread, we realised our stomachs were already full. Nevertheless, when the main course arrived, we made a good fist of clearing our plates. It would have been rude not to!

Even though we were sitting rather too close to the toilets, with our food perched on a tiny table, we thoroughly enjoyed our first meal in Ireland. The service was excellent, and our waitress was happy to fill in for the conversations we had avoided outside. "Oh you're English. Are you on your holidays? You're most welcome. Buying a house are you? Good idea! I have two in Bulgaria and an apartment in Spain." It seemed the booming Celtic Tiger economy had brought benefits for everyone. We left a generous tip, I expect she had several mortgages to pay.

Back at our B&B, we bid Mrs Menopause a hearty goodnight and headed up to bed. Even with the windows closed, our room was still freezing. The radiator was stone cold and I suspected it would stay that way. To stay warm under the damp sheet and threadbare blanket, we remained almost fully clothed. I even wore a woolly hat to warm my threadbare head. We huddled together platonically, under the enormous wooden crucifix and the watchful eyes of a dozen pictures of Jesus, and quietly reflected on our first day in the country that could soon become our new home. On balance, we decided things were going well. Lesley's breathing soon became deep and regular as she drifted off to sleep. Perhaps it was the cold, or the wonderful clean air, or the two pints of Guinness I'd consumed, but I was soon deep in the arms of Morpheus as well.

I was woken by a violent pounding on the door. It took a moment to find the light switch in the unfamiliar surroundings, and when I checked my watch I was shocked to discover it was ten to one in the morning. Such an insolent disturbance could only mean one thing – there must be a fire! I shook Lesley into some semblance of wakefulness and threw open the door before it was knocked from its hinges. Fully expecting to see another guest, or a member of the emergency services, I was somewhat taken aback to find our Mrs Menopause, wearing blue hair rollers, a pink dressing gown, fluffy slippers, and carrying a tray.

"I thought you would enjoy some tea and biscuits." She gave me the tray and a warm smile.

"Thank you," I said. "That's very kind." What else could I say?

With my heart pounding and adrenalin flooding our veins, there was no prospect of sleeping for a while. So, we sat up in bed and drank the tea. At least it warmed us up a bit.

This far west in the depths of winter, it doesn't get light until almost 9 am, but the Guinness and late-night tea was taking its toll on my bladder. At 7 am I had to get up. The room was freezing and by the time I crept back into bed, so were my feet. Lesley did not appreciate my stealthy efforts to reheat my chilly appendages, and kicked me away with commendable gusto. Suitably chastised,

I was ordered to make the tea. After hunting around for a few minutes, I risked waking my wife again, but this time I used a gentle shoulder shake.

"Waaat?" she mumbled into her pillow.

"There's no kettle," I said.

She turned over and blinked. "Don't be silly. It'll be in a cupboard. Try under the television."

I looked around the room. "There's no television."

Lesley sat up and looked around. "I didn't notice that," she admitted.

"Me neither. Anyway, I had a good look. There's no kettle." I shrugged apologetically.

"Tea when we're asleep, and no kettle when we're awake." She pulled the blanket over her head. Lesley isn't really a morning person.

To fill the time, I decided to shave and take a shower. At least we could both be washed and dressed and warm, ready to attack breakfast at 9 am. Inevitably, the water for the shower was barely warm. I figured the immersion heater was set to a timer that didn't take account of mad British tourists. Wide awake and freezing cold, we sat up in bed wearing our coats and hats, and read our books whilst we shared last night's leftover biscuits.

To be fair, breakfast was a magnificent feast, even though it was almost an hour late. Lesley attacked hers as if she were hollow. The legendary 'Full Irish' is made with bacon, sausage, baked beans, black pudding, hash browns, mushrooms and toast, along with pints of strong Barry's tea. I opted for a huge bowl of porridge, followed by scrambled eggs on toast and lashings of tea. By the end, we were warm, fit to burst, and ready for our first day of house hunting. Thank you, Mary!

***

I had to run the car for twenty minutes before enough frost had melted from the windscreen to permit safe driving. Thanks to our tardy breakfast, we were running much later than I had anticipated, and we still needed to visit Ennis to buy those maps. Although my carefully calculated itinerary was now a vague and wishful guideline, something that would normally drive me to distraction, I felt surprisingly calm. Perhaps the relaxed attitude of our host was rubbing off on me.

We successfully navigated our way into Ennis, through what could have been the town's rush hour, but more closely resembled British Sunday afternoon traffic during the World Cup finals. After leaving our hire car in a near-empty carpark by the River Fergus, we headed uphill towards the town centre. As luck would have it, I spotted a man busily rubbing away at a lottery scratch card with his thumbnail, so I asked him for directions to a newsagent. He was happy to oblige, but after a short walk we discovered newsagents do not stock Ordinance Survey maps. However, the assistant was very helpful and suggested we tried a nearby bookshop, which he was confident would satisfy all our orienteering needs. Although he seemed genuinely happy to have helped, I still purchased a couple of KitKats and a bottle of orange juice to alleviate my guilt. As they seemed so popular, I even toyed with the idea of buying a couple of lottery scratch cards, but again I resisted.

The bookshop was exactly as described, and with maps in hand, we headed back towards our car, pausing only when Lesley spotted a high-street estate agent. I didn't mind a few moments of window shopping, particularly if we gained a better insight into the current value of Irish properties, but our schedule was already in tatters, and I definitely didn't want to go inside. This was something that I shared with my wife, only to discover that I was talking to a complete stranger, albeit one wearing similar clothes.

"Have you misplaced your wife?" the lady asked with a smile.

"She must have slipped away while I wasn't looking," I explained sheepishly.

"Is that her," the lady pointed, "inside the shop?"

She was right. Through the window, I could see Lesley having an animated conversation with one of the estate agents.

"Oh, bugger!" I said.

"Never mind, dear." She patted me on the shoulder.

"I'm sorry. Thank you."

I quickly went inside, keen to catch my wife before she made a unilateral offer on a castle, or a chicken farm. By the time I had navigated the entrance, the auctioneer was searching through a filing cabinet and Lesley was standing, fists on hips, like King Canute daring the waves to approach.

"You left me outside!" I whispered.

"I wanted to ask about houses," she replied, oblivious to my abandonment issues.

"What's wrong?"

"He…" she hissed with bitter inflection, "can't understand that we don't want a new house. I think he was considering having me committed."

"Oh dear." I looked at my watch, pointedly. "Right! Let's go."

"Wait a minute, he's just getting a few property papers."

"We're late!" I insisted.

Lesley gave me a look that suggested my presence was temporarily unwelcome. While I waited outside, I phoned Alan and apologised for the delay. He was unperturbed, and I suspected he had again forgotten our appointment. Nonetheless, he told me there was no rush and gave me the precise coordinates needed to find his house. I unfolded my new OS map, propped it against the window to stop it from flapping in the breeze, and traced the two sets of numbers to a point of intersection, where I drew a little circle and wrote 'Alan'. At that moment, Lesley came out of the door clutching a handful of property flyers. As I struggled to refold the map, she paused to frown at me before striding off towards our car.

"Come on, hurry up!" she commanded.

Who am I to disobey?

9. The Lottery

The trip to Alan's house and office could best be described as 'interesting'. The roads were slick with frost and along the way we saw three cars that had failed to cope with the slippery conditions. Fortunately, apart from a few dented egos, nobody seemed to be injured, but clearly, road gritting was reserved for the wealthy parts of Dublin.

A few miles into our journey, Lesley pointed at a signpost.

"Ooh! Spancilhill!" she exclaimed. "I read about that. There's a famous song about Spancil Hill. They hold a horse fair here. It's one of the oldest in the country."

"A famous song about a horse fair?" I asked.

"No, silly! The song is about the people from here who emigrated to America."

"But not horses?"

"It might mention horses, I haven't heard it," Lesley said. She turned her head. "Who was that?"

"Who was who?" I asked.

"In that car. Someone waved."

"I didn't see."

"Well, not so much a wave, more of a raised finger," she said. "There! So, did he!"

"Oh yes," I said. "I saw, but I didn't recognise the driver."

"There's another!" Lesley exclaimed.

"Perhaps it's some sort of local tradition. Here, watch this."

As the next approaching car drew close, I raised my right index finger. This drew an immediate and equal response from the other driver. I repeated the action with the next car and received the same response.

"It's like we're in a secret club," Lesley laughed.

I found myself watching for this finger gesture and trying to reply before the oncoming car passed by. I wasn't always successful, which felt somehow embarrassing, but I also felt mildly annoyed when my greeting wasn't reciprocated. After a couple of miles these gestures suddenly stopped.

"How strange," I observed. "It seems we've passed out of the secret club zone."

"It does, doesn't it?" Suddenly she pointed. "There's one!"

"Bugger! I missed it!"

And so the game began again, only to inexplicably peter out when we passed the next village.

Around twenty minutes later, we turned off the main route and onto a small single-track lane. It was no more than a mud track, with a centreline of grass, like a Mohican hairdo.

"DOG!" Lesley suddenly bellowed in my ear.

A scruffy black collie had shot out from behind a wall, almost colliding with our front bumper. I swerved the car as much as I could, and almost drove into the ditch. Seconds later, we were attacked on the other side by another dog. I squealed and swerved again. Unperturbed, the dogs began a determined chase which lasted for almost half a mile.

"Welcome to Ireland," I said, quoting the sign we had admired as we left Shannon airport.

We found Alan's place to be exactly where I had marked it on the map. His office was towards the rear of his property, overlooking a small garden, given mainly to grass and a few sorry looking shrubs. He was on the telephone, apparently in the midst of an animated conversation. When I politely tapped on the window, he waved in acknowledgement and gestured for us to enter.

He was a tall, slim fellow, aged about forty and casually dressed, with an equally casual manner that could easily be mistaken for indifference. After so many telephone conversations, it was nice to put a face to the voice.

"Look, I'm on my own today, and horribly busy," he said, apologetically. "But my girlfriend's here tomorrow, so I'll have time to show you some properties then."

"Oh," I said, trying to mask my disappointment. "We were hoping you could tell us about these properties."

Lesley waved a handful of papers and raised her eyebrows quizzically.

In between numerous interruptions to take telephone calls from clients in America and Germany, Alan reviewed our selection and marked them on our lovely new maps with a fat felt pen. Most of the properties were local to his office in East Clare, but one from his portfolio and two from another agent, were miles away towards the west coast. Without any discussion, several property papers were unceremoniously ripped up and dumped in the bin.

"That's sold…that's rubbish…you won't like this one…" he mumbled, and so the carnage continued.

Alan agreed to show us several properties the following day but suggested we set off for the remainder of this day on our own.

"Go for a drive," he suggested. "Discover Ireland, view some houses, and have a pub lunch. It's a good way to start your week. Come back and see me tomorrow morning."

He selected one paper from our list of 'probable' properties, and pushed it across his desk.

"I spoke with these people earlier, they'll be expecting you this afternoon," he said. "It's a good bit west of Ennis, so a viewing will use up the rest of your day. OK?"

"OK," we agreed.

Alan's phone rang again, he answered, seamlessly switched to speaking German, and with a casual flick of the fingers, waved us on our way. So, equipped with our maps, property details, basic directions and borrowed wellington boots, we set off in search of our new home in Ireland.

***

Even though I was mentally prepared for a repeat of the earlier dog attack, it still came as rather a shock. I surmised that these farm dogs were more proficient at attacking cars than I was at avoidance. So my plan was to drive sedately forward whilst pretending to pay them no attention, until they lost interest. Unfortunately my instincts got the better of me, and after I had involuntarily braked and swerved, our forward progress was so slow that the second dog was able to block our path. I tried cautiously edging forward, but with both dogs somewhere under the front bumper, barking and snapping at the wheels, our progress was tediously slow. Common sense told me I should just drive on, trusting that these experienced canine assassins would get out of the way, but I just couldn't do it. As we finally ground to a halt, Lesley, with typical aplomb, climbed out and marched to the front of the car.

Open mouthed in shock, I watched as my wife, in full mummy mode, proceeded to give the two terrified dogs a 'damn good telling off'. Lesley squared up to the growling dogs and delivered a robust verbal admonishment, which she emphasised with much finger wagging and gesticulation. Suitably chastised and with their tails hung low, the poor pooches quickly crept away to the comparative safety of a barn.

"I've never seen such badly-behaved dogs," she said, as she returned to her seat. "Sometimes they just need to know who the boss is."

"Err," I said, still somewhat flummoxed.

"Close your mouth, dear. Drive on."

The frost had disappeared, as had the crashed and broken cars, so we made good time to Ennis. I chose one of several vacant parking spots on a side street, just off the market square. We did the 'remember where we parked' thing, and set off in search of lunch. Just up the street we saw a tidy looking eatery called O'Brien's Sandwich Bar. What could be better?

It was obviously a modern operation, perhaps part of a chain hoping to cater for the younger, upwardly mobile business customers, whilst remaining authentic enough to attract hungry tourists. Painted in soft pastel shades, but with enough deep green highlighting to confirm its Irishness, the room felt clean and inviting. There were several blonde-wood tables, with matching chairs, along with a scattering of couches and seats arranged around low tables. To the rear were two doors leading to the toilets, they were marked *Mná* for women and *Fir* for the men. On the wall behind the marble topped bar was a large blackboard displaying the menu, and a second, smaller board enticing us with the daily specials. The toasted sandwiches and spicy wraps smelled delicious, but after a little debate, we both chose the soup of the day with tea and, to ensure we didn't run out of energy during the house hunting trip, we agreed to add something sweet.

"Even during an eclipse, you should never look directly into the bun!" I joked as we examined the delectable display of cakes and sugary delights before us.

For a small sandwich bar, they certainly had a most impressive range of cakes and desserts. There were muffins, scones, pastries, cookies, and several types of cake. We left numerous finger marks and nose prints on the glass front of the counter before making our choice. Lesley opted for hot apple pie with cream, and I chose one of those swirly Danish pastries, sticky with sugar and raisins. As it was lunchtime, there were few empty places, so we chose to sit on high chairs at the long bar that faced the windows. Because the building had been converted from what was once a shop, the large display windows gave plenty of natural light and provided nosy tourists with an excellent vantage point from which to observe the good people of Ennis.

While we waited for our food, Lesley and I chatted about nothing in particular and watched the world go by. In comparison with England, the pace of life here was noticeably slower, and the people who passed by seemed happier and more polite. They were quick to step off the pavement to make room for others and glad to stop and chat.

My wife was a little concerned our two dogs would fret because we hadn't left them with the usual kennels, and I was worried our homicidal chickens might attack our friend when she came to collect the eggs. I made reassuring noises about how nice the heated kennel was, and suggested that our dogs were probably having a better holiday than we were. They would certainly be warmer at night. As far as the chickens were concerned, although we had given our friend ample warning during her training session, Lesley decided it would be wise to buy an appropriate gift to compensate her for the inevitable injuries.

The sandwich bar was doing a roaring trade, with plenty of lunchtime foot traffic. Most of the seated diners were, like us, casually dressed. Rain jackets, jumpers, and jeans were prevalent, along with a scattering of wellies, so much so that a business woman, who came in wearing high heels and a smart designer business suit, looked particularly out of place. A moment later, the fashion meter swung to the other end of the scale. The young woman who came in next was wearing 'runners', short white socks, and a thin black belt. Despite the cold, she wore two wide, elasticated bands of white cloth to cover her dignity, and little else. With her fake tan glowing as tangerine as an Umpa Lumpa and her bleached hair piled high like blonde candyfloss, she was a head-turning sight. Lesley and I watched in mild disbelief as she completed her purchase and carried her coffee and bagel into the street, doing a good job of ignoring how the cold bit at her bare midriff. The man sitting to my right heard our British tuttings and added his own comment.

"She's from Limerick. The young girls all dress like that there," he said. "I think they're trying to attract the Orangemen from the North."

It was a witty riposte, albeit an unlikely one as 'Orangemen' is a byname for a Northern Irish Protestant fraternal organisation and probably not too popular in such a Catholic country. Nevertheless, we all laughed.

With our map unfolded, we enjoyed our delicious bowls of vegetable soup, with soda bread and shared a pot of tea, while we decided which route we would take.

The Ordnance Survey map of County Clare is covered with a mind-blowing mass of little squiggly lines, almost like a Victorian maze, which on closer inspection is the rural road network. Only a few roads travelled across the map with any sign of confident purpose and these major roads were coloured red and given numbers, although the actual roads seemed unaware they were expected to be major thoroughfares, or display numbers.

More numerous than the red roads on the map were yellow ones. These jolly little lines travelled in all directions, like a spilled packet of spaghetti, occasionally connecting two red lines for no apparent reason. Whereas the red lines indicated A-class regional roads, the yellow lines represented B-roads and they were usually around four metres wide, or less, and resisted all attempts at identification. Alan told us that the 'B' stood for "Bloody hell, we're lost again!" Branching off from the B-roads were hundreds of grey lines that the map key indicated as 'other roads'. Alan had described these as being barely passable, impassable, or non-existent. The grey lines were usually subdivided, sometimes several times, into branch roads, becoming ever more difficult to find and navigate. Inevitably, nearly all the properties we had selected were hidden at the end of one of these branches.

Although we were full of soup and tea, and keen to see our first property, we took a casual stroll through the town on the way back to our car. Along the way, we saw an eclectic variety of shops. There was an old-fashioned stationers, selling fountain pens, reams of coloured paper, staples and multitudinous other items. Nearby was a bookshop – not a well-known retailer with magazines and school supplies, but a small family run bookshop selling only books and nothing else. On one street, just yards apart, we saw three butchers' shops, all apparently thriving in the Celtic Tiger economic boom.

As we turned the corner, I cast my eyes ahead in search of our hire car. It took me a moment to figure out which one was ours, primarily because it was partly obscured by the impressive bulk of a traffic warden. Lesley spotted him at the same time as me.

"I think we're about to get a ticket," she said.

"It's free parking," I replied. "There are no signs or parking meters."

We were still several yards away when I noticed the warden reaching into his breast pocket for a pad and pen, so I pointed my key and blipped the alarm. He stopped and looked around in time to see my waving hand.

"Hello there," I said, jogging the last few yards.

"Oh! You're tourists," he said, as if that explained everything.

"Have I transgressed?" I asked, doing my best to look innocent. I don't know why I bother, it's a ploy that has never worked.

"You don't have a voucher," he said, tapping the windscreen with his pen.

"What voucher?"

"A parking voucher," he repeated. "You're not displaying a valid parking voucher."

I looked around in genuine confusion. There were no pay-and-display signs, or machines to dispense tickets, and no indication of parking restrictions. I scratched my head – the bit with hair.

"I'm sorry, I don't understand. As you rightly said, we're tourists."

He looked at me, as if I were a simple child. Then he smiled.

"Don't worry, this happens all the time." He pointed at a shop window a few yards away. "Look there."

It took a few moments to visually sort through the jumble of multi-coloured adverts and flyers, but there in the centre, slightly askew, was a hand-written A4 poster declaring, "Parking vouchers here."

"Honestly, I didn't see that," I said.

"It's true," Lesley added.

The warden sighed. "Wherever you park in the town, you must enter a shop and purchase a parking voucher. Then you must scratch the card to reveal the time that you arrived, and display it on your dashboard. Failure to do so will result in a fine."

Suddenly the penny dropped. There was no obsession with lottery scratch cards here, the people I had seen rubbing at their cards with coins were buying parking tickets. The traffic warden was a kindly and understanding fellow, and we were fortunate to avoid a parking fine, particularly as this was our third transgression. Suitably educated in the mysteries of Irish parking, we made our apologies and set off towards the west.

The first house on our list was near to a place called Derryshaan. It was situated halfway between Ennis and the port town of Kilrush. As we had a little time in hand before our appointment, we decided to take the scenic coast road, through Killadysert and along the northern bank of the Shannon estuary to Kilmurry McMahon. At that point we planned to stop and ask for directions. It was a typical Irish winter day, frosty and calm with a crystal clear blue sky. The air, flowing in from the west over thousands of miles of the Atlantic Ocean, was so pure and clean that breathing suddenly seemed like a forgotten pleasure. The coast road is relatively unused and we saw only two other cars during the forty mile drive, which was fortunate, because the views were so spectacular we both spent most of our time looking out of the side windows. Our lunchtime tea soon started to take effect and we switched our attention to searching for a service station with a toilet. There were none.

"Come to think of it, we haven't seen a garage since we left Ennis," I said.

"Or a shop," Lesley commented. "How are we for petrol?"

"Just over half a tank," I replied. "I'll fill up when we get back to town, but I can't wait that long for a pee."

"Likewise." Lesley was squirming in her seat. "How far is it to this house?"

"Probably half an hour yet, but I'm not going to swan up there and immediately ask to use their toilet."

"Pull over up there." My wife pointed ahead. "I've got to go."

"Me too."

At the side of the road there was a gap in the drystone wall, where someone had fitted a rusty farm gate. I parked the car as far off the road as possible, without getting stuck in the mud, and we jumped out. We were on a slight bend in the road and on the side of a gentle slope where the land to our left swept down towards the Shannon. Apart from a scattering of low stone walls, the grassy fields around us looked windswept and barren. There wasn't a single tree or bush visible within a mile of where we stood.

"We'll just have to go behind this wall," Lesley said.

The gate had been secured in place with some bright orange nylon cord. Whoever had tied the rope, did not intend for the gate to be opened with ease, as they had knotted it eight times. Eight times! I couldn't believe it. Despite my bursting bladder, I counted the knots to make sure. My calculation was correct. What breed of fiendish escapologist livestock were they breeding here to require eight knots on a gate? Ironically, one knot would have done the job. The rope was old and frayed and so slick with ice that it was impossible to undo.

"You'll have to climb over," I suggested. "You go first, and I'll keep watch."

I helped Lesley over, which wasn't too difficult. The wall was only three feet high. No sooner had she attained a squatting position...

"There's a car coming!" I warned.

Lesley jumped up, rearranged herself, and assumed the casual pose of a tourist taking in the scenery. The car barrelled past a moment later. The driver gave us a toot of his horn and a friendly wave.

"All clear," I said.

My wife glanced around until she was satisfied with the level of privacy, before returning to her task. As she bobbed down for a second time, I heard another approaching engine. I called a warning and Lesley stood up and rearranged her clothing a second time. She repeated her nonchalant pose, and the driver of this second car also gave us a toot and a friendly wave.

"We've hardly seen a car all day, now there's two in as many minutes. They must be queuing up around the corner."

Unlike me, my wife was struggling to find the humour in the situation.

Nevertheless, I persisted. "Third time lucky."

It occurred to me we were being very British about this. Surely people from other countries had to pee in the open sometimes? I heard another vehicle approaching.

"There's someone coming!" I shouted.

"I don't care," Lesley replied, and she didn't.

After the motorcycle had passed, I confirmed my stubborn Britishness by walking 50 yards further into the field, well out of sight from the road, where I could water a pile of rocks without being disturbed. Thus relieved, we returned to enjoying the beautiful scenery for the remainder of the journey. In due course, we found the village of Kilmurry McMahon and headed to the post office to ask for directions.

The first person I encountered was an ancient and weather-beaten woman, in an equally ancient and weather-beaten car of indeterminate manufacture. She had on three coats, fingerless gloves and was wearing a knitted hat that may, at one time, have been a tea cosy. As I approached, I noticed she appeared to be trying to reattach her car door with a piece of baling twine and, assuming she was the victim of a recent automotive disaster, I offered my assistance.

"Ah, you're grand," she replied. "The fecking thing falls off every time I open it. It's been like it for years. I'll just stick my arm out of the window and hang on till I get home."

Peering through the mould on the cracked windshield, I could see two bottles of holy water and statues of Jesus and the Virgin Mary on the dashboard. There also appeared to be a bale of hay and a goat on the back seat.

"Have you far to go before you get home?" I asked.

"Only a few miles, but I'll be shopping in Ennis first. Are ye lost?"

I explained we were looking for a local property that was for sale and showed her the details, in the hope she could provide directions.

"Don't know it," she said and pointed to a nearby building. "Try the postmaster."

After much clanking and the issuing of alarming quantities of oily smoke, she started her car and, still holding her door, drove off at a terrifying speed. Feeling slightly shocked, I entered the post office and, proffering the property details, asked for directions.

"I don't recognise that house," the friendly postmaster said. "Whose house is it?"

I shrugged. "No idea. All I know is we are to meet Mary or John there, in half an hour. I don't even have a phone number for them."

"That's a bit of a problem," he said scratching his head. He called to a man by the door, "Here, Paddy, do you know where this is?"

Paddy also asked who the house belonged to, before recruiting the support of a third person. Within a few minutes, no fewer than eight people were involved in the discussion, all of them animated and excited by the challenge. After some lively debate, they decided the property was probably McNamara's house. With the ownership established, they coerced another local into giving me directions.

"Here, Seamus. Tell this feller how to get to McNamara's house. You know, where John Kelly lives."

Seamus seemed delighted with his newfound responsibility and, after pulling up his trousers and squaring his shoulders, he began his directions.

"Right. You go down this road and then you go that way, right?" he said, pointing left. "Then you go on a ways, until you can't go no further, then you go that way, right?" Pointing left again.

"You mean left," I offered helpfully.

He went quiet for a moment. "Yea, that's right, left – right?"

"Eer, yes I think so," I said.

"Right then," he said with renewed confidence. "Now, when you get to the crossroads you go that way – right?" He waved his hand to the right. "Kelly's place is up the end of that lane, you can't miss it. Ten minutes, tops." He smiled confidently and the others joined in smiling and nodding in support.

I thanked my new friend for his help and, armed with our directions, set off on the short trip to the house. About forty-five minutes later we arrived at the crossroads, which turned out to be a six way junction with each road looking identical to the others. All were helpfully devoid of any road signs.

"I think we're supposed to turn right here," I said scratching my head.

Lesley shrugged. "All roads lead to Rome," she said, helpfully.

"We may go there next. Perhaps they can give us better directions."

Lesley squinted at the map. "It's up that road," she waved vaguely somewhere to our right.

I chose a lane at random and astonishingly we arrived at the correct house two minutes later, just half an hour late.

At that time in the UK, prospective house sellers were being subjected to an avalanche of television programmes, providing advice on the best ways to present your property for sale. Much was being made of the importance of clearing personal clutter, painting everything with neutral colours, completing maintenance projects, tidying the garden and making the kitchen smell of coffee and fresh bread. Ireland had yet to catch up with this trend, so it would be fair to say we were slightly taken aback by the first house we visited.

It was a fairly large bungalow, sitting in seven acres of meadow at the top of a gentle rise which provided panoramic views south to the Shannon estuary. We parked at the rear of the bungalow, near several outbuildings and cowsheds, and sloshed our way through three inches of mud and dung on our way to the back door. A portly lady wearing an overcoat and an apron was waiting for us.

"You 'ere to see around?" she enquired. "Better come in then," she said without waiting for a reply. We stepped into a back kitchen area that contained an ancient, oil burning range, a dining table and an enormous picture window. We stood looking out towards the estuary. To the right, we could see the smoke from a distant power station.

"Lovely view," Lesley said politely. "I see the house comes with seven acres. Is this the land at the front?"

"My husband deals with all of that, and he ain't here. But in any event, it's 29 acres now."

"29 acres!" I squealed. "But this says seven." I flapped the property details at her.

"We been and decided we don't want the other land no more, so it's got to go with the house – or we won't be selling."

Crossing her arms below her bust, she brazenly told us the new asking price, which was almost double what we had expected, and edging dangerously close to the top end of our budget. After a little prompting from Lesley, the lady led us through the house on a quick tour. By the time we reached the back bedrooms, I was beginning to ponder if they had recently been burgled, or the victim of a mini tornado, as most of their belongings appeared to be on the floor, with discarded clothing several inches deep in places.

"That's my daughter's room – she don't clean up much," she observed helpfully.

The dear lady took us around the house and garden for the next half hour, before setting us loose to explore the mud and rushes, which made up the remainder of the 29 acres. Overall, it was a nice property and had the potential to become a pleasant home. However, there were three obvious problems. First, the new asking price would be pushing our budget to the limit. Second, 29 acres is a lot of land, particularly when you are used to owning no more than a large garden, but it wasn't a deal-breaker. Finally, as you travel west in County Clare towards the coast, the land flattens and the trees thin out, leaving a rather barren and wild outlook. We both suspected the area could be 'hard living', particularly during the winter months. Nevertheless, we had a positive feeling about this, our first Irish property.

As we headed away from Derryshaan, I noticed we were being chased along the road by a car with madly flashing lights. Initially, I thought the driver just wanted to get past to attend to a farming emergency, or to beat the evening rush at the pub. But it transpired that he was, in fact, our prospective neighbour. He took a few minutes to grill us on our opinion of the property, the area and how much we were willing to pay, before getting to the point.

"If you buy it, can I keep grazing my cows on the land?" he asked.

"I expect so – if we buy it."

"That's grand." He smiled, and as an afterthought added, "For free, mind you." He gave my hand a mighty shake and waved us on our way.

***

By diligently following the map, we successfully navigated our way through the mass of squiggly lanes and eventually found our way to the Kilrush road, where we turned east and headed back towards Ennis. Ten miles later and the vista had changed considerably. As we drove away from the sea, the flat featureless landscape was broken by gentle hills and dotted with bushes and small wooded areas.

"The views down to the Shannon estuary were pretty spectacular," I said, "but I think I'd miss seeing trees every day."

"You'd get used to it," Lesley replied. "Anyway, there were some trees at the far end of the land."

"They weren't terribly big."

"They were deciduous trees," she said. "Without their foliage they look quite small. I think that will be a pretty little wood when the summer comes."

"You could be right." It was dark. I looked at my watch. "It's getting late. Shall we go into Ennis and look for somewhere to eat?"

"I suppose so." Lesley reached for a sheet of paper from the back seat. "How are we doing on your itinerary?"

"Actually quite well," I laughed. "Since Alan ruthlessly destroyed half of the houses on our 'Must See' list, we're ahead of plan. At this rate we're going to run out of places to visit."

"Really?"

"Let's see how we get on tomorrow."

We parked in the pay and display carpark of Dunnes stores, an Irish retail chain of food and clothing shops. I'm not an enthusiastic shopper, but I was impressed by their range of foodstuffs and the quality on display. Before heading into town, I bought a few packets of biscuits and some orange juice to help us through the long, cold mornings before breakfast was served. I would have bought a kettle and some beverage supplies, but my suggestion was overruled by management.

Walking along O'Connell Street in search of a nice place to eat, we detected the unmistakable aroma of Chinese food. It seemed distinctly out of place – something I did not expect to find in the west of Ireland. Nonetheless, it was a long while since we had eaten Chinese food, and we were salivating. We literally followed our noses until we found the source of that delectable smell. It turned out to be a relatively new and extremely smart restaurant. As we were the first customers of the evening, we were treated like royalty, although it is entirely possible that they give all their patrons the same excellent attention. In any event, we were starving, so we dined like kings on their magnificent fare. I even managed a pint of Guinness.

Stuffed to the gills and pleasantly drowsy from the wonderful country air, we arrived back at our digs around 11 pm. As we came through the door, Lesley took a quick left turn and disappeared into the guest lounge. I soon discovered why. There was a roaring peat fire in the hearth. The room was empty so we appropriated the two wing-backed chairs nearest to the fireplace. Although the fire was throwing out heat like a furnace, the remainder of the room was still freezing.

"This is odd," Lesley commented after 15 minutes. "I'm roasting all along one side, but my other side is freezing."

"I'm the same," I whispered. "We need to rotate to balance the heat. Let's swap seats."

"That's better," Lesley said, cooking her other side. She closed her eyes. "Perhaps we can sleep here."

"Best not," I responded.

"But it's warm in here." Lesley gave me a pleading look.

I ignored it.

I had a disturbing thought. "This is a nice house, and quite new, but the insulation must be dreadful for it to be so cold."

"Good point," she conceded. "It's odd though, given how cold it is here."

"We'll have to watch out for problems like that. Perhaps they have different building regulations here. We'll ask Alan tomorrow."

A few minutes later, Mrs Menopause came in carrying a huge tray, loaded down with food.

"Hello, Mick and Lesley," she said. "I thought you'd like some tea and sandwiches before bed."

I looked at my wife in horror. It was almost midnight and we had recently eaten an enormous meal.

"Thank you," Lesley said. "That's so kind of you." What else could we say?

"You're most welcome," Mrs Menopause replied. "I'll leave you to eat. I have a few chores to do."

These sandwiches were the size of roof tiles. Made from thick slabs of ham, fitted between two slices of roughly cut white bread, the result was a two-inch thick doorstop. In other circumstances, these 'stomach-liners' would have been memorably delicious. What a shame!

"I can't eat this," I whined, "I'm full up."

Lesley cautiously lifted one edge of the bread.

"I don't like mustard," she said.

"We can't just leave them."

"I know," my wife whispered.

"Put some in your handbag," I suggested.

"I would, but they wouldn't fit," she hissed. "These things are enormous."

As luck would have it, we were saved from upsetting the kindly Mary Menopause by the arrival of two very hungry American backpackers. These lovely slim girls attacked the free food as if it was, well…free food. In a matter of minutes, they had cleared the plate and drunk the tea. In thanks, we allowed them to join in our rotational roasting game of musical chairs. After all the stresses of the last few months, it was delightful to sit with strangers in such an oasis of calm and converse about nothing in particular, for no apparent reason.

Our second day of house hunting took us inland to East Clare. There is a beautiful and wide valley running from Ennis and the River Fergus, slightly northeast for around 30 miles, to Mountshannon, on the north shore of Lough Derg. The valley is bordered by Gappaghabaun Mountain to the north and Slieve Bearnagh to the south, which rises to some five hundred metres above the valley floor. The land is green, fertile and yet sparsely populated, containing only a dozen or so small villages, interspaced with farms and the occasional cottage. During the warm summers, the lush grass provides excellent grazing for many sheep and cattle, and in the winter months, the mountains are usually topped with snow, although the lower land can still remain largely clear. This area is characteristic of the beautiful scenery of East Clare. We had several likely properties on my list, so I had arranged for Alan Sykes to show us the houses in the north of the valley in the morning, while in the afternoon we would again go solo to view those in the south.

After another scrumptious breakfast, we headed towards Peppers Bar in the tiny village of Feakle, a pub famous for its traditional Irish music sessions and *Céilí* dancing (pronounced kay-lee), where we met with Alan. It was another beautiful and frosty Irish morning. The air was sweet and fresh, and the sun was warm on our faces as we discussed our itinerary. Before setting off, Alan shared a little of his valuable local knowledge.

"In case you haven't realised, one delightful feature of rural Ireland is that the roads have no names or numbers *and* there are no post codes," he said. "Individual houses are named, but most of them share that name with several others in the same area."

"We had a lot of trouble finding Derryshaan yesterday," Lesley admitted. "Even the postmaster didn't know where it was."

"Did he ask you who lived there?" Alan asked.

"Yes. How did you know?"

"Experience!" He smiled and held up a finger to emphasise his point. "It's quite simple, once you know how the system works. Each area has a townland, like Derryshaan, which is the local name in Irish for a particular hill, valley, road, bog etc. Assuming you buy a house in rural Ireland, it will probably be named after the local townland, along with twenty or so others."

"Sounds almost fool proof," I jested.

Alan ignored my gentle attempt at sarcasm and continued his lesson. "Second to that, your address will also carry the name of the local post office, even if it closed twelve years ago and your post is now handled by another post office."

"Really?" Lesley asked.

"There's more. Your address will also show the county that the house was in when it was built, but this may not necessarily be the county it's in now." He smiled, but he wasn't joking. "Many of the borders of Clare and Limerick were changed a few years ago, but the addresses weren't."

"Good grief," I said.

"And finally," he added, "for international post, your address would show Ireland, or The Republic of Ireland, or Eire."

"So houses in Ireland are all known by the owners' names?" I asked, looking for a simple solution.

Alan pulled a face. "Not quite!"

"Go on…"

He pointed across the street to the local post office.

"To save any confusion, when you first take ownership of your new home you should seek out the local postmaster and inform him which of the twenty or so identically named houses you now live in. He'll tell the postman and you'll be sure of getting your post."

"I think that's nice," Lesley said. "Really quaint."

"It is," he agreed, "but…owning and paying for your house may not make it yours in the eyes of the locals. We've lived in our place for ten years, but people still call it Bill Harris' house. Which is an Irish peculiarity as Mr Harris himself was actually English, the second of five owners, and he only lived in the house for nine months. How DHL and FedEx manage, is a mystery. I've never seen the same driver twice. I wonder sometimes if they go out on a delivery and just never come back!"

Lesley and I both laughed. Quirky Ireland was definitely growing on us.

As Alan climbed into his car, Lesley asked an important question. "What's the thing with the finger waving while people are driving?" She gave a short demonstration to illustrate her point.

"Aah! A peculiarity of County Clare," Alan exclaimed, with a hint of pride. "Unlike us Brits, they have an uncontrollable urge to acknowledge the presence of other people."

"And that's why they wave?" Lesley asked.

"Pretty much," he said. "In general, in rural parts of County Clare, passing drivers will subtly raise the right index finger, no more than two inches, but without removing the hand from the steering wheel. That's how you say 'Hi' to other motorists or pedestrians. Around here, it's somewhat of a local tradition."

"But not everyone waves," I pointed out, remembering our own finger waving experience.

"That's true," he admitted. "Not all motorists will comply. Some may be visitors from the city. Others might be tourists. Unlike you, they get confused and stare blankly, or panic and wave their entire hand. That is only an acceptable gesture, when returning an identical wave from the first generation of your immediate family. To be honest, the finger waving can be a mystery. It seems to start and stop for no apparent reason."

"Well, I think it's nice," Lesley said. "It would be lovely to live somewhere where our only worry was who we should wave at."

"Very true," Alan said. "Right, let's get moving. As I know where we're going, you can follow me."

"Okay," I said.

"By the way," he added a final observation as he started his engine. "To try and see further around corners, some of the locals have a disturbing habit of driving on the wrong side of the road. It can make life rather interesting!"

He shot off in a cloud of blue smoke, before I even had a chance to climb back into our car. Like most men, I consider myself to be a decent driver, but on the narrow and icy lanes, in an underpowered rental car, it took all my skill just to keep him in sight. For a while we lost contact, but I pressed on regardless, and a few miles later we found him taking photographs of an ancient rusty tractor. Despite being an enchanting example of vintage farm machinery, this wreck was obviously still in daily use. The cab was missing, there was an old sock acting as an air filter, and a timeworn wooden kitchen stool had been attached with baling twine to seat the driver. Alan seemed very proud of his discovery and took several 'artsy' pictures for his collection. I was impressed with the mechanical longevity of the tractor, in Britain such a wreck would long since be consigned to the scrapyard.

A few miles further up the road, he pulled over so we could view the first property. After our previous experiences with estate agents in England, where descriptions like 'convenient for commuters' means people use your back garden as a short-cut to the railway station, and 'scope for improvement' would turn out to be a derelict chicken coop, Alan's approach was a breath of fresh air.

"You won't like this one, it's horrible – been on the market for ages," he said as he marched up the path.

He was correct. It was a nasty, dank little cottage, balanced precariously on the side of a hill so steep we almost needed ropes and crampons on the approach. We quickly agreed with his assessment and moved on to the next house, all the time wondering how that property got onto our 'must see' list. The next two visits were equally depressing, both being muddy fields that had no services and just outline planning permission for more jelly-mould houses.

Just as we were starting to despair that our entire trip might have been wasted, Alan pulled to a stop at the crest of a hill and we climbed out of our cars. Although it wasn't obvious to us while driving, we had climbed to a height of around 800 feet. There before us was a spectacular view looking south, down across the valley. Even though our viewpoint was not particularly high, the slope was steep and the valley floor below so flat as to give the impression that we were much higher and able to see for hundreds of miles. It was utterly breath-taking. The sun was in our faces, low in the sky behind Slieve Bearnagh Mountain, which I could imagine being the aged remains of an exploded volcano.

Ten miles to our extreme left we could see part of Lough Derg and the village of Scariff, where a single column of white smoke rose vertically into the morning sky. The valley floor was predominately green, occasionally obscured with patches of light mist, and dotted with lakes glistening in the sunlight. To our right, the land was flat for 30 miles, leading out towards Limerick city. Just visible in the haze was the Shannon Estuary and some distant smoke arising from Moneypoint power station. We stood in silent awe for a few moments until Alan broke our reverie.

"Some view, hey?"

"Spectacular," we both agreed.

"Can you imagine waking up to that every morning?" he asked, as his sales instincts finally kicked in.

It was immediately obvious that the next house was much closer to what we were seeking, albeit rather more basic than we had hoped for. It sat in a dip at the base of a hill, by the side of a stream and surrounded by mature trees. The property had around half an acre of vegetable garden to the front and, up the very steep hill at the back, another six acres of pasture. There was a house, a barn and a new garage that had been partially converted into a small guest apartment.

Alan rapped loudly on the door. After a short delay, it opened and we met the owner, a softly spoken Englishman. Painfully thin and rather stooped, he wore brown corduroy trousers, a threadbare cardigan that may once have been green, and fingerless knitted gloves. We exchanged pleasantries, but he seemed painfully shy, or perhaps self-conscious, and at the first opportunity he stepped away. Taking no further part in the conversation, he sat on a high-backed wooden kitchen chair, and stared morosely into the fire. I wondered if this house was some part of a failed project he was now being forced to sell. A wave of sadness and depression washed over me. I wanted to walk over and put my hand on his shoulder. I wanted to apologise for taking his dream away. I wanted to say that everything would be alright, but I didn't. Lesley called for me to follow, snapping me out of my downward spiral.

The house was concrete built, with a rusty corrugated metal roof. It was about 80 years old and typically Irish in its construction. There were just two downstairs rooms, divided by a single wall containing the chimney and fireplaces. The room on the left was a living room that contained the stairs and the other was a kitchen and eating area. The floors were dry bare mud with some straw sprinkled around, and overhead I could see rafters and the bare floorboards of the rooms above. The upstairs was a copy of the living space below, being two rooms divided by a central chimney and lateral wall. One of the rooms contained a bath, sink and toilet, enclosed by a curtain to create the illusion of privacy. The other room seemed to be the only bedroom. Electricity was provided to lights and sockets through a series of disturbingly antique wires, which hung precariously from nails along the walls and rafters. I reached over to experimentally flick a light switch, but stopped when Alan put his hand on my shoulder.

"Probably best to leave that alone," he said.

The only obvious source of heating was a few peat briquettes burning on the hearth below the chimney, which stubbornly refused to accept any of the smoke. We thanked the vendor as we stepped outside, but he was either ignoring us or transfixed by the dance of the flames as they licked around the peat fire.

"He's a quiet one," Alan said, once we were out of earshot. He gestured at the house and land with a sweep of his arm. "So, what do you think?"

"It's a lovely location," Lesley said, guardedly.

"Lots of potential," I added.

"I thought this was exactly what you were looking for," Alan said. Clearly, he was a trifle disappointed.

"Well…it is," my wife admitted. "I guess it's just a bit overwhelming to see how much renovation we'd have to do."

"On the other hand…" I put my 'Mr Practical' hat on. "We could live in the apartment above the garage while the work was being done."

"It might be a bit cramped. Where would we put all our stuff?" Lesley's voice suggested more statement than question.

"I guess we'd have to put it in storage. It could be months, or longer."

My wife pulled a sour face. "I don't like that idea. Even if we got one of those containers. There's bound to be mould, and think of the cost."

I turned to Alan for some advice. "How hard would it be to get planning permission to repair this place?"

"As long as it's within the boundaries of the existing property line, you can do what you like," he said. "And there are no building regulations to speak of, you won't have to call out a Council Inspector like you would in England. That's why I don't trust the new build houses, dreadful quality."

"Something to remember," Lesley said. "Luckily we're not looking for one."

I nodded towards the house. "Do you think he'll come down a bit on the price, given how much work there is to do?"

"Quite the opposite," he said, looking rather uncomfortable. "When I spoke to him yesterday, he mentioned that he now wants the buyer to pay all of his legal expenses and moving costs."

"What?" Lesley exclaimed. "That could run into thousands!"

Alan shrugged. "What can I say? He's run out of money."

"We couldn't possibly commit to covering his costs. Is that sort of thing normal here?" Lesley asked.

"Not really," he replied, "but very little in Ireland is normal. Let's just say it's an irregular request."

"Well, it certainly puts this house firmly in the 'we'll think about it' pile," I said. "Sorry Alan."

And that was the end of that.

Although frustrated at the lack of progress, we were undaunted as there were still several more houses for us to see before heading home. But from here on we would be flying solo. We thanked Alan for his help and the guided tours, and waved goodbye as his car roared off, leaving behind another cloud of blue smoke.

12. Jelly Moulds and Churches

Through careful planning, or by happy coincidence, our agenda for the afternoon matched my itinerary exactly. We had several properties to see in the south of the county. Alan had kindly marked them on our map and even added a few comments to ensure we didn't get stuck on an unmade road, or lost in a wood. In search of lunch, we made our way back through Feakle, and followed the aptly named River Scariff toward the comely market village of the same name. Turning south, we drove slowly past the hulking bulk of the wood pulp factory, the only sign of industrialisation we had passed since our first day. For the next two miles, the road was much wider, with the houses set well back, giving the area a more European feel.

Soon we entered the little village of Tuamgraney, where we parked outside the Mc Kernan Woollen Mill and museum. It was a small building, but an impressive operation nonetheless. Although we didn't have the time to visit, Lesley still spent a few minutes looking at the scarves and hats in the window. As I am somewhat less interested in crafts, knitwear, and fashion, I supplemented her education by reading from a tourist sign.

"The village name Tuamgraney in Irish is *Tuain Greine*, 'The Tomb of Grain' or 'Graney' – referring to the legendary Grain, daughter of a local king who drowned in the lake," I said.

"Good to know," Lesley mumbled.

"And…" Undaunted, I continued reading. "The Oldest Oak Tree in Ireland is in Raheen Woods, just outside the village."

"Perhaps we can go for a walk, if we come this way again." She pointed. "There's a pub. Let's eat."

The pub seemed a little dark and uninviting, but the staff were friendly and the food was delicious and surprisingly cheap. We were both tempted by the prospect of homemade soup and bread, but you can have too much of a good thing, so we opted for toasted sandwiches with chunky chips and a salad to ease our conscience. As we drank our tea, Lesley pointed to a sign on the wall.

"Only one *Bodhrán*," she read. "That's the second time I've seen that sign. I wonder what it means."

"Perhaps it's something to do with politics," I suggested. "You know, like 'Free Nelson Mandela' or 'Your country needs you'. We should ask."

"Best not. We might offend someone."

Ever the diplomat, I asked our waitress as I paid the bill. She smiled, clearly used to answering this question.

"*Bodhrán* (or BOW-ron) is an Irish word which simply means drum or tambourine," she explained. "We have several trad music sessions here every week. They're great craic – you should come. There's always lots of instruments being played, like fiddles, guitars, and flutes, but we only allow one *Bodhrán* drummer per session. Otherwise the roof would come off!"

Refreshed, reinvigorated and educated, we set off in search of the last few properties on our list. For some reason, the radio in our hire car refused to play anything other than the local station. Awash with holiday spirit and goodwill, we were amused by the uniquely unusual cover versions of popular songs, which they seemed to play almost all the time. We even made a decent fist of joining in with a little community singing. But, despite being a long-time fan of American country music, Lesley just couldn't stand the Irish version, and insisted I turned the radio off each time a song was played. All of this paled into insignificance when we heard the local radio 'Death Notices' for the first time.

During my travels, I have witnessed a variety of different approaches to marking the passing of a loved one. I've seen organised wailing and mass browbeating at funerals in Africa, joyous dancing and drinking at a Scottish wake, and the reserved and respectful 'close friends and family' of an English cremation. We were, of course, used to seeing the occasional obituary in English newspapers, paying respectful acknowledgement to the passing of some local gentry. However, hearing the list of local deaths being read out on the radio as casually as the shipping forecast, was an entirely new experience for us.

"I presume it's a tradition that predates modern communications," Lesley suggested. "A way of keeping people informed."

"It does sound rather like he's reading the soccer results," I observed, "but I guess he could easily cause offence, so he keeps his voice expressionless."

"I wonder what the descriptions mean," she asked. "They keep saying, suddenly, quietly, peacefully or unexpectedly."

"It may be a code," I suggested. "Perhaps 'peacefully' means drunk, and 'unexpectedly' translates to she didn't have a will."

Lesley glared at me. My black humour had failed to find a receptive audience again.

As we headed south, our route took us through a succession of small villages, each with its own church. Although a few were of a familiar design, small, stone-built churches with arched windows and a spire, many were of a more modern and slightly incongruous design. However, we found them to be quite attractive, and a useful aid to navigation, particularly as they were disproportionately large, brightly painted and generally taller than many British city cathedrals.

The next three sites were all prospective building plots, something we were not particularly keen on, as building a new home while waiting to move in would leave us temporarily homeless, and potentially significantly poorer. But, as there were so many plots available, we had agreed to add a few to our itinerary. During one of our many phone conversations before arriving in Ireland, Alan had explained the reason behind this sudden excess of small land packets.

"With the spiralling property prices, many land owners are seeing the opportunity to make a quick buck," he said. "They're carving off any small plots that have road access and chancing their arm on the price. Most of these are being snapped up by rich overseas clients, who are going to sell them on when the prices rise. It's always worth a look. You may find something you like."

Unfortunately, although the weather was nice, the house hunting that afternoon was a disappointing washout. First, we visited a field with outline planning permission for a small jelly-mould house, followed by a field with full planning permission for a large jelly-mould house, and finally, a field with no planning permission at all, but several scrap cars. None of the sites had access to electricity, or telephone, and the views were all uninspiring – a difficult thing to achieve in such a beautiful country. Despite this small dissatisfaction, our spirits remained high – with even a hint of an upward trend. We may not have found our dream home just yet, but our early experience of Ireland, the landscape and the people was very positive.

Our final viewing – at the behest of an Ennis estate agent – was a newly-built jelly-mould house. Although it wasn't the age or style of property we were looking for, we had decided to see a 'new build house', if only to discover what all the fuss was about. Facing a busy main road, the house was at one end of a long row of concrete-grey, indistinguishable jelly-moulds, each built on an identical three-quarter acre plot of grass and gravel. We had declined the auctioneer's offer of a formal viewing, preferring to save some time by visiting the site and looking through the windows. If we were inspired by what we saw, the option remained to revisit with a key for a closer look.

Although the property was advertised as completed and ready for sale, there were no kitchen or bathroom fittings at all, just bare wires and pipes, and dusty looking concrete floors. Alan had warned us this was standard practice in Ireland, as most buyers preferred to add these personal touches themselves.

"It's going to cost a decent chunk of money to install a kitchen and two bathrooms," Lesley said.

"Don't forget the floors," I added.

"This land is completely waterlogged. I'd struggle to grow anything here without proper drainage."

"The build quality seems very poor, considering the price being asked," I said, poking my finger into the gap around the back door.

"I'm sorry," Lesley said. "I did my best to remain unbiased and positive, but this really isn't my dream home."

"I'm sure someone will be very happy here, but it won't be us."

We demonstrated our displeasure at the wasted time, by emptying our bladders out of sight behind the garage before setting off towards the welcome prospect of hot food and a nap by the fire.

Our serpentine route towards Ennis, brought us through the small town of Sixmilebridge where we stopped for a while to take in the sights. According to the tourist booklet Mrs Menopause had kindly provided, the town takes its name from the 400-year-old bridge, which spans the O'Garney River where it flows through the village. During the 18th century, the town was a busy river port, trading soap, rapeseed oil, and produce from the brewery and water-powered mill. The stone bridge, which must be six miles from somewhere, is still in use, which I found to be most impressive given the amount of traffic it has to handle. In homage to the heritage of the town as a milling centre, in the centre of the river is a large limestone statue of a shirtless man walking unimpeded through the water, whilst carrying the heavy tools of his labour.

The large and steeply sloping town square, has many old and interesting buildings. Their great age was evidenced by the dates carved in the stone panels displayed on their walls. At the bottom of the hill, alongside the river, is the derelict and imposing bulk of the old mill. Although it was dark and foreboding, there were signs that a major renovation was about to get underway. I imagined this magnificent building could soon become offices and apartments. Our circular walk brought us back to the brightly painted Duck Inn, where we took a few minutes to feed the ducks and geese that gather alongside the pink pub on a small duck pond. On the pond floats a beautifully crafted duck house, an exact replica of the pub. I am not sure if the ducks appreciated the effort that had gone in to providing their accommodation, but we certainly did.

The shocking pink colour of the pub reminded me of something Alan had mentioned. Apparently, the residents of County Clare had recently discovered the joy of coloured masonry paint, something they had taken to with commendable enthusiasm. Although many traditional Irish stone cottages were still protected with a white lime wash, new houses had been constructed of concrete blocks and covered with cement render, leaving them a depressingly dull grey colour. In the moist and humid Atlantic air, this concrete quickly becomes streaked with red algae. Upon discovering the power of coloured masonry paint to brighten up their homes, the good people of Clare wondered what colours they should use. Not for them the mid-tones and pastel shades of those town folks in Dublin and Cork (locally pronounced Cwork). No, the brave people of Clare unflinchingly chose the most audacious colours imaginable, colours previously only reserved for safety jackets, warning signs and perhaps hot air balloons. Presumably the owners were not satisfied with that singular insult to the eyes, as on some houses, two colours, which cannot naturally exist together in nature, combined on the same building. This produces a mind-numbing effect, only safely replicated by hyperventilating whilst snorting fresh lemon juice. When we saw one of these ocular monstrosities for the first time, my response was to inadvertently stamp on the brake pedal and shout, "Holy crap – look at that!"

***

Although Ennis is a relatively small town, wherever we decided to eat we were pleasantly surprised by the quality of the food on offer. On this occasion we returned to Poets Corner and finished another delicious meal with a sweet. Lesley chose hot apple pie with custard, and I opted for sherry trifle – in honour of all the jelly moulds we had seen that day. As the bar had a convivial atmosphere and an open fire, we were in no rush to return to the cold of our B&B, so I went to the bar to replenish our drinks.

These days, Lesley is almost teetotal and I don't drink much alcohol either. Perhaps we used up our quota when we were younger. Although I still enjoy a glass of decent red wine with a meal, my stomach is easily upset by alcohol and I don't particularly like the dizzy and uncontrolled feeling of drunkenness anymore. When I visit a pub with friends, I will usually order an orange juice and act as the nominated driver, so drinking Guinness in Ireland was a new experience for me. The flavour is quite different to any beer served in England – much smoother and nuttier. When I mentioned this to a barman, I was surprised to discover that the flavour of Guinness in Ireland can vary from county to county, but the quality is ensured by a fleet of testers that tour the country in dedicated Guinness vans. Only in Ireland!

While I waited for our drinks, I fell into conversation with another patron at the bar. Lesley soon joined us, having given up the table to another hungry customer. Declan was a tall and physically dominating man who had recently retired from the Irish police force, or *Garda Síochána*. Aged around sixty, he had thick, wavy grey hair and hands the size of dinner plates. But his voice was calm and kind, and his lilting Irish accent perfectly complemented his humour and the irreverent twinkle in his eye. On hearing of our tentative plans to move to the Emerald Isle, he said we would be most welcome, and proceeded to administer some sage advice about safe driving in Ireland.

"First, you need to take notice of the road signs – and then ignore them," he said waving his arm energetically, and liberally christening those around with splashes of Guinness. "The country is changing from using miles to kilometres on all road signs, and to me it seems like the local council staff just went out with a crayon, crossed out miles and wrote kilometres. On Monday, one sign near us showed Ennis 14 miles and by Tuesday, the new sign in the same spot read Ennis 14 km."

"We noticed the same thing this week," Lesley agreed.

"And we're all expected to drive in kilometres-an-hour, which is bloody stupid, because everyone's speedometers are still in miles-an-hour. People are so busy trying to read the small kilometre digits on the dial that they're not looking where they're going!"

"Yes," I said. "I must admit it's difficult to see the dial, and even harder to do the calculation."

"It's easy, just multiply by point six-two," he said, proving he was less drunk than I thought, or perhaps showing a natural capacity for alcohol.

"Ah! Good to know," I said.

"Another peculiarity in parts of Clare is that the introduction of the horseless carriage has not changed people's desire to stop and chat. It's quite ordinary and acceptable to find two vehicles facing in opposite directions, completely blocking the road as their occupants talk through the open windows."

"We've seen that," Lesley said, rather proudly.

"If you're delayed again, during your visit to our fair land, please do not toot your horn or enquire as to the cause of the delay. On encountering such an obstacle, it is best practice to switch off your engine and wait patiently, while perhaps reading the paper or learning to play the tin whistle." He added a comment, with genuine seriousness, "I know someone who carries one in his car for this reason alone."

"I find it strange, that the pace of life here in Ireland is slower than England," I said, "yet the driving can be so unsettlingly fast."

"Ah ha!" He raised a finger to indicate he had an answer. "We in Ireland have a very relaxed attitude to things like learning to drive, road safety, speed limits, drink driving, and vehicle maintenance." In common with all Irish police officers, he pronounced vehicle *ve-heck-al*.

I bought Declan another drink and nodded for him to continue his history lesson. I noticed he was taking care to pronounce his words without excessive slurring.

"The Irish are generally resistant to rules. For a long time, passing a driving test was optional and unrelated to whether you drove a car or a 40-tonne lorry," he said, adding a little hiccup. "I believe in the UK, drivers can practishe driving a car on a provishional licence. Is that correct?"

"Yes," I said. "Provided they're insured and accompanied by an experienced driver."

"Well, a while ago in Ireland, the government deshided it would be nice if all drivers proved they could drive by passing a test. Shortly after, they realised they were woefully short of test centres, testers and instructors. So, they issued the existing driversh with licences immediately and required any new driversh to pass the test."

"Fair enough," I said.

Declan toasted my accord with the dregs of his Guinness, before raising his eyebrow pointedly.

I nodded to the barman – again.

"However…" As Declan continued, his speech was becoming a little incoherent. "Sh–till short of t–hest centres, they decided that anyone who failed the driving tesht, would be issued with a *shecond provisional licence*, which would allow them to drive un–accompanied *indefinitely*, provided they continued to dish–play a learner plate." He let out a large belch.

"Good grief," I exclaimed, genuinely shocked. But there was more to come.

"Now, I'm *sshure* the Department of Transport expected drivers to return diligently for retesting at their… earliest convenienshe, but few, if any, ever did," he slurred. "Now, more than half of Irish driversh have never taken, or have failed to pass, the driving teshht."

"Well, that explains the standard of driving we've seen," Lesley added. "Some of it was really very scary."

Declan waved a finger in disagreement, before taking another huge swig of beer. His eyes were noticeably unfocused.

"Adherenshe to driving lawsh hash to be equally balanced with the Irish need for flair and shtyle, particularly in the rural areas." His words were now so slurred as to be almost unintelligible. "In the countryshide, it is entirely acceptable to drive at shpeed using a mobile phone, whilst map reading, applying makeup, drinking coffee and eating a breakfast roll."

"What's a breakfast roll?" Lesley asked.

"A breakfast roll ish required morning shush…shustenance for all commercial drivers and oshifers of the law," he said, draining his beer. "It ish a full Irish breakfast, with all the trimmings, including runny eggs, looshely contained within a French stick." He took a deep breath and attacked his final sentence with great care. "They are available all day at most good garages. I fanshy I shall have one hon my drive home!"

With that he bade us farewell with a wave of his car keys, and weaved his way towards the carpark.

13. Unreasonable Demands

We began our last full day in Ireland with another hearty breakfast and a discussion.

"I've been thinking," Lesley said.

Those three words again, sending chills down my spine. What was it this time? Did my darling wife want me to go back to my old job? Was I about to become the proud owner of a horse? Or a barge? Whatever she wanted, I feared it would not bode well.

"Yes, dear?" I asked, dreading her next words.

"Well, the thing is..." Lesley let the thought hang while she buttered some toast. I knew better than to interrupt her contemplative pause, instead I suffered in silence while I waited for the other shoe to drop. Once the marmalade had been evenly spread, she continued.

"...we haven't really seen any houses that we actually loved."

"We still have another two days to–"

"I know, but I was thinking," she cut in, rather firmly.

"Go on," I said, somewhat apologetically.

"We both quite liked the first house we saw," she said.

"You mean the one out west that looked like there had been a burglary, Derry something?"

"Derryshaan," she corrected.

"That's right, Derryshaan." I shrugged. "What about it?"

"I was thinking that we should put in an offer."

"Really?" I was a little taken aback. "I thought you were a little so-so about it."

"Well I am a bit," she admitted, "but it's not a horrid place. We could move in straight away, and it's large enough for all our furniture."

"The land's large enough, that's for sure! Don't forget it has 29 acres now." I was going to cross my arms and assume a defensive posture, but my scrambled eggs were getting cold. "What would we do with it all?"

"We could keep a few cows...or some sheep." She gave me her 'little girl' smile. "You could get a tractor. It'd be fun!"

"Why the sudden change of heart?" I asked, naturally suspicious of her intentions.

"I don't really know." She shrugged. "I keep thinking of the view from the front room window. I could see all the way down to the Shannon. It was a nice house. I think we could be happy there."

Lesley smiled. Clearly, she was genuinely taken by the house. I had to agree with her thinking. Even if it didn't have the 'wow' factor we were looking for, Derryshaan was a house we could easily make into a home. Just one with a very big back garden.

"Well...I suppose you're right," I said.

Lesley clapped her hands.

"What do you want to do?" I asked. "We still have other properties to see, and we've only just put our house on the market. It could be months before we're ready to buy."

"Alan said the buying process over here is much the same as England," she explained. "There is no actual commitment until we pay the deposit. So, our offer is only an offer. We can always withdraw if we see something better, or change our minds about moving."

"That's unlikely, unless we win the lottery," I commented with heavy irony. "How much shall we offer?"

"Call Alan," Lesley tapped my mobile phone with her knife. "Ask him if they will take €10,000 under the asking price."

"I suppose this will give us a feel for the housing market," I said, wiping some marmalade from my phone. "Let's see what he says."

Our plan for the day was to visit Corofin, a small village on the edge of the Burren National Park, a little to the north of Ennis. We had only one house to visit that day, after which we would have lunch and spend the afternoon sightseeing. A large chunk of the morning was taken up with telephone calls to and from Alan Sykes. Lesley and mobile phones are not happy bedfellows, particularly when the signal is patchy. We found ourselves making frequent stops in lay-bys, and farm entrances, or wherever else we could get a signal, while still pushing on towards our destination.

During our discussions with the vendor's wife, we had made it abundantly clear we would be selling our house and moving to Ireland and would require the sale to be completed, and the property vacated, by May or even earlier if possible. Furthermore, we would be cash buyers, which put us in a strong position – or so we thought. After much discussion with Alan, we made a generous offer, at slightly below the asking price. Within minutes, it was firmly refused, so we made a counter offer on the asking price and this was accepted, but with one proviso. The vendors said they were quite happy to complete the sale by March, as they needed the money to buy a plot of land and build their new house. And then they dropped their bombshell.

"WHAT?" I asked, in disbelief. Lesley did her best to explain again what Alan had said, but I wasn't convinced. "That can't be right. You must have misunderstood."

"I swear, it's what he said."

"But that's complete madness," I exclaimed. "It's a totally unreasonable demand."

"That's what I told him," Lesley said, her voice tight with suppressed anger. "You heard me."

"It's unbelievable!" I shook my head. "It just can't be right."

"It's what he said," Lesley replied firmly, her lips were tight with dissatisfaction. She tossed the phone onto my lap. "If you don't believe me, you can speak to him yourself!"

"It's not you I don't believe…"

Lesley was staring out of the side window, her arms tightly crossed, and my words were falling on deaf ears. I pulled the car over at the first spot where we had a mobile phone signal, and called Alan. He answered on the first ring.

"Alan. It's Nick," I snapped. "What the hell's this proviso these people want? Surely they can't be serious."

"I'm sorry, Nick, but they are," he said. I could hear his frustration mirrored my own.

"They seriously want to remain in the house for a year or more, after we buy it?" I asked.

"Apparently so," he said. "They intend to use the proceeds from the sale to build another house."

"I don't care what they want to do with the money," I said, rather louder than was necessary. "I'm not going to buy their house and rent it back to them for a couple of years while we…what…live in a caravan somewhere?"

"Aah! There's another thing," I could hear him sucking his teeth. "I didn't tell Lesley this, but…they don't expect to pay rent."

"Oh, you are joking!"

"I wish I was," he said, his voice failed to hide his sadness and frustration. "I've put a lot of work and money into marketing their house. I've met with them several times, and today is the first time they've mentioned this plan."

"But it's a ridiculous suggestion." Feeling as if my head were about to explode, I pinched the bridge of my nose between thumb and finger. "Surely they must realise nobody will even consider buying their house under these circumstances?"

"Well…although it's not common practice," Alan said, "such an arrangement is not considered unusual in West Clare."

"We consider it to be very unusual." I looked at Lesley for confirmation, she gave me a short nod of agreement. "I'm sorry, Alan, someone may buy their house, but it won't be us. You can tell them we've withdrawn our offer."

Alan had nothing further to say, other than another apology. Lesley and I climbed out of the car and took a moment to breathe and relax. As we held hands and looked out across the fields, I could feel the tension and anger falling away.

"There's still two more properties to see," I said, trying to keep our spirits up.

"Perhaps after we've seen this bungalow, we should go into Ennis and trawl the estate agents," Lesley suggested.

"We can do that in the morning. We've got one house to view tomorrow, and plenty of time before our flight." I gave her hand a squeeze. "It's a lovely day, let's enjoy ourselves."

"OK." She smiled for the first time in an hour. "I'm looking forward to seeing the Burren. It's quite famous."

I checked my watch. "We'd better get moving. It's almost twelve. The estate agent said he'd meet us at the house."

"Auctioneer," Lesley corrected my repeated use of the incorrect term.

"Ha! I'm starting the think the Irish *auctioneers* are no better than the British lot," I complained.

"I know you don't mean that. Alan's doing his best." Lesley gave me a nudge in the ribs. "Play nicely."

"Must I?"

"Yes you must," she said. "Come on, let's go."

"OK."

The house we had arranged to view was a 1970s bungalow, one of several of a similar style scattered along a busy side road, a short distance outside the little village of Corofin. We eventually found the correct property by slowly driving along the street and squinting at houses until Lesley spotted the auctioneer waving at us. He directed us through the low, wrought iron gate, and indicated I should drive up the short, sloping driveway and park at the front of the house. The front garden was predominately laid to lawn along with a few mature shrubs and a small flowerbed.

"Nice view, isn't it?" Sean, the auctioneer, said, launching into his sales pitch. "The lake has some great fishing, I'm told."

The house was around ten feet above the level of the road, and maybe a hundred higher than the lake, which was visible through the trees.

"How far away is the lake?" Lesley asked.

"Not far," he said. "I'd say you could walk there and back in under an hour."

"A lovely way to spend a summer evening," I said.

Sean said something in reply, but I couldn't hear over the sound of a huge lorry driving by. It was a dumper, piled high with crushed rock. Seconds later an empty lorry of the same design passed in the opposite direction. I felt the sound rumble through my feet and into my chest.

"Goodness! What a noise!" Lesley exclaimed.

"There's a couple of quarries near here, but don't worry, you'll soon get used to the noise," Sean said. "Come on. Follow me."

He took us in through the front door and began the tour. Although the bungalow was unoccupied and unfurnished, someone had tried to keep it clean and presentable for prospective buyers. The pattern of the carpets and wallpaper stopped being fashionable in 1979, along with the kitchen units, the avocado green bathroom suite, and the matching sinks with plastic backsplash that were fitted in all three bedrooms. As there was no central heating, electric storage radiators had been added at strategic points around the house, and there was a three-bar electric fire, with flame effect plastic coal, sitting proudly on the low-level stone fireplace. The view through the large single-glazed window at the front was of the road, trees and the distant lake. To the rear was a small paved courtyard.

"Where's the garden?" Lesley asked, waving the estate agent's papers. "It says here there is an acre of well-maintained garden."

"Does it?" Sean asked, obviously perplexed. Lesley showed him the details. "Ah, yes. It's this way."

He took us through the back door, across the courtyard, out a gate and along a passageway leading to a large grassy field.

"Here it is," Sean said, gesturing dramatically with his arm.

"Here what is?" I asked.

"The garden," he answered, again gesturing with his arm.

The view before us was a depressing sight. The 'mature garden' mentioned in the property details, was no more than a large square of muddy grass, surrounded on all four sides by the rear fences of the 30 or so houses overlooking the field. Well-trodden footpaths leading to back gates, temporary goalposts, piles of rubbish and rusting washing machines, and a dejected looking donkey tied to a wooden stake suggested this was less of a private garden and more of a communal area. I flinched as another lorry rumbled by behind us.

"This is it?" Lesley asked in astonishment.

"I'm afraid so." At least Sean had the decency to look embarrassed. "It could be made into a very nice garden," he suggested weakly.

"I doubt it," Lesley said, her frustration overcoming her diplomacy. "You'd always have people watching you out of their windows.

"I suspect anyone who stopped people accessing this field would quickly become very unpopular with every one of these neighbours," I added.

Sean's shoulders slumped in defeat. "I suppose you're right."

"This is not really what we're looking for," Lesley added.

"My wife is right, it's not quite what we're looking for. Thanks for showing us around, Sean," I said, looking at my watch. "We'd better get on. It's time for lunch."

We shook hands with Sean, before climbing into our car and setting off towards the village. I felt sorry for him, he was an honest and affable fellow, trying his best to offload someone else's problem. I understood his frustration and wished the house was more to our liking, but it wasn't. We were equally disappointed and in danger of becoming depressed. Although we were putting a brave face on the situation, with only one more house to see before our flight home, our trip was looking like it would become a failure.

A short drive took us into the village where we parked in the main street. After our careful searching identified no secretive parking signs, we decided it was probably safe to leave our car where it was. To be on the safe side we entered a newsagent to check the local rules. The lovely assistant was rather amused by our enquiry and assured us parking in Corofin was indeed free. I expressed my gratitude with a wild gesture of financial excess, investing a euro to purchase a lottery scratch card. In keeping with our house hunting luck so far, we didn't win. I was unceremoniously dumping the remains of my scratch card into the bin when my mobile phone rang. It was Alan. I answered, putting the phone on speaker mode. He sounded even more upbeat than normal.

"I was just wondering why you didn't choose to see Glenmadrie." he asked.

I was puzzled, and looking at Lesley's face, so was she.

"We've never heard of it," I said.

"You must have seen it," he said. "It's the feature property on my website."

"The big yellow house?" Lesley asked. She had conducted most of our internet window shopping.

"Yes, that's the one!"

"I thought it was your office," she said. There was more than a hint of excitement in her voice.

"No, no!" he laughed. "It's this month's feature property, by far the best house I've got on my books just now. You really must view it before you return to England."

I looked at Lesley and we shared a nod of agreement. "I suppose we could see it tomorrow, in the morning. If there's time," I said. "Where is it?"

"It's not far," Alan replied. I could hear another phone ringing in the background. "Can you meet me in Feakle again, at eleven?"

"Err, I guess so, we've–"

"Grand, I'll see you tomorrow" The phone clicked and he was gone. I looked at Lesley and shrugged.

"I remember it!" she said, her eyes wide with excitement. "It was a beautiful, big yellow farmhouse. It looked so lovely, I never dreamed it was actually for sale."

"Apparently it is," I said. "Perhaps we can end our visit on a high."

And with our spirits once again raised, arm-in-arm, we set off in search of lunch.

14. Boulders and Butterflies

Although the village of Corofin has a population of under 500 people, its location on the edge of the Burren, and being near to Lake Inchiquin, makes it a popular waypoint for walkers, anglers, tourists, and anyone seeking a pleasant lunch in convivial surroundings. Corofin is also home to several festivals, most notably the North Clare Agricultural Show, the Corofin Traditional Festival, and the Corofin Festival of Finn with its infamous World Stone Throwing Championship and Ireland's Best Beard & Moustache competition. Inevitably, none of these events were scheduled to take place during our visit, but we made a mental note to check them out should we ever return.

As well as the newsagent, the short street that ran through the centre of the village had all the required shops – except for a candlestick maker – and several pubs. We randomly chose one at the north end of the village and stepped through the door. Perhaps the higher proportion of tourists visiting Corofin made the patrons more used to strangers entering their favourite watering hole, or possibly they were just thirsty and focused on the job at hand. Whatever the reason, unlike some other pubs we had visited, in England and Ireland, we were not subjected to the usual head turns and blank stares. Externally the building had seemed relatively small, but I could immediately see that the pub was considerably deeper than I had imagined, extending well beyond an enormous central stone fireplace, into a second seated dining area at the back. The large windows to the front of the building provided the space around the entrance and bar with plenty of natural light, and had the added benefit of making the large rear seated area seem more secluded and private. Overall, it was a pleasant room, with a nice, welcoming ambiance.

We took a few minutes to inspect some of the many framed photographs displayed around the walls. They all captured joyous moments of celebration, music and dancing. Many of the photographs featured the same smiling blonde lady, in various poses of fun and enjoyment. Clearly the good people of Corofin, visiting tourists, and the owners of this bar, knew how to have a good time.

"Hi! I'm Sarah. What can I get you?" an English accent asked. I did a double take. The blonde-haired woman at the bar was unmistakably the same person who appeared in many of the pictures.

"Are you serving lunch?" Lesley asked.

"Sure. Grab a table at the back, and I'll bring you a menu," she said. "Would you like some drinks?"

"Could we have a pot of tea?"

"No problem," she replied, adding a dazzling smile. "You're English. Are you on your holidays?"

"Sort of. Actually, we're house hunting," Lesley said. "We're hoping to move here."

"Oh, that's nice. I'm sure you'll love it here. The people are so nice. How's the search going? Have you found the right house yet?"

I pulled a face. "Not yet. It's a little harder than I imagined."

"I suppose you're looking for an old 'second-hand' house?" Sarah asked, and seeing my surprise added, "It's a British thing."

"Not much luck so far, but we have another couple of promising prospects yet to see," I said, trying to remain positive.

"Don't worry, love," she spoke to Lesley, "it will work out."

"Let's hope so, in case not," my wife said, slipping into her native Birmingham slang.

"Have you tried Alan Sykes at Clare properties?" Sarah asked. "He's very good and he specialises in old houses and farms."

"Funny you should say that…"

Even though she was busy, after our delicious lunch, Sarah took a few minutes to introduce us to her husband, Eamon, who was the chef. A large and obviously muscular fellow with tattooed forearms, initially he seemed quite physically intimidating, but when he spoke, his soft Lancashire accent and wry sense of humour belied that impression. As we chatted, Eamon and Sarah told us they had quite recently taken over the business, after many hard years running pubs in the tough East End of London. Used to regular knife fights, and even gun battles, between warring gangs from the inner city, they overreacted spectacularly when faced with their first drunken brawl in sleepy Corofin.

"We now know that in most village pubs in the west, bar fights are extremely rare," Eamon said. "And they can usually be stopped

113

by someone shouting, 'Ah! Paddy, would you cut that out – here, have another pint!' or something similar."

"But we didn't know that," Sarah added. "We were well-versed in the art of dealing with violent confrontation."

"The trick is to get in hard and fast and convince people of the error of their ways," Eamon whispered. "So, when the fight started, I launched myself across the bar brandishing a baseball bat and screaming blue murder."

"Well, you should have seen their faces," Sarah laughed. "They were totally shocked at what they saw as a completely unnecessary reaction to a friendly scuffle."

"Suddenly everyone in the bar was asking *us* what the hell we were thinking!" Eamon added. "They said, 'This is just a friendly fight, there's no need for violence!' I couldn't believe my ears!"

We all laughed.

"Mind you," Sarah whispered, "we haven't seen a fight since!"

Lessons learned all around, I expect.

On our way back to the car, we took a short detour along a side road and up a gentle slope, to see a group of holiday cottages. They were biscuit-tin-pretty, traditional Irish thatched cottages, painted lime-wash white, with thick red gloss paint on the window surrounds and the half-and-half kitchen doors. Sarah had mentioned they were available for medium-term rental, and I was starting to formulate a cunning plan.

"Perhaps, once we've sold our house, we could rent one of these cottages for a few months while we look for our dream home," I suggested.

"We'd have to store our furniture and live out of suitcases." Lesley pulled a sour face. "I suppose it's an idea, but I'd much prefer to move over once we've bought a house."

"Only a thought," I said, defensively.

My wife patted my arm. "Never mind, dear…"

We set off driving north, in an anticlockwise loop, pausing for a short walk once we reached the Burren National Park, before driving on to see the spectacular Cliffs of Moher. The word Burren comes from an Irish word *Boíreann* meaning a rocky place, which is very apt as much of the area is made up of exposed natural limestone pavement. It was formed around 350 million years ago, from sediment, when a tropical sea covered most of Ireland. My initial impression was of a barren landscape, looking as if a mighty hand had swept away all the soil and trees, leaving behind only the bedrock for as far as the eye can see. The mighty hand was probably a glacier, during the last ice age, which scoured away much of the top soil. This erosion process was completed by thousands of years of rain, snow and ice. However, nature abhors a vacuum. Every crack and crevice in the limestone is now alive with a dazzling array of flora and fauna. The area is also rich in wild birds, insects, feral goats and wandering tourists. It's a great place to visit, with breath-taking views from the bald hill tops, of the green pastures below and the mysterious 'disappearing lakes', which fill and drain into underground rivers at seemingly random intervals.

One thing we had noticed about Clare, in comparison to other places we had visited, was the lack of any cohesive tourist planning. The result of this delightfully quaint omission is that tourists like us get to roam far and wide in the hunt for elusive attractions. By Irish standards, at 250 square kilometres, the Burren National Park is huge, so with limited time and no clear guidance, we were unsure where to begin. In the end, we drove around aimlessly for 30 minutes just admiring the views, before climbing over a drystone wall and walking for a bit longer. With so many huge chunks of limestone to negotiate, our walk soon turned into a careful climb. We were both wearing street shoes and keen to avoid turning an ankle or damaging a knee, so after a few hundred yards, we paused to take in the views before returning to the car. Prior to setting off, I read from the tourist pamphlet Mrs Menopause had given us.

"In 1651, an officer in Oliver Cromwell's army observed of the Burren that there was not water enough to drown a man, or wood enough to hang one, nor earth enough to bury them."

"That says a lot about Cromwell's opinion of the Irish," Lesley said.

I added my own comment to that of Cromwell's dissatisfied officer. "And there's no broadband or mobile phone access either!"

I didn't get a laugh.

As we negotiated our way along miles of single track roads, heading west, Lesley kept me entertained by pointing out the groups of feral goats, which are famous in the area, and some of the strange and unusual houses that were partially hidden up driveways and behind hedges. Even though none were displaying for sale signs we paused a few times to peer through the windows at several of these architectural peculiarities.

"Well, I don't think we need to worry too much about planning permission and building regulations," I said, as we looked at a property thrown together from a baffling array of random parts. "I imagined this was the result of an amorous encounter between a gypsy caravan and a tree house. It's the third 'unique' property we've seen in as many minutes."

"They certainly are a little unusual." Lesley smiled "But quaint," she added.

"A little too quaint for my liking."

"Mine too," she agreed.

We found our way to the main road that led to the coast, and soon entered Lahinch. Like many seaside towns during the off season, Lahinch looked rather depressing and forlorn, particularly as the weather was taking a turn for the worse, with low glowering clouds and sleety rain. I imagined it would be a very pleasant and busy place to visit during the summer, but today even the illustrious golf links looked cold and uninviting. Turning north, we pressed on up the gradual hill towards the cliffs. As we climbed upwards, the straight road soon gave way to a succession of long sweeping bends. This was annoying for the car and coach drivers, but manna from heaven for the hundred or so motorcyclists we saw scraping their knees and footrests to eke out every ounce of enjoyment and adrenalin from their rides along this legendary bikers' road.

At the highest point of the hill was a small sign informing us that we had arrived at the famous Cliffs of Moher. To our right, beyond the coach park, the land gradually fell away to the distant valley floor in an irregular series of small fields, drystone walls, and cottages. But to the left, the grassy hill blocked any view of the cliffs and sea, as it climbed steeply towards the cloudy sky.

We left our car in the small carpark, staffed by a pleasant gent in a garden shed. He wore a smart trilby hat, a matching tweed jacket and fingerless gloves. His happy, toothless smile was genuine and his pride obvious as he welcomed us into his domain.

116

As we exchanged a miniscule amount of cash for a parking space and unlimited access to the cliffs, he directed us to the visitors' centre, suggested the easiest route for walkers to take, and pointed to where we would find the best views. With our gloves and scarves on, and our coats tightly buttoned against the cold wind and sleety drizzle, we trotted across the carpark towards the visitors' centre. This was an ancient wooden shack, reminiscent of a village cricket pavilion, selling refreshments and the usual range of Irish-themed trinkets for tourists. The food was good, the service friendly and the toilets were spotlessly clean, despite the number of coach parties passing through that day. Before we braved the cold, Lesley read from the guidebook she had just purchased, along with two key rings and an Irish bookmark.

"The Cliffs of Moher are one of Ireland's busiest tourist attractions," she recited. "These spectacular and much-photographed cliffs, run for more than five miles along the coastline of County Clare. At their highest point the cliffs are over seven hundred feet tall. The name Moher (pronounced Moo-har) comes from the word 'Mothar' after a promontory fort demolished during the Napoleonic wars to make room for the signal tower, called O'Brien's Tower, which is now on the high point of the cliffs."

"That's fascinating," I said. "Let's go and see."

"Hang on a sec, there's more," Lesley said. "On a clear day, the views are spectacular. Looking north you can see the Aran Islands, Galway Bay, and as far as Connemara. To the south, you will see Loop Head."

"And on a day like this, the wind will flail the skin from your face and the crashing waves will send salt spray all the way to the top of the cliffs," I added.

The steep walk up to the cliffs was along a soil path interspaced with steps fashioned from wide slabs of granite. Despite the worsening weather, local traders and musicians, all trying to earn a crust, stood in groups alongside the path. Near the top, in the most exposed spot imaginable, we saw a young girl in traditional Irish costume playing a full-sized harp while a veritable blizzard of sleet and salt spray slapped her blue-tinged face. I couldn't feel my toes with two pairs of socks on, so how she was able to play the harp so beautifully was a mystery to me. Grateful, we gave generously.

Reaching the top of the path was like approaching the edge of the earth. The view before us was truly breath-taking. Far away, towards America, sunshine on the distant horizon bisected the cloud from the sea. Closer in, there was a fishing boat fighting bravely through the rolling whitecaps, pursued by a thousand wheeling seabirds. I cautiously stepped forward and looked down. There at my feet was a vertigo-inducing seven-hundred-foot drop, plunging down the sheer rock face to the sea. At the bottom, there was a mass of swirling foam, where the rocks were pounded by the unrelenting Atlantic waves. My head spun, and the sensation of falling forward was enhanced by hundreds of snowy white gulls, dancing on the updraft and diving towards the sea below.

"Whoa!" I exclaimed, stepping back and inadvertently treading on someone's foot. "Some view?"

"It's stunning, isn't it?" Lesley said. The wind was whipping her face so hard, she looked like she was riding a motorbike without a helmet.

"Let's walk on, before we freeze," I suggested.

Along the cliff edge there had been a few half-hearted attempts at erecting safety fencing, but these were roundly ignored. Although the edges of the cliff are worn and unstable, hundreds of visitors were defying certain death in the pursuit of the perfect photograph. There was a flat sandstone ledge, about one hundred and fifty by fifty feet, which hung out above the water, accessible by an unofficial path. It sat twenty feet or so below the cliff top and was so level and perfect, it could be mistaken for a concrete viewing platform.

I agreed to walk down for a better look, but bravely refused to go nearer to the edge. These cliffs may be as old as time, but the Atlantic is patient, destructive and unrelenting. The signs of erosion were plain to see. Even as we stood on the sandstone shelf, when the waves smashed against the cliffs far below, I could feel the ledge jumping from the shock of the immense impact. Most disturbing to those of us with vertigo and vivid imaginations, was the row of unsupervised children dangling their legs off the edge of the platform and enjoying the view, whilst eating their sandwiches and crisps.

118

Second only to the Guinness factory in Dublin, these cliffs were Ireland's busiest tourist attraction, but with its cricket pavilion visitors' centre, garden shed parking attendants, and common sense approach to health and safety, we found such an uncommercial set-up to be wonderfully quaint and delightfully Irish.

***

That night, as we sat by the fire talking with the backpacker girls, the strangest thing happened. I noticed a butterfly flapping about near the ceiling. A few moments later it was joined by a second, and then a third. Within 20 minutes, there were perhaps 30 butterflies flying around, all having appeared from thin air – or so it seemed. After some discussion, we decided the butterflies had taken refuge for the winter, through the open windows, and had been temporarily woken by the heat from the fire. Since then, I have seen the occasional butterfly woken in similar circumstances, but never nearly so many – it was a truly magical and beautiful moment. In retrospect, although we had yet to find our dream property, I believe that it was on that evening, sitting by the fire, enjoying the easy company of strangers and laughing at the dancing butterflies, we decided we would move to Ireland.

15. The Last Hope

The final day of our trip began with another scrumptious breakfast at the capable hands of Mrs Menopause. Once packed, we settled our bill, said our goodbyes, promised to return, and set off along icy roads towards Feakle village. Alan was waiting outside the post office, and without leaving his car, waved for us to follow him. Perhaps conscious of the slippery conditions, he drove rather more sedately than before. After several twists and turns, and long stretches of single track roads, I was starting to suspect he was lost when he indicated and promptly made a sharp right turn into a long gravel driveway.

"Now this is more like it," Lesley said, as we passed a large garden on the approach to a long, yellow farmhouse.

"Very nice," I commented.

This was Glenmadrie, the house we excluded from our list mistakenly believing it was either an advertisement on the website, or Alan's office. As we climbed out of our cars, Alan handed us the property papers.

"Why is there a 20-foot yin and yang sign on the wall?" I asked.

"The owner is a musician," he explained. "He's rather New Age, as you'll see."

The double front doors were built from thick planks of oak, held together with iron bands and roughly hammered rivets. I imagined they had been liberated from a medieval church. After a short search, Alan found the keys hidden behind a loose rock in the wall.

"The house is empty because the owner is away somewhere in South America. He's keen to sell," he added with a smile.

He led us into what can only be described as a cowshed, attached to one end of the house. It was dark and dank, with a bare mud floor partially obscured by piles of rubbish.

"*Here we go again,*" I thought.

Alan described the property as an 'English' house, meaning the unconventional layout would not appeal to many Irish buyers, and would probably only ever be owned by a nutty English couple, or perhaps a German family.

"That's lucky," Lesley said.

From the cowshed, Alan led us along a lengthy brick built conservatory and through a second external door. We were in a large, square courtyard, around 30 feet long, facing a drystone wall. The buildings along the three sides of the courtyard all had low arched windows, giving the feeling of a cloistered walkway. Even though the weather had caused some of the roofing to collapse, I liked what I saw.

"As you can see," Alan said, "this courtyard faces almost due south, so it will get the sunshine for most of the day."

He took us back through the conservatory and into the house, or he would have done, had he not hit his head on the lintel over the kitchen door.

"That door's so short, it's a wonder you didn't break your jaw," I joked.

Lesley could pass through unscathed, but Alan and I both needed to duck – he rather more than I. The kitchen was dark, with a low ceiling made of rafters and the naked floorboards of the room above. There were no kitchen units, just a large larder painted dark purple, a makeshift sink and work-surface, and a shiny red cooking range. In one corner of the kitchen stood a homemade metal spiral staircase disappearing up through the ceiling. It was painted to match the psychedelic purple of the larder, but was otherwise completely out of place in a cooking area.

"Why?" I asked pointing at the offending article.

"I think this part of the house was once the cowshed," he explained. "When it was first converted to habitation it remained separate from the rest of the property, so they added this," he kicked the spiral staircase with his shoe, "to access the two floors above."

Alan took us into the living room.

"This doorway was knocked through in 1977." He pointed at the date carved into the stone above the door. "But I guess they never got around to removing the spiral staircase."

"It would have to come out," I said. "If there was a kitchen fire, the staircase would act as a chimney. Anyone upstairs wouldn't stand a chance."

"You're right," Alan said. "Although now it's probably holding up the floors."

121

"This room is nice," Lesley said, trying to insert a positive note.

The living room was an impressive size, with a polished wooden floor, stone walls, and a low, slatted wooden ceiling. A huge stone fireplace protruded almost a third of the way into the room. I noticed some printed words on several of the wooden strips covering the ceiling. When I tapped one with my finger, it wobbled slightly and I was rewarded with a small shower of dust.

"I think the wooden strips on the ceiling are teak," Alan said. "Probably from old tobacco cases. You'll find a lot of things in the house are recycled or repurposed."

"We're all for recycling," Lesley replied.

"I believe this staircase was once in a local church," Alan commented, as he led us to the first floor. "It's probably over a hundred years old."

The large master bedroom had a row of four leaded glass windows with views to the south and up the hill to the land. The floor was made of polished pine floorboards, and the sloping ceiling, like much of the upstairs, was covered with the same repurposed teak strips. The colour scheme throughout was certainly New Age, with a heavy emphasis on dark blues, purple, and red. Although the lack of pastel shades was unfamiliar to us, the result was not unpleasant on the eye.

"It's going to be a bugger to paint over this lot," Lesley said, ever the practical one when it came to decorating. The floor beneath our feet creaked alarmingly as we walked. I could see several signs of active woodworm.

"I wouldn't worry about painting," I whispered. "Most of this will need to be ripped out."

The bathroom was small, practical, and very purple, with a toilet balanced on a chunk of wood, and a stained bathtub with no side panel. Through gaps in the floorboards, I could see the room below. Alan walked us through a large central bedroom which also acted as a corridor to the rooms above the kitchen. I almost tripped when we encountered a short slope where the floor level changed by several inches. I looked at Alan. He shrugged and did his best to explain the anomaly.

"At one time this part of the property was a traditional Irish thatched cottage. Where we're standing, a wall and chimney would have bisected the house. Sometime in the 1970s, the central wall was removed and a new chimney added. You saw it downstairs."

"The different floor levels would have been on either side of the original dividing wall?" I suggested.

"That's right."

"Rather than bodging the gap with a slope, why didn't they just put in a new floor?"

"They probably didn't have the money," Alan shrugged. "My wife would call this a 'higgledy-piggledy house', the product of the incomplete thoughts and unfinished ideas of several underfunded owners. It has great potential though."

"I like it," Lesley said. "It feels nice."

"It does feel nice, and it certainly has potential," I said. "But it's going to cost a pretty penny to renovate."

There were two rooms above the kitchen, but on separate floors, accessed by the rickety spiral staircase. Both had very low ceilings and the floors had been constructed from a mixed batch of recycled floorboards and sky blue chipboard. Much of the flooring did not reach the granite stonework of the walls, and in several places, there were gaps as wide as my shoe. The lower room housed a partially constructed airing cupboard, a workbench, a collection of dead spiders, and an interesting display of rodent droppings. The upper floor was no more than a half loft, with a ceiling so low, even Lesley needed to crouch.

"I think this bit was a sort of sleeping loft for the owner's children," Alan explained.

"Perhaps that's why the ceiling's so low," I suggested.

We carefully negotiated the spiral staircase, which rocked alarmingly with three people on it, but remained upright. Back downstairs, we walked through the conservatory and around the courtyard to see the final room of the house, which was only accessible through a rough wooden external door. It was a large room, with a low plasterboard ceiling, supported by a single horizontal tree trunk. This makeshift beam was two feet thick, freshly varnished, and riddled with woodworm. The room smelt of fresh paint, new carpet, and damp.

"This part of the house was recently converted to act as a music room," Alan said. He pointed to the large, bright yellow double doors. "I think it may once have been a garage, or a store room."

"It's the best room in the house," Lesley said. "We could easily fit all our belongings in here while the renovations are done."

"This would need to be fixed first." I pointed to a large area of damp and mould on the south-facing wall. "There's water getting in somewhere."

"That's nothing to worry about." Alan tapped the wall with his knuckle. "It's probably just a broken gutter or something. It'll be an easy fix."

Outside again, we began a tour of the land. Alan strode on ahead, giving Lesley and I the opportunity to share our thoughts. We agreed Glenmadrie was by far the best house we had seen, and a definite 'maybe' despite the renovations required to put it right. But there would be a lot to do if this building was to become a home.

Whereas the property showed potential, the land and location delivered the 'wow factor' we were hoping for. Set high in the hills to the south of Lough Graney and several miles from other habitation, the house sat in four acres of land and was truly remote. Although it obviously had not been cultivated for years, the soil was of decent quality and fertile, having once been used as a goat farm. Alan led us up a steep hill to a high point from where we could see the entire property.

It was a beautiful late December Irish morning, with crystal clear skies and a pleasantly mild breeze blowing in from the east. The sun was bright and surprisingly warm. Alan directed our attention to the north, beyond where the house sat, looking yellow, sturdy and permanent.

"That small wood, beyond the buildings, is part of the property, and marks the northern boundary. Along with the trees around the perimeter of the meadow and quarry, you should have enough firewood to keep you warm until global warming really kicks in."

"Did you say quarry?" Lesley asked.

"Yes," he said, pointing his thumb over his shoulder to the south. "It's over there in the corner."

We walked over and cautiously peered in from the top edge. The flat gravel floor was about 30 feet below. The quarry was shaped like a horseshoe with the open end facing east towards the setting sun, which was presumably why the base had recently been levelled to allow the construction of a fifty-foot-high oak pyramid. To my practical mind, this wooden monstrosity spoiled a spectacular view. I couldn't help thinking the money could have been spent far more wisely by treating the house for woodworm. But that was only my opinion.

"Around a hundred years ago, limestone was quarried here and turned into quicklime, by baking it for days in a furnace," Alan said. "You can still see the lime kiln at the top of the quarry. It's an important historical feature, which will be marked on the ordinance survey map, along with old churches, monuments, and the like."

"Quicklime and slaked lime, produced in reaction with water, were important chemicals back then," Lesley said. She had recently finished an Open University course. "They were used in farming, agriculture, the manufacturing of iron and steel, as well as in medicine and as an ingredient in cement."

"I'm impressed," Alan said. "Some lime kilns were still in use as late as 1950, when they stopped being commercially workable."

"That pyramid's a bit of a joke," I commented.

"Actually, it is a bit of a local joke," he admitted. "It's called Foley's Folly, after the owner."

"It will have to go," I said.

"Good firewood," Lesley suggested.

Alan and I nodded in silent agreement.

Turning in a circle, Lesley and I slowly scanned the surrounding countryside, gradually taking in the outstanding views. To the rear of the property was a steep hill, planted with young pine trees, and beyond were hundreds of acres of mature forest. To the south I could see a series of low hills, leading down to a distant valley. Looking to the east, we had unrestricted views across miles of pristine moorland dotted with huge glacial boulders, looking like discarded toys in a giant child's bedroom. I took my wife's hand.

"Isn't it beautiful?" I said.

She squeezed my hand in agreement, but added a reminder. "There's another house to see before we fly home. We'd better get moving."

We thanked Alan for the tour, and promised to call him with our thoughts when we were back in England.

***

The final house on our itinerary was a disappointment for all the wrong reasons – we really liked it. Over lunch Lesley and I had agreed we were very taken by Glenmadrie and should make an offer. We loved the views, the remote and secluded location, and we both felt the house held great potential, despite the obvious flaws. Now, after a week of disappointment, we were suddenly presented with not one, but two properties to choose from.

Ballymallone was in the possession of a delightfully eccentric elderly Dutch widow who spoke very little English. As we spoke no Dutch at all, the meeting was conducted almost entirely in mime. We arrived by appointment, dead on time at 3 pm, to find her amiably drunk, and by the time we left at 4.30 she could barely stand. She had a nice house, recently converted from the remains of an old barn, with five acres of fertile land, sitting high on a hill overlooking the village of Scariff. The property was built on several levels with many quirky rooms, full of character and charm. Because of the recent renovation, there would be no need to decorate. We would be able to move in without even breaking into a sweat. As if that wasn't good enough, the property included a second, smaller house a few yards away, which would provide immediate revenue through rental income. While this was financially attractive, I was worried moving abroad to get away from it all, only to end up living so close to a neighbour and tenants, would somewhat defeat the purpose. However, the benefits of a guaranteed income, along with a ready-to-occupy and fully decorated house were obvious. So, there it was – everything we had been looking for, beautifully presented in the last house of our visit.

I was sad to turn my back on the potential of Glenmadrie, with its wonderful views, particularly so soon after we had decided to make an offer, but Ballymallone seemed to have everything we had wished for. And yet there was a part of me that felt strangely empty. If this was our dream home, why did I not feel more elated? Lesley suggested we were just coming down from the emotional high at the end of the trip. She was probably right. Through a series of hand gestures, mimes, and hugs, we told the Dutch lady we wanted to buy her house. To avoid any risk of confusion, we called Alan and confirmed our offer. As his language skills were far superior to ours, I handed over the phone, and after a brief exchange, the sale was agreed. We left our smiling host in a cloud of gin, as she slowly slid from her kitchen chair towards the floor, and happily made our way towards England.

After acclimatising to the pace of life in Ireland, I was struck by how busy and bad tempered everyone in Colchester seemed to be. We stopped at a local supermarket for some milk and bread. As we waited to pay, I foolishly tried to pass the time of day with a lady in the queue, only to be cut short with the comment, "I'm sorry, I don't know you." So it was not surprising that Lesley, who hadn't smoked a single cigarette since we had set off for Ireland, was back on the evil weed just moments after we set foot back in Britain. However, arriving home was not without its benefits. Our two dogs were delighted to see us, alternating between barking madly, running around in circles, and leaping up like they were on springs to give us our welcome home kisses. The chickens were typically unimpressed by our return, and possibly more aggressive than ever.

Soon we were settled in at home, with our feet up and drinking tea while we caught up on life back in the real world. I was sorting through a pile of junk mail and utility bills when I noticed an unstamped envelope of high quality vellum. Inside was some positive news from our neighbour.

"It's a letter from Richard," I said. "He says he and his wife want to buy our chickens."

"Oh, that's nice!"

"And our house," I added.

"Well," Lesley said with a big smile, "it looks like we had better start packing."

Richard, our neighbour, was offering to buy our house as a new home for his elderly parents. It was to be an immediate cash sale, for the full asking price, less only the estate agent fees we would be saving. The only provisos to his offer were that our asking price needed to be assessed as being fair, by three independent valuations, and the sale be completed without a forward chain. In other words, we were to take his money and get out.

The following day I met with Richard and accepted his offer for the house. We immediately contacted our respective solicitors to start the ball rolling and I also informed our estate agent we had sold the house privately. Richard wanted to complete the purchase so quickly so they could make an early start on the structural changes necessary to prepare the house for his elderly relatives. With dizzying speed, all the necessary inspections and property searches were completed, contracts were drawn up and signed and the deposit was lodged with our solicitor. Barring any last-minute hitches, we would move out on March 12th. Whereas this was excellent news for us in moving the project forwards, it created a logistical challenge, as we had to pack our lives into boxes and arrange safe storage with a firm that could deliver to Ireland at a reasonable cost.

After some research, I found a removals firm who could store our belongings and deliver them safely to our new home, at a cost that was only slightly more than that of the first moon landing. Next we acquired dozens of one metre triple-ply cardboard boxes and started packing. Each box needed to be labelled and the contents listed separately, or so Alan had told us, in case the lorry was inspected by customs when arriving in Ireland. Lesley did a magnificent job of packing, although the task was made a little easier because we already had a pile of boxes in the garage. These were yet to be unpacked from our previous house move, several years before, and only needed to be added to our list.

Once she had packed and taped the first box, Lesley asked me to move it to the dining room at the front of the house, where the completed boxes were to be assembled. I grabbed the box and went "ooff" but it didn't move. Next I spread my legs, bent my knees and with a straight back made an "eeeffe" sound, but to no avail. Finally, I tried going blue in the face and heaving with all my might, until the veins in my neck looked like hosepipes and sweat dripped down my back. The box stubbornly refused to budge.

"What the hell did you put in it?" I asked, lying on the floor and watching little white dots dance before my eyes.

"Just the records and a few books," Lesley replied.

"Not all the records?" I asked in horror. We still had our vinyl collection of over 100 albums.

"And a few books to fill up the box," she explained in a matter-of-fact tone.

"But I can't even move it," I complained. "It must weigh a ton."

"Oops!" She shrugged and gave me that little girl smile that I love her for.

After that, we redistributed the weight more manageably across three boxes, and agreed that just because she could lift a box herself, it didn't follow that two strapping removals men could also lift it. Within a week the packing was completed, except for the items we required each day for cooking, eating, dressing, and a Christmas party for Lesley's mother, Muriel, and Joanne, our daughter.

Typically, Lesley and I wouldn't be inclined to have a big Christmas bash, unless it was for the benefit and enjoyment of others. When Joanne was a child, Lesley would scrimp and save to buy small gifts throughout the year that would make suitable Christmas presents. These were secreted in nooks and crannies around the house, ready for the big day. I am confident several of these gaily wrapped presents still lie where they were hidden, like a squirrel's forgotten winter hoard, covered in dust and waiting for another family to discover them. At our previous home, each Christmas, Lesley and I dressed as Mr and Mrs Santa Claus and visited the elderly and lonely to offer mince pies, mulled wine, and the best wishes of the local community association. But with Joanne grown up and living with her flatmate, during the years since we moved to a 'posh village', our Christmases had become increasingly low key, bordering on the non-existent. However, as this was our last Christmas in England for the foreseeable future, we decided to have a slap-up dinner, with all the trimmings. I even put up some decorations, and bought a box of Christmas crackers.

It was a lovely and festive day. In the morning, Joanne brought Muriel over by car, and after tea and cake, we drove to Dedham village where we planned to take a walk with the dogs. Unfortunately, because of the recent atrocious rains, the river had burst its banks, flooding much of the surrounding countryside. We could only stare morosely at the rushing waters, then stand alongside Dedham lock and point towards the spot where the 'Hay Wain' once stood, back when John Constable was still alive and painting.

We took a circular route home, so we could ogle the exotic houses and posh country estates that would always be beyond our budget. Back home, the cooking range had done a magnificent job of slowly cooking the turkey and roasting the vegetables, and with the addition of some kale, cabbage, peas, and bread sauce, we were ready to feast. After we had eaten our fill and the plates were cleared, I served my secret recipe American Cheesecake. It is rich and delicious, but runs at 1,000 calories a slice, which I didn't mention at the time. Well, it was Christmas. Fit to burst, we pulled our crackers, wore paper hats, read silly jokes, and raised our glasses to remember our absent friends. Joanne proposed a toast to wish Lesley and me the best for our new adventure.

"Although everyone will be sad to see you move away, we all wish you the very best," she said. "Anyway, you're only an hour away, so I'm sure we'll all be visiting so frequently that in future, you'll probably see more of us than you do now. Cheers!"

When Brandy reminded us why we don't usually feed her on turkey and leftover cabbage, by cracking a fart so offensive that it almost discoloured the wall paper, we retired to the living room where we watched the Christmas edition of *Strictly Come Dancing* and fell asleep in front of the fire.

New Year's Eve was a quiet affair, except for Richard's annual spectacular fireworks display, which rattled the windows for two hours and terrified our poor dogs.

"I won't miss this every year," Lesley complained.

"These days the fireworks in England seem to start at the beginning of October and last right into January," I observed.

"It's a crazy waste of money."

130

"Rather than buying so many fireworks, Richard could have just paid a bit more for our house," I joked.

"Do they have fireworks in Ireland?" Lesley asked.

I shook my head. "After so many years of terrorism, I expect they don't like things that go 'bang' unexpectedly."

"Twit!"

***

The year started quietly, as our plans to move gradually took shape. My lists grew longer, but many of the required ducks were dutifully lining up into rows, to the point where I was starting to feel rather confident everything was going to work out splendidly. And then it didn't.

I was sitting at my desk, laboriously adding to the master list of all our worldly goods, which would accompany the removal van to Ireland, when the phone rang. It was Aidan Houlihan, the Irish surveyor (called an engineer in Ireland) who we had appointed to inspect and approve our new home.

"I've got some bad news, Nick," he said, getting straight to the point. "I'm afraid you can't buy Ballymallone."

"Why ever not?" I asked.

"There's no planning permission."

"For what?"

"For the new house," he said, gravely. "She had no planning permission to build a house on the site of the old barn."

"None whatsoever?" I asked.

"I'm afraid it's worse than that."

I closed my eyes and covered my face with my hand as I waited for Aidan to deliver his bombshell.

"Go on," I said.

"Do you know about Statute Barred and what it means?" he asked.

"Yes, Alan mentioned it," I replied. "If something has been built without planning permission, if it's been there for more than six years, the council can't make you take it down."

"It's eight years, but otherwise you've got the gist of it," Aidan said. The soft warmth of his accent only served to remind me of Ireland, and the implications of what I suspected he was about to say.

"Can't she get Statute Barred planning on Ballymallone?" I asked.

"She should have, but the idiot engineer she hired has cocked it up!"

My heartbeat was becoming irregular and I imagined my blood pressure would be soaring. I took several slow breaths and tried to relax.

"What happened?" I asked quietly.

"Normally, a competent engineer would recognise the situation and apply for planning permission for a new window, or something," he said, "and at the same time register the remainder of the planning infractions as being Statute Barred. It's quick, easy, inexpensive, and almost fool proof."

"But not in this case..." I suggested.

"No. This idiot applied for full *retrospective* planning permission, instead of Statute Barred. It was tantamount to saying 'We admit to building *an entire house* without permission, please forgive us'. As you can imagine, the answer from the council was a firm no," Aidan said. "They've ordered her to demolish the house."

"Oh my God! The poor woman must be mortified!"

"She is," he said. "Her only hope is to sue the engineer for gross incompetence."

"What happens now?" I asked, with a heavy heart.

I could almost hear Aidan shrug. "You forget Ballymallone and look for another house."

"We might have something in mind, but I need to phone Alan," I said. "Thanks for being on the ball, Aidan. I'll get back to you."

Lesley had been in town when Aiden called. She was window shopping for curtain material suitable for Ballymallone. So it was an hour later when I shared the bad news. Her reaction surprised me.

"That's OK," she said, brightly. "Perhaps it's fate, or something."

"I thought you would be upset," I said.

She shook her head. "Ballymallone was a nice house. I suppose I should be upset, but somehow I'm a little relieved." She shrugged in confusion. "I don't know why."

As unexpected as her reaction was, it was a relief to me. I was upset to hear of the planning problems at Ballymallone because I thought Lesley had set her heart on owning the property, and I felt sorry for the lovely Dutch owner. Now I realised the prospect of a ready-to-use house, and the guarantee of a regular income, had blinded us to our true feelings.

"You're right," I said. "Perhaps it *is* fate. I feel much the same."

Lesley could see the property papers for Glenmadrie sitting in the centre of the desk. She guessed what I had been doing and smiled.

"Did you phone Alan?"

I smiled and nodded.

"Did you make an offer?"

I raised my eyebrows and smiled even wider.

"And?"

"He just called me back. The offer was accepted. We're buying Glenmadrie!"

Lesley did a little dance and we hugged. This time there was no doubt about the decision, and we were both elated. Ireland was the right country for us, County Clare was spectacular, and the house felt right. Glenmadrie really was our dream home.

***

Although our house sale and packing was progressing almost flawlessly, the road leading towards our purchase of our dream home was proving to be narrow, poorly signposted, and full of dangerous potholes. The March 12th deadline for our sale was looking more certain every day, and we had no intention of rocking the boat by asking for a delay. But our progress towards completing the purchase of Glenmadrie was painfully sluggish, even by Irish standards. The first pothole we had to negotiate was communication, or 'Miss Communication' as I had started to label this vexing difficulty.

The problem arose because the vendor was still somewhere in South America and only able to communicate with his solicitor and estate agent by fax, something that happened sporadically at best. Although our initial offer to purchase Glenmadrie was accepted, several issues with the property and legal process soon came to light. In each case, we had to get assurances from the vendor that he would make changes, or agree to adjust the purchase price. Normally, such exchanges are quick and easy, but in this case, Miss Communication had other ideas. For example:

- On Monday, I emailed Alan about problem A, and he faxed Mr Vendor at his last known location.
- On Tuesday, I telephoned Alan about problem B, which was almost solved, save for a small adjustment to the wording. He spoke with the vendor's solicitor and faxed Mr Vendor again. He also sent a second fax to a different South American fax number where Mr Vendor may or may not be residing temporarily.
- On Wednesday, Alan emailed to report problem C that he had just been made aware of. I asked him to fax Mr Vendor and to ask again for a response to problems A and B.
- On Wednesday afternoon, my Irish solicitor telephoned to report that he had just received a completely unsatisfactory reply via Mr Vendor's solicitor regarding problem B. He suggested that we withdraw from the sale. I ask Alan to fax Mr Vendor again to enquire what the hell he is playing at.
- On Thursday, Alan calls to say that Mr Vendor has agreed to a small price reduction to solve problem B. I reply that I am confused, because my solicitor had received a message from Mr Vendor's solicitor with an unacceptable demand. I tell him to fax again and ask for clarification.
- An hour later, I receive an email from my solicitor. He confirms Mr Vendor is prepared to reduce the price, but by a different amount to what Alan was told.
- At 4 pm on Friday, I receive another communication from my solicitor. Apparently, the unsatisfactory response to problem B was meant as a satisfactory solution to problem A. The price reduction Alan told me about was to solve problem C, and the second price reduction was to compensate us for problem B. He also mentioned he had just discovered problem D, which

could scupper the sale. Fortunately, by that time the pub was open.

By early February, most of the packing was done, the movers were ready and waiting, and we were in an unstoppable plunge towards homelessness. At times our frustration with the legal process and Miss Communication almost reached boiling point. It was all Lesley and I could do to avoid taking our stress out on each other. Apart from phoning or emailing Alan and our solicitor, there was little we could do but wait, feed the chickens, and walk the dogs.

As if things were not complicated enough, Ireland was in the process of introducing a streamlined house buyer's process. In theory, the vendor would produce a pack with all the legally required documentation, and with a deft flick of the wrist, the buyer's solicitor would check that everything was in order before approving the sale. Unfortunately, the new regulations were still in their infancy, with many aspects yet to become law. Consequently, there were some differences of opinion between the opposing legal teams.

Our solicitor, probably with the best of intentions, wanted to apply all the new regulations with an excess of alacrity. Whereas, the vendor's legal representative, being more relaxed about these things, was only prepared to apply the current legislation. For a while during February, convinced the whole project was probably about to go belly-up, we even started house hunting again, but our hearts weren't in it. Fortunately, each day we saw some small indication of progress towards the sale. It was enough to keep our hopes above water, but only just.

The final pothole we needed to negotiate was the removal of rubbish. After we moved into our house in England, we had to spend several thousand pounds to clear glass, asbestos and other rubbish from the garden and outbuildings. This was the kind of unbudgeted expense we were keen to avoid in future. Given the remoteness of Glenmadrie, the lack of local waste and recycling services, and the scrap cars and piles of rubbish we had seen during our visit, we were conscious of the likely cost of a similar exercise. We pushed firmly for the site to be cleared before we moved in.

This was the point where Miss Communication really came to the fore, particularly regarding Foley's Folly, the 50-foot pyramid residing in the quarry. I would have been happy for the pyramid to remain, as it would have been a welcome source of firewood, but Mr Vendor was clearly very attached to his folly, or so we thought. With the help of Miss Communication, he became convinced we were being bloody-minded about his precious pyramid. So he responded by insisting that it remained in situ for the next six years, to be maintained by us, at our own expense. Furthermore, he wanted the right to remove the pyramid, at his convenience, and without any prior notice. It was a crazy idea and we refused point blank, indicating that this issue had now become a ridiculous 'deal breaker'. In the end, he agreed to arrange for his magnificent folly to be disassembled and removed before the sale was completed.

I never met the vendor, but I am sure he was a nice chap; I never heard a bad word said about him. But as our frustration grew at the lethargic communication process, I found myself loathing the man. I created mental images of him sitting on some sunny beach in Mexico, drinking his afternoon cocktails and laughing heartlessly, like a pantomime pirate, at our latest desperate request for essential information. As ridiculous as it sounds, I think that if we had met back then, God forgive me, I would have punched his lights out. Of course, he was probably equally frustrated by the poor communications and our seemingly endless list of asinine questions and demands.

However, all's well that ends well, and by mid-February we had finally reached a stage where we could push on with the purchase. Or so we thought.

17. The Legal Crisis

We had appointed Daragh, a reputable solicitor in Ennis, to act on our behalf in the purchase. He was a professional and thoroughly likeable chap who had our best interests at heart, but he seemed determined to present every possible reason he could find to stop us from buying Glenmadrie. Although he made some good points, the difficulty was that he simply couldn't understand why two nutty English people wanted to waste their money buying an old farmhouse when we could afford to buy a shiny new jelly-mould, just like his. This problem came to a head at the end of February when he received our engineer's survey report.

Admittedly, Aiden's report was honest to the point of being impolite, but he was a direct and down-to-earth individual, the sort who considered comments like 'You don't sweat much for a fat girl' to be a factual compliment. So his largely negative official report, laced with damming observations such as 'the guttering is a thriving habitat for all forms of wildlife' and 'much of the flooring is rotten and requires replacement' had to be taken in the context of us being cash buyers planning a substantial renovation. But for our Ennis solicitor, this litany of property faults was the last straw.

Daragh sent me an almost tearful email, citing all the problems with the property and the errors he had discovered in the associated paperwork. The final line of his message made my heart sink. "Despite my best advice, you seem determined to push ahead with the purchase of this unsuitable and uninhabitable property. In the face of such an irresponsible attitude, I cannot continue to act on your behalf in this matter."

Lesley and I were truly shocked. I had never been sacked by a solicitor before, in desperation I telephoned Alan, the estate agent.

"Don't worry, Nick," he said, brightly. "I know Daragh well, he's sound enough. He's just a bit of a jobsworth sometimes."

"He says he won't act for us anymore," I said. "And in that situation, neither will any other solicitor. The sale will be off."

"*Don't worry,*" Alan replied with more confidence than I felt. "This isn't the first time he's done this. Your best bet is to sit down man-to-man. He just needs a little reassurance."

"Really?"

"Sure. Once he sees you're genuine, and unlikely to sue him in the future, he'll be happier to continue."

Although I was marginally comforted by Alan's advice, I wasn't convinced he was right. Daragh seemed to be pretty firm on the matter, but what was there to lose? So I fixed up meetings with Aiden at Glenmadrie, and Daragh at his office, and booked a seat on the next available flight to Ireland.

Lesley had done a magnificent job with the packing, and our lives were now neatly itemised and boxed in cardboard, ready to go into storage. Despite a couple of last minute queries about planning and the boundary of our home in England, the sale was progressing smoothly and on schedule. On the other hand, everybody in Ireland even remotely connected to our house purchase seemed hell-bent on sending me to an early grave. With the purchase of Glenmadrie so hopelessly stalled, it looked like we were soon going to be homeless, as well as unemployed. Hardly the bright future we had dreamed of. If Alan was right, and our solicitor's discomfort with this house purchase was partially due to doing business by phone and email, rather than face-to-face, someone needed to be on hand in Ireland to keep things moving along. It was Lesley who proposed a solution.

"If the purchase of Glenmadrie is going to drag on for weeks, I think you should move to Ireland."

"That could prove expensive," I observed.

"Not really," she replied. "I was thinking about what would happen after the 12th, when we have to move out. I could go and live with my mum, and you could move to Ireland. That way you'd be on hand to resolve any issues. In the long term it would be quicker, and save money."

"Makes sense," I admitted. "But where would I stay? Hotels or B&Bs would cost a fortune. It's a shame we haven't still got the caravan... I could try and rent one of those holiday cottages we saw at Corofin."

Lesley nodded. "That could work. Pop into the pub when you're over and have a meal. See if you can arrange something for after the 12th, assuming Glenmadrie isn't ours by then."

"OK," I said, "that sounds like a plan."

So I went back to Ireland, all the time worrying we would never buy our Irish home, and thinking, "*What a shame Ryanair don't do frequent flyer miles.*" At least Jules, the outrageously camp flight attendant, recognised me and immediately left me in peace, abandoning any attempt to sell me the most expensive sandwiches in Europe. After another smooth flight at the steady hand of our fifteen-year old pilot, and his twelve-year old friend, we landed ahead of time and I bade a relieved farewell to Jules and his two Latvian beauty queen assistants. The girl at the car hire firm also remembered me and provided a free upgrade from my base model car to a monstrous V8 4X4, which was great fun to drive, but seemed to consume petrol faster than a rugby team can drink beer.

An hour later, I booked myself into a hotel on the outskirts of Ennis. It smelled vaguely of damp, dust, and garlic. A curious mix of aromas, which made me question what the kitchen was cooking. After I'd dumped my luggage in my room, I stopped in Ennis for a delicious lunch of vegetable soup and a sandwich, before setting off to meet with the people I was ostensibly paying money to, so they could stop me from buying a house.

I had arranged to meet our engineer at Glenmadrie, so we could discuss his horrific survey report. When I arrived, he was sitting in his car with his head back, listening to classical music. The door was wide open and despite the throaty rumble of my V8 engine, I could hear the unmistakable sound of a soaring aria from *Madam Butterfly*. Although this was the first time I had met Aiden face-to-face, it didn't matter, he was instantly likeable. He was perhaps a few years older than me and of a similarly average build and height, but Aiden had rather more hair, honest, brown eyes, and a warm, welcoming smile. His handshake was professionally firm, and he used his left hand to hold my forearm and emphasise his greeting. My salutation was more apologetic.

"Sorry I'm late," I said. "I got lost. It's only the second time I've been here and this time I came from a different direction."

"Not a worry." Aiden dismissed my apology with a wave of his hand. "I was just enjoying the fresh air. It's a lovely spot to kick back and relax."

"We like it."

"I'm not surprised." Aiden slowly turned a full circle to look at the views. "This is a fantastic house, with unique views."

"That's not what you said in your report," I chided.

139

He pushed his fingers through his thick brown hair and looked rather embarrassed. "Well, you know, I have to write all that stuff. It's for my insurance. But I can assure you, this is a great house. There's nothing much here for you to worry about."

"Thanks, Aiden," I said. "That's very reassuring. Unfortunately, my solicitor doesn't see it that way. He's more inclined to believe the written word."

"Daragh?" Aiden exclaimed, his face showing in ill-concealed hint of disgust. "If he had his way everyone would live in a newly-built house, with a sterile stainless steel kitchen and artificial grass in the garden."

"That's as may be, but when he saw your report he refused to let the sale proceed. If I can't change his mind, we'll never be able to buy this house."

"I'm sure he'll come around." He nodded and gave me a reassuring pat on the shoulder. "Let's have a look at the house, I'll show you what I've found and tomorrow you can tell him you're confident there's nothing to worry about. He *will* come around."

"Okay." I smiled, feeling a little more hopeful.

As we toured the property, Aiden showed me the areas of wood rot, damp, and woodworm infestation he had identified in his report, and dismissed each point with a shrug of his shoulders and comments like, "That'll be easy to fix," and, "That's nothing to worry about." Strangely, despite the dismissive nature of his comments, I found myself feeling evermore concerned about the scale of the impending renovations.

"Gosh, there's a lot to do here," I exclaimed. "It's a huge job, and it's going to take a long time to get it all done."

"It is, but it will be a fantastic home once it's finished."

I smiled. "We think so."

"How are you planning to do the work?" Aiden asked.

"We're hoping to find a good builder," I said. "Can you suggest one?"

"Not really." He huffed dismissively and pulled a particularly sour face.

"You've had problems?"

"You could say that," he laughed. "Perhaps I should explain. The problem is there's too much money in building work. Most of the good builders are working flat out and making a fortune, and those that aren't are of dubious quality – to say the least."

He leaned against the wall and crossed his arms.

"I'll give you an example," he said. "I'm the engineer for a new-build development near Ennis. It's my responsibility to visit the site every few days and inspect the work. I was there a couple of days ago and I asked the foreman if the builders had installed all the insulation I'd requested. He assured me they had. I told him he was mistaken, but he again said they had. He even swore on his mother's grave that the space behind the plasterboard was stuffed full of insulation."

"But you thought he was lying?" I suggested.

"I knew he was lying."

"How so?"

"If they'd installed the insulation as I had instructed, the rubbish skips would have been full of the bright orange wrapping it comes in. So I knocked a hole in the plasterboard to check, and you know what?" Aiden asked.

"It was empty?"

"Damn right," he snapped angrily. "They hadn't installed any at all. It was lucky I spotted it when I did, before too many walls were fitted, otherwise it would have cost thousands to put right."

"What did the foreman say?" I asked.

Aiden gave a scornful grunt. "He said that in his opinion, insulation was a waste of money and we should have left the walls and loft as they were because nobody would have noticed."

"Good grief." I was truly shocked.

"He didn't care." Aiden shook his head. "The problem is, there's more work than there are builders. Some blocklayers are getting two or three euro for each block they lay, the quick ones are earning 600 euro or more a day. As I said, the builders are getting so much money just now, and naturally the good ones are all working and booked far in advance."

"So we may have problems getting a builder to do our renovations?"

"I'd say that's almost certain." He looked me up and down. "Are you handy?"

"Sorry?" I asked, confused by the colloquialism.

"Are you any good at building work?" he asked. "You Brits are supposed to be experts at do-it-yourself."

"Not really." He may as well have asked if I had a talent for juggling hand grenades. "I've done some decorating and carpentry, and fitted a shower and a kitchen, but nothing like this."

"Get a book," he suggested.

"I'd be afraid of cocking it up."

"Believe me, Nick, your worst is probably better than the best efforts of the builder nobody else wanted." He put a reassuring hand on my back. "Think of all the positives. You won't have to wait for a builder. You'll save a fortune, and you'll be sure the insulation has been fitted."

"Good point," I said, warming slightly to the idea. "I'll think about it."

We finished our tour of the property and returned to our cars. Although his report was comprehensively negative, when we looked at each item separately, the faults all seemed minor and repairable, albeit with the liberal application of money and effort. Overall, I was feeling much more confident about the meeting with my solicitor. Aiden's final comment to me was prophetic.

"Gosh, what a beautiful spot this is, Nick," he said, looking out over the moor. "You and Lesley would be fools to miss the opportunity of living here."

He was right.

I waved Aiden on his way and, with nothing else to occupy my time for the remainder of the day, spend an idle hour taking some photographs of the house and land. It was a good opportunity to dream a little, and visualise how the house might look once we had finished the renovations. Although unoccupied, I could see someone had been keeping an eye on the place. The heating was on at a low enough setting to keep the pipes from freezing, and there was a new toilet roll in the bathroom. Conversely, despite a specific agreement with the vendor, it was obvious no effort had been made to remove the rubbish in the outbuildings, or the junked cars in the driveway. Inside the house, the half-completed decorating and building work remained untouched, lying under a thick layer of dust and cobwebs. As I walked around to the quarry I was disappointed to discover the pyramid was still obscuring what was otherwise a beautiful view.

Although I had no rock climbing experience or equipment, for some reason I took it into my head to try and climb the rock face at the highest part of the quarry. You may imagine, in the spirit of mountain climbers, that I attempted to scale the east face of Glenmadrie quarry 'just because it was there', but actually it was 'just because I'm an idiot'. Nobody was about and I was wearing wellington boots and a long cashmere coat, hardly state-of-the-art climbing equipment. The rock face is about 50 feet high, almost vertical, and it was slick with ice and crumbly with loose shale. About halfway up I thought, *"Nobody's about and I'm wearing wellington boots and a long cashmere coat."* I found myself stuck, unable to go back down and, because of the risk of falling, unwilling to climb further up. In my mind I was transported back to a time when, as a child playing alone in the woods near our house, I had climbed a high embankment and become stuck. Now, again I found myself similarly paralysed, not so much by fear but rather by my analysis of the situation. If I tried to climb down when unsure of a decent foothold, I might slip. Conversely, climbing higher increased the risk of damage should I tumble. The safer option seemed to be staying put and waiting for help, but the quarry is very remote and help from a random passing stranger seemed unlikely. In the end, I remembered what I had done as a child – I climbed upwards, focusing only on the next handhold, one step at a time.

When I reached the top of the quarry, I lay in the tall grass and laughed out loud at the absurdity of the situation. Although the wall was not particularly high by climbing standards, it would have been a substantial fall, sufficient to break a leg or knock my silly head off. In the middle of winter, an injured person lying at the foot of the cliff would have died of exposure and shock within an hour. Perhaps I learned an important lesson that day. Sometimes when things seem hopeless, focusing steadily on the next step will keep you moving forwards, towards your destination. However, such insight didn't stop me from being an idiot during the following years, by falling off ladders, getting electrocuted, climbing the quarry again, or just taking long walks across the moor without telling anyone where I was going.

***

The following day proved to be a turning point in our quest for a new life in Ireland. My meeting with Daragh couldn't have gone much better. Despite his strange passion for newly-built jelly mould houses, I found him to be personable and utterly professional. As Alan had predicted, once we were face-to-face Daragh's intransigence dissipated like mist in the sunshine. During a professional discussion, I accepted he was only trying to protect Lesley and me from unwittingly making a mistake. And he recognised we were determined to buy Glenmadrie, unless there was some deal breaker we had yet to be made aware of. So I acknowledged each of his objections and politely dismissed them and, after careful consideration, he agreed to continue to act on our behalf in the purchase of Glenmadrie. We were back in business and there was more good news to come.

I had previously telephoned the managers of three different golf clubs local to County Clare. None of the courses had a resident professional offering golf lessons, and they all agreed to meetings with me, albeit with varying levels of enthusiasm. During that hectic afternoon before my flight home, I drove about a hundred miles, visited each of the courses, and had three interviews. The proprietors of one course, a lovely married couple, were immediately very keen on the proposal. They recognised how my business could be complimentary to theirs, adding value and bringing in some extra customers − or perhaps they simply felt sorry for me. In any event, after some discussion, we agreed terms, and as quickly as that I was no longer unemployed. In my head, I imagined another of our ducks stepping helpfully into line.

To make my trip even more successful, I found a traditional Irish thatched cottage in Corofin I could rent weekly for a reasonable off-season rate. I paid the deposit and made my plans to move to Ireland on March 13th.

Feeling elated, and convinced everything was now going to be okay, I set off towards Shannon Airport and another Ryanair flight home. A few miles from Ennis, I encountered a police checkpoint where a young Garda, with the confidence of officialdom, waved for me to stop.

Lacking the sophisticated computer systems linked to number plate recognition cameras commonplace in the UK, the Irish police rely on checkpoints and visual inspection of window stickers displaying certificates of taxation, insurance, and road worthiness. These checkpoints pop up in the oddest of places. Incredibly, the first one I encountered was on the motorway between Ennis and Limerick. It is a testament to the tranquillity of Ireland's unpopulated roads that such a bottleneck barely registered as a hindrance to my journey. I laughed at the idea of two police officers checking the tax discs of every car on a British motorway, and cringed at the thought of the ensuing chaos and recriminations. But this was Ireland, and here such checks are conducted with dedication in all weathers, and a touch of humour.

As I rolled to a stop, the young Garda checked my windscreen stickers and, as all was in order, he started to wave me on. Suddenly he spotted something amiss and held up his hand. Cautiously, he approached my open window.

"Excuse me, sir," he said in a strong Clare accent. "Is this your ve-hackle?"

"Err – no, it's rented from Shannon Airport. Is something wrong?" I asked, wondering if I had been driving too cautiously for the Irish roads.

"No, sir, everything appears to be in order. Except...I notice you were listening to the radio."

"Yes, I was," I replied cautiously.

"And singing, were you?"

"Not very well, but yes, I was," I replied, trying to think where I could get a copy of the Irish Highway Code.

"Barry Manilow – wasn't it?" he asked with a devilish gleam in his eye.

Slightly embarrassed I replied, "Yes, I'm afraid it was."

The Garda looked past me to the next car and with mock severity said, "Well, sir, I believe it is a reportable offence, but I'll let you off with a warning this time. Don't let it happen again," and he walked away. You've got to love Ireland!

Just a couple of days later, Lesley and I were on a flight back to Ireland. This time we had to sign papers with the solicitor, apply for our PPS numbers, which were necessary to pay stamp duty on the house purchase, and to open an Irish bank account. To prove we weren't international terrorists, or money launderers for South American drug cartels, we had to bring a substantial pile of documents, old bank statements, utility bills, and several other forms of identification. Fortunately, we had only needed to empty a couple of Lesley's carefully packed boxes to locate all the required bumf. After meeting with our solicitor, and yet again assuring him we were indeed willing to deliberately waste our money on a derelict hovel when much nicer new houses were readily available, we pushed on to the bank and the simple task of opening an account.

At the time, banks in Ireland were reminiscent of those in England during the 1950s – as large as churches and of similar architecture. There were no security cameras, guards, or walls of bullet-proof glass, only a counter piled high with money and a kindly old lady to give it out. Once the sale in England was completed, we expected to deposit a substantial amount of cash into our new Irish bank account. Although this was not a fortune, it was much more money than we had ever had in one place. We therefore had a reasonable expectation of some courteous treatment, or at least some respect on a par with our British banking status, where we had an account called 'Platinum with Knobs On' or something similar. But it was not to be.

The first bank teller we spoke to seemed genuinely surprised we wanted to open a bank account, but she quickly gathered her wits and directed us to join the queue for the enquiries desk in the back corner of the building. There were three customers ahead of us, and during our wait we entertained ourselves by comparing this bank with the high-security British equivalent.

"With all that money laying on the desk, I'm surprised they don't get robbed every day," Lesley said.

"When I was over the other day, I was listening to the car radio and they were talking about thefts from the cash-in-transit vans.

Apparently, they've had a spate of violent robberies, and in some cases the families of the cash van drivers have been kidnapped."

"Oh that's awful!"

"It is," I agreed, pointing to the vaulted ceiling and the open-plan cash counters. "So, enjoy this vintage experience while it lasts. They'll be upping the security pretty soon."

"What a shame. Look, it's our turn."

We stepped forward and I addressed the smiling information desk assistant.

"Hello. We're moving to Ireland and we need to open a joint bank account."

"Oh!" She rocked back as if I had terminal halitosis. "Are you sure?"

"About moving to Ireland?" I asked. "Yes, we are."

"No." She giggled and smiled shyly. "I was referring to the joint bank account. I'm afraid it's not particularly common for a wife to share her husband's bank account."

"Really? How odd," Lesley said.

The assistant leaned forward and spoke behind her hand in a dramatic stage whisper. "They're mostly old farmers here. Wives are rather an underclass."

"We're buying a house together," I explained, "so we need a joint account."

"We've got all our papers," Lesley added, dangling her handbag helpfully.

The assistant pointed to a battered and ancient school desk standing in the centre of the banking floor, surrounded by people queueing for the bank tellers.

"If you'd like to wait over there, I'll call Mary. She deals with all new accounts."

We bumped our way apologetically through the queues to the school desk and waited expectantly. I checked my watch, it was 3 pm.

"I wonder what time they close."

"Don't fuss," Lesley ordered. "There's plenty of time."

"I think they shut in half-an-hour."

"*Don't fuss!*" Lesley hissed.

A few minutes later we met with Mary, a particularly sour-faced young maiden. Without comment, she occupied the only

147

chair, leaving Lesley and me to stand facing the desk, all the time feeling like naughty school children. Around us, queuing customers could hear our every word, and probably read our old bank statements at the same time.

"I believe you want to open a bank account?" Mary asked, looking at her watch.

"Yes please," I replied. "We need a joint current account."

Mary looked at her watch again, before staring at me over her half-moon glasses.

"You're English." It was more accusation than observation.

I almost countered with, "And you're Irish." But Lesley quickly cut me off. "Yes, but we're moving to Ireland. We're buying a house."

Mary completely ignored Lesley, but checked her watch again.

"Couldn't you come back tomorrow to make the application?"

"I'm sorry if it's inconvenient, but we need to complete the application today," I said. "We need the account number for our solicitor."

Mary gave a dramatic sigh. "Very well, I'll do it now, *if I must!*"

As Lesley and I stood side by side, facing the schoolmistress's desk and surrounded by curious customers, I began to feel a bit like Oliver asking for more gruel. I was confused and rather irritated by Mary's obvious suspicion and ill-concealed contempt, particularly as we were attempting to entrust her and her employer with all our money. Nevertheless, we pressed on regardless. We were after all, foreigners in a foreign land. However, things became even more tense when we reached the subject of joint accounts.

"Are you sure you want a joint bank account?" Mary asked me conspiratorially.

"Yes, *we* would," I replied pointedly.

"Are you sure?" she asked again. I imagined she was stabbing frantically at an alarm button concealed beneath the desk.

"Yes, I, I mean, we – are sure, thank you."

"Well, if you're sure, I suppose it's okay," she said, looking at the application form with a frown.

I glanced to my right at Lesley, who stood stiffly, staring at the desk. I thought she looked a little pink in the face.

148

Mary continued to fill out the application form. As she approached the section requiring details from Lesley, I took half a step back, to allow her better access.

"Now, sir, what is your wife's name?" she asked, looking at me, over Lesley's shoulder.

"She," I said pointing at Lesley, "is called Lesley."

"Yes, sir, thank you, sir. And what is her date of birth?"

I answered, and again did the pointing thing. Lesley had now gone a nasty red colour.

"And what was her maiden name?"

Lesley stepped forwards and answered, through tightly clenched teeth. I noticed she was now rather purple around the neck.

"And how are you spelling that, sir?" Mary asked, seemingly unaware of the approaching storm.

I was about to answer, when Lesley placed both hands on the desk and leaned forwards, until she was nose-to-nose with the unfortunate clerk.

"I – AM – RIGHT – HERE," she said slowly and rather loudly, by way of confirmation.

As if a gunslinger had just walked into a Wild West bar, all conversations stopped and several people turned to look in our direction. In the distance, I clearly heard the unmistakable sound of a pencil falling onto a tiled floor. There was an awkward moment of silence, and I imagined the two women facing off in the street and preparing to draw their weapons, as a tumbleweed blew by in the background. Finally, the clerk pulled a face, rather like someone whose finger had just gone through the lavatory paper, and, with a stiff smile she pretended to notice Lesley for the first time.

Fortunately, the form filling continued without further incident, although my finer senses detected some air of tension between the two women, as they verbally circled each other like feral cats. I wisely avoided standing between them. By four o'clock, the bank appeared to be closing. All the curious onlookers had been shooed out, and there was a man guarding the door. Once Mary had finished filling the forms, she added copies of all of our documents, issued our new account number, and pointedly wished me good day. Lesley and I laughed together as we made for the exit.

"We're lucky she didn't call the police to arrest me," Lesley joked as we stepped through the door. Outside, the street was empty except for an armoured personnel carrier, two jeeps and about twenty soldiers, all fiercely brandishing rifles.

"Christ! Perhaps she did!" I said in shock as we slowly raised our hands. There was a moment of tense silence combined with some extreme stillness.

The officer, bravely standing behind his men, gave an exasperated sigh and spoke loudly but clearly, as if he was addressing a group of school children. "Excuse me, would you two please move out of the way?"

Following the recent spate of security van robberies, cash collections were now being conducted by the army – or so we had just learned. The heavily armed soldiers watched us suspiciously as we sidestepped our way cautiously along the front of the bank for 20 yards, before bursting into giggles and running towards the car park.

With our administration visit completed we had some time to spare before our flight back to England, and so after a meal in Ennis and another freezing night at our regular B&B, we revisited Glenmadrie with a camera and tape measure. I had in mind most of the structural changes I wanted to do at the house, but I needed to take some more accurate measurements so I could draw up my plans and get a decent idea of the kind of budget we would need.

At the same time, Lesley wanted to measure up the windows to see if our current curtains could be reused. We had only recently bought posh new drapes for our house in England, but with 20 windows in Glenmadrie to cover, we could damage our limited budget quite quickly. Luckily Lesley is such a dab hand at sewing that she decided most of our curtains could be altered to fit the new house, with the rest being made from material bought in the sales.

We spent a valuable couple of hours quietly walking around the house and grounds, getting a feel for the place and noticing the little things that would pass unseen in other circumstances. Once we had completed our photographs and measurements, and finished imagining everything we wanted to do with the property, we reluctantly decided it was time to move on. It was obvious we were both falling in love with Glenmadrie, and we were at risk of becoming seriously disappointed should the sale fall through unexpectedly. For the sake of our sanity, we had to try to maintain some emotional distance, at least until the house was ours.

As I was thinking this could be the last time we ever saw Glenmadrie, I was suddenly struck with an overwhelming urge to test the plumbing. Lesley rolled her eyes and waved me on my way, content to have a final walk around the land while she waited. When I came back outside, she was nowhere in sight, so I stepped into the courtyard to enjoy a few moments of solitude. I was struck by how quiet it was, and yet how noisy. The wind was rustling the trees, water was running in a stream below, thousands of birds were chattering, and in the distance, I could hear the roar of a mighty waterfall. In my experience, wherever I went in Britain, one could always hear indications of civilization: the noises of trains, cars, people or music were always present. But in the 50 square kilometres around Glenmadrie there were just ten other houses, all but one were on the road to the next village. Here, perhaps for the first time in many years, I was experiencing real solitude.

But what was that noise at the periphery of my hearing? Was it the squeak of a rusty gate swinging in the wind, the baying of a feral goat, or the call of a rare eagle? No, it was my lovely wife distantly calling for my help. I tried to locate the source of her agitated cries, repeatedly shouting her name, but without success. Each time she called, the sound was whipped away by the wind, or bounced back from the distant cliffs, confusing the direction and source. Suddenly I was certain my wife had accidentally fallen into the quarry and was at that moment lying injured and bleeding, pathetically crying out for my help. I turned left and ran across the meadow towards the quarry, but after a hundred paces I noticed her voice seemed more distant. Was I heading in the wrong direction, or was Lesley getting weaker?

A mighty bellow of "N-I-I-CK?" from the rear, confirmed I was indeed on the incorrect track. I turned back towards the house shouting for Lesley, but without receiving a response. Still unable to locate my wife and unsure of what to do next, I stood in the driveway scratching my head in frustration. Just then I heard another shout, this time from much closer. I yelled back and finally received an immediate response. Homing in on Lesley's calls, I had to walk for several yards further before spotting where she was standing, 40 feet away and 15 feet below me, hidden amongst the trees on the edge of the wood.

"Where have you been?" she demanded sharply. "I've been shouting for ages."

"I was looking for you," I replied, "but I couldn't figure out where you were. Anyway, what are you doing down there?"

"I wanted to see what the wood was like. I went in over there," she said pointing far to her left, "and walked through that bit, then down that bank and over that log – until I got to here."

"Oh, okay," I said. "What's it like then?"

"Rather muddy actually," Lesley replied with a smile, looking down. "Especially this bit."

I stood, hands on hips and searched the terrain for a moment. "I think you're standing in the percolation area for the septic tank. That's probably why it's so muddy."

"Yes, that would explain it," she said tersely. "Anyway, can you help me please? I seem to be rather stuck."

As she was slightly hidden by a small tree, I moved a little to one side for a better view. Finally I could see the full scope of her predicament. The intrepid explorer was holding a low branch and balancing precariously on one foot, with the other wellington boot firmly stuck in the mud, just out of reach. A bright pink sock was dangling limply from the toes of her other foot, like a slightly effeminate warning flag.

"Stay right where you are," I said, not being one to miss an opportunity. "I'll get the camera."

Lesley gave me a stern glare. "It's in my pocket."

Duly warned, I slithered down the bank and cautiously squelched through the muck to her rescue. While she rested her hand on my shoulder, I managed to extract her wellington boot from the sucking sludge, and after refitting the sock, return the boot to her foot. Using each other for balance, we took a few careful steps until we reached the safety of firmer ground. Despite her gratitude, Lesley refused to repeat the pose for our photo album, so we cleaned our muddy boots as best we could, and set off for a leisurely trip to Shannon airport. As we drove past Lough

Cullaunyheeda, I paused our journey for a few moments so we could take in the peace and the beauty, and marvel at the solitude.

"Look at this place," Lesley whispered, awestruck, staring at the half-mile of calm water before us. "There's not a boat, or a yacht or a fisherman in sight."

"If this was England," I said, "it would be difficult to see much of the water because of the number of people water-skiing, swimming, fishing, and roaring around on any number of motorised boys' toys."

Ireland may have been missing out on a large chunk of the recreational water hobbyist market, but that was fine with us.

When we arrived at Shannon Airport, we joined a bizarre ritual we were to witness many times over the next few years, until it stopped without explanation. At the entrance gate to the airport was a small glass-sided cubicle, like a toll booth. Sitting inside this draughty enclosure was an airport policeman tasked with challenging the intentions of each driver. This poor unfortunate soul, or an equally unwilling colleague, was present in all weathers and around the clock, presumably as some form of cruel and unusual punishment for a hideous crime.

The road, guarded by the checkpoint, had only two possible destinations: the airport or Shannon Golf Club. Every time we flew from the airport, or collected visitors, the unfortunate policeman would step out into the wind, rain, sleet or snow, to ask us, "Where are you going?" The answer was always the same. "The airport," while pointing at the big place behind him, full of terminal buildings and shiny flying machines. The poor, blue-faced policeman would look over his shoulder in surprise, as if noticing the airport for the first time, and say, "Oh – that's okay then," and on we would go.

I am unsure what the real intention of the checkpoint was. Perhaps they hoped some fiendish master-plan to blow up the pro's shop at Shannon Golf Club would be thwarted when the terrorist accidentally announced his intentions to the lonely policeman. Of course, the villainous evil-doer could have simply put the bomb in a wheelbarrow and walked past the checkpoint unchallenged, on the opposite side of the road.

We successfully navigated the checkpoint, only to discover Stansted Airport was closed by a blizzard and our flight was cancelled. Luckily, I guessed our long-delayed flight was going to be cancelled before the announcement, and jumped the crowd to secure seats on the first trip the next day, as well as the last room at the airport hotel. While others less fortunate than us had to sleep on cold, hard, plastic seating in the airport departure hall, we ate well and, despite our best efforts to resist, became quite drunk in the company of a generous businessman from Manchester. Anaesthetised by our libations, we slept deeply in a warm, comfortable bed, and woke refreshed but a little hungover, in good time for our flight home.

Back in England, the snow had turned to beige slush, so our journey to the kennel to collect the dogs, and onward to our house, was uneventful. Nice as it was to be home, we both agreed we were missing Ireland already and looking forward to starting our new life there.

The day after we arrived back at our home in England, I was walking our two dogs when I realised Brandy, the oldest dog, was unwell. As a spritely ten-year-old, she was robustly fit and keen to lead the daily walks with her niece, Romany, trotting along behind. But on this day, as we circumnavigated her favourite field, Brandy was lagging far behind, very obviously out of breath and unable to keep up. Curtailing our walk, I headed back to the house at a much slower pace than usual. Once we were home, Brandy had a long drink of water and flopped onto her bed in the conservatory with a satisfied grunt.

"You're back early," Lesley said, coming in from the garden.

"Brandy wasn't well. She was struggling to breathe, so I brought her straight back."

"She looks okay now." Lesley tickled Brandy's ear, the little dog returned the favour with an affectionate lick.

Romany did a little dance, eager for some attention.

"Yes, she does," I admitted, giving Romany a pat on the head. "But if you'd seen her earlier… I almost had to carry her."

"Really?" Lesley looked at me with genuine concern. The symptoms were worryingly familiar.

I nodded.

"Perhaps you should call Jane."

Jane Finch was a professional and knowledgeable vet who knew our dogs well. As we were planning to move abroad, both Brandy and Romany had just had a full check-up with updated inoculations, as well as being microchipped, so this sudden onset of illness was unexpected. After a comprehensive examination, Jane declared Brandy to be fit and well. However, she decided to keep the little dog at the clinic overnight just as a precaution. Perhaps she was mindful of Brandy's sister, Tammy, who had suffered a long and painfully slow decline in health from a mystery lung condition that finally took her life. This same vet had previously spent a considerable amount of our money in her unsuccessful battle to save Tammy and I presumed she wanted to take early action to ensure Brandy was kept healthy. Despite what had happened to Tammy, we were confident Brandy was in excellent hands.

The following morning, I called the surgery to find out what time I should come down to collect my dog. Jane answered the telephone, her voice cracking with emotion.

"Nick, I'm so sorry, but Brandy is dead."

"Oh no!" Feeling like I'd been slapped, I sat down.

"I'm so sorry." I could hear she was crying.

"What happened? Do you know?"

"Not really," she sobbed. "I checked her last thing and she was fine, but when I came in this morning… Well, she was curled up as if she was sleeping. I think Brandy suffered a heart attack during the night. She died painlessly in her sleep."

"The poor thing." There was little else I could say.

"We may never know what happened, unless you want me to perform an autopsy?"

"No, I don't think so." I couldn't bear the thought of someone cutting up our baby.

"It's possible she may have had an allergic reaction to the microchip or the inoculations," Jane said, looking for some explanation where there was none.

As often seems to be the case when bad news needs to be delivered, it fell to me to tell Lesley. I was of course deeply upset by the loss of our beautiful dog, but my heart would break for Lesley. She sobbed uncontrollably onto my chest while I hugged her as tightly as I could. After I had collected Brandy from the vet and tearfully driven my way home, we laid her body on her bed in the conservatory. Poor Romany seemed genuinely confused when Brandy wouldn't wake up, and in an effort to ease their mutual sadness, Lesley sat alongside Romany and the body of her friend, while I prepared a grave in the garden.

Later that evening we wrapped Brandy in a blanket and, along with her favourite toy, buried her next to where her sister Tammy lay. That night, Romany sat by the grave in the pouring rain for over an hour before, with obvious sadness, she finally answered our calls to come indoors. The loss of such a close companion can be very difficult to get over. Brandy was so central to our lives it felt as if we had lost a close family member. I was deeply upset Brandy had died, but a dreadful pain boiled up in my chest whenever I saw the terrible sadness in my wife's eyes. Lesley seemed particularly affected, perhaps because Brandy's death was so sudden and unexpected, but also because she knew we would be moving away so soon.

The following week was a blur of sadness, tears, and the worry our sale would unexpectedly fall through at the last moment. As much as we liked our house, now it was just a constant reminder of our loss and we wanted to leave. Brandy had been with us since the day we moved in, loyally alongside through all the renovations of the house and the garden. Now, despite her passing, the memory of her enduring presence was in every room. Outside, things were no better. Every inch of our garden and every walk we took reminded us of Brandy, her liquid chocolate eyes, her soft golden coat, and her happy smile.

Suddenly moving day was upon us. It was March 12th, 2004, everything was ready and we were waiting for the order to hand over the keys. Once we had packed our respective cars with the things we needed for the next few weeks, everything else was loaded into the removal vans and they departed – hopefully to be seen again in Ireland, very soon.

After putting so much work and love into the house and garden, it was inevitably going to be an emotionally painful day. Lesley and I took a few quiet moments to walk around the property for the final time. After we fed the chickens, we walked slowly along the path that looped through the orchard and around to the vegetable garden. When we reached the point where we could see the entire property, we stopped and reminisced quietly about all we had achieved together in the last few years while renovating a rundown cottage into a beautiful and desirable family home.

Although this was supposed to be a happy and positive move, there was naturally considerable sadness and some apprehension as well. As we stopped beside the flowerbed where Brandy and Tammy lay, I gently pulled Lesley towards me and we hugged each other and shed a tear. Our moment of quiet reflection was rudely shattered by the ringing of my mobile phone. It was our solicitor calling to report we were currently trespassing. He told me the sale transaction was complete, the cash proceeds had been transferred to our bank account in Ennis. We should now hand over the keys to our neighbour and vacate the property. After exchanging pleasantries with Richard, we left him with our house and chickens, and set off to our new life – Lesley temporarily to her mother's house, and I towards Ireland.

***

My schedule took me to Holyhead port, where I would overnight at a hotel before taking the early ferry to Dublin and on towards Corofin. Travelling east to west, I would drive across the entire width of England, Wales and Ireland in around 14 hours. One of the first steps towards living without debt was buying an affordable and reliable car I could maintain myself. Ten days previously I had purchased a 1.8 litre Ford Escort that was priced competitively, as it had some slight accident damage. A local garage had replaced the front wing and one headlight, and given the engine a full service, changing the timing belt, oil, filters, and so on. Although I had already driven a few miles in the car, the trip to Ireland was going to be a major test of reliability.

The journey to Holyhead on a busy Friday afternoon, driving an unfamiliar car, with a broken seat, from which I could barely see over the dashboard, left little time for contemplation or reminiscences. However, my stress levels were at manageable proportions, partly because I wasn't rushing to catch a ferry, which was fortunate because for the majority of the journey the traffic was murderous. In some ways the torture of driving with a numb bum, in Birmingham's rush-hour traffic, whilst watching my wiper blades' lethargic efforts to rearrange the dead flies on the windshield, lifted my slightly apprehensive spirits. I had anticipated being giddy with excitement, but found myself feeling a little uneasy, perhaps because the house purchase was still up in the air, and perhaps because I was leaving Lesley behind.

During the quieter moments of that hellish drive, I gave much thought to those people we were moving away from. I knew I would miss seeing so much of our ever-supportive daughter, my two sisters, both our elderly mothers, and our friends. But I was glad we would only be an hour's flying time away. Furthermore, it was conceivable our new home would encourage friends and family to holiday in Ireland, or visit for long weekends. I had high hopes of having more quality time with those people we love, but would otherwise miss so much.

I had visited the friendly folk in south Wales while on holiday, and we had considered moving to the area before Ireland came into focus. However, I had never before visited north Wales and, despite being forewarned, I was shocked by some of the venomous anti-British graffiti decorating many of the bridges on the route into Holyhead. Given the recent history between England and Ireland, I started to worry unnecessarily that perhaps I had made an awful error of judgement and we would soon be hounded from our new home by hordes of angry xenophobic villagers.

After an uninspiring meal and an uncomfortable night in a lumpy motel bed, I drove through the morning mist to board the early ferry. As the ship powered its way towards Ireland, with the rising sun on my back and the salt spray in my face, I held tightly to the railing of the observation deck and whooped like a ten-year-old, to the obvious consternation of the other passengers.

As Dublin and the sun-kissed Wicklow Mountains came into view for the first time, I thought of my father and how he must have felt in 1943 when, after four years of struggling to survive in prisoner of war camps, he had sailed into Liverpool harbour to begin a new life. Perhaps, like me, he may have had concerns about being an immigrant in a foreign land. Like me, he may also have believed the worst had now passed, and things were only going to get better.

Without a Satnav, I had to rely on a map and my uncanny sense of direction, so I was lucky not to end up in Iceland. Although Dublin is the capital city of Ireland, it is only the size of a small English city like Colchester or Norwich, but much more difficult to navigate. Every available signpost was strewn with jumbles of jolly road signs pointing the way to exciting places like Dundrum, Blackrock, Palmerstown and Coolock, none of which I had any immediate plans to visit. Nowhere did I see any directions for the N4, which I did want to visit, or, more helpful still, a bloody big arrow pointing 'West This Way'. Where there were street signs, they were helpfully placed just past the junction, as if to say, "Ah now see, you should have gone down that one!" Other signs seemed to lack any real confidence, only pointing vaguely towards where you might need to go, and one, more confident, sign pointed to a shop doorway. I wondered if it was even more lost than me and was suggesting I ask in the shop for directions.

Being a man, I am genetically unable to admit that I am lost, or to ask for help, although I am delighted to offer copious and detailed directions to anyone else, even if I have no idea of where I am at the time.

Mercifully, Dublin's streets were quiet for a Saturday morning, which was a good thing, as I constantly found myself in the incorrect lane. Unlike England, however, even when I indicated my intention to change lanes at the most inopportune moment, the other cars immediately made space and sent me on my way with a jolly wave. On occasion I felt the need to justify my erratic navigation by shouting, "Sorry, I'm English," but I soon started to wonder if people thought I was just apologising for being English, which is not such a bad idea sometimes. In the end, I decided my obvious yellow GB licence plate was excuse enough and kept my mouth shut. Eventually, I navigated my way through the labyrinth of confusion that is Dublin, and found a suitable road heading west.

As I travelled further out of the city, the traffic thinned noticeably, making the drive ever more pleasurable by the minute. Soon I could relax and enjoy the drive towards a new life. Most of the larger roads in Ireland have the usual white lines in the centre, but unlike England they also have a yellow stripe on the left marking a second lane for tractors and slower traffic. We drive on the left in Ireland, the same as the UK, but I was unsure of the etiquette in the use of this lane. I wondered if it was reserved only for farm traffic, or were elderly farmers driving a car permitted to use the slow lane as well? I saw tractors, bicycles, some cars, a lorry, and a pony and trap using the lane. Yet on other occasions they stubbornly stayed on the main part of the road and held up the traffic.

A couple of times, when being aggressively tailgated by a large, speeding lorry, I crossed the yellow line to make room for them to pass, only to find myself bouncing around alarmingly on the unmade surface. During another attempt to politely allow some homicidal lunatic to pass, the yellow lane suddenly disappeared without warning, as the road crossed a small bridge, leaving me trapped between the uncaring lorry and a stone wall. For a moment, I revisited my long-discarded Catholic schooling and sought divine guidance to slow my car on the loose gravel. God must have been with me that morning, or perhaps it was the ghost of Henry Ford. In any event, I negotiated the bridge without any damage to my vehicle and took a moment to swear loudly at the back of the lorry as it disappeared into the distance. After that incident, I stubbornly stayed in my lane, forcing any driver determined to break the speed limit (more than me) to overtake in the conventional way.

However, the excitement wasn't entirely over because Ireland also has an impressive collection of some of the biggest and deepest potholes it has ever been my misfortune to drive into. A paranoid person would suspect some shady government department, in an effort to bolster the profits of the Irish motor industry, had deliberately placed potholes in positions most likely to surprise the unsuspecting motorist. They seem to appear in the most inconvenient and unlikely places, for example, on the inside of a bend, at the top of a hill, or whenever you cannot swerve to avoid one due to a bus travelling in the opposite direction.

The most insidious of Irish inventions is the water-filled pothole. These are cunningly disguised as one of the other puddles your car has been laboriously splashing through all day, but are actually a massive pit, filled to the brim with oily, black water. So, there I was, merrily driving along on a normal Irish road, slick with rain and dotted with puddles. My car was filled to the brim with the things I needed to live in a rented cottage for a few weeks. To relieve the boredom of the long journey, I was attempting to touch the end of my nose with my tongue. The puddles went splash, splosh, splat, and then KERBANG! Suddenly most of my belongings were on the front seat, the car had developed a pathological desire to turn left, I was choking on a boiled sweet and my glasses were jammed under the brake pedal, along with the end of my tongue.

I must have been somewhere near the village of Moate when I stopped at a garage for petrol, tea and a pee. Noticing they had a deli counter, I asked the nice lady if she could make me a sandwich.

"Of course, my dear, and what would you like in it?" she asked.

I looked hungrily at a magnificent display before me, containing every conceivable sandwich filling, but not wanting to mess up the inside of my car any more than was necessary, I opted for simple and safe.

"Oh, just a cheese salad please," I replied.

"Would you like a nice bit of ham with that?" she offered sweetly.

"No, thanks very much, I'm a vegetarian," I explained.

"Oh, you poor dear," she said as if I was afflicted with some incurable disorder. "Some chicken then, just to give it a little flavour?"

"Thanks for the offer, but cheese salad will do me fine."

"You're English, aren't you?" she asked.

I said I was.

"I suspected you were," she said with a smile as if my nationality explained my outrageous diet. "Are you on your holidays?"

"No, I'm moving over here to live," I replied proudly.

"Are you?" She looked me up and down. "Well," she said, "you are most welcome." And she meant it.

While she prepared my sandwich, I looked around the shop for a few minutes and collected some items I fancied for evening snacks, along with the makings for breakfast the following morning. When I came to pay, I discovered my sandwich comprised an entire French stick, piled high with what must have been a pound of cheese, half a jar of pickle, a small lettuce, and umpteen slices of tomato and cucumber. In shifts between meals, it took almost three days to eat – magnificent! Although my grocery purchases were a little costly, even compared to a village shop in England, the petrol was 30 percent cheaper, and my sandwich was an incredible bargain at just €2. Refreshed and refilled, I was soon back on the road again and making good progress towards Corofin. At Loughrea I turned left from the N6 towards the seemingly drab, concrete grey, village of Gort, where I needed to consult a map for the first time in 150 miles. Here I struck out across country on single track roads and into the setting sun, past the amusingly named Lough Bunny and several other Loughs, along the southern edge of the Burren, finally arriving at Corofin, tired but elated.

After a few phone calls I managed to track down the holiday home manager, who gave me the key to the cottage and showed me around. The guided tour didn't take very long. The cottage was quite traditional, with a two-part front door opening directly into a sitting area with two rocking chairs, a slate floor, and an open fire, providing the only source of heat and entertainment. A galley kitchen had been squeezed into the corridor leading to two small bedrooms and an even smaller bathroom. Lukewarm water dribbled out of the shower, thanks to an ancient and somewhat temperamental immersion heater, which ate money faster than I could feed it into the electric meter. After I had unpacked my belongings and linen, made up the bed and called Lesley to let her know I had arrived safely, I decided it was time to eat.

The cottage was rented through the same charming bar and restaurant in the centre of Corofin Lesley and I had eaten at during our house hunting trips around Christmas. Not being inclined to visit pubs often, we had very much enjoyed the friendly welcome and pleasant atmosphere. They had an excellent menu, and we found the food to be delicious and keenly priced, so it was no surprise to discover it was rated in the top ten pubs in Ireland. Despite having eaten a third of my enormous French stick lunch, I found I was ravenous and in a celebratory mood, so I opted for my favourite – a veggie pizza and side salad.

While my meal was being prepared, I sat by the fire drinking a pint of Guinness and felt the stress of the last few years draining away. For the first time in almost 30 years, all my bills were paid, I had ample money in my pocket, no debt to service, and I was no longer concerned about my career prospects. Although there might be some dark clouds approaching from just over the horizon, at that moment everything was looking pretty rosy. Perhaps it was the beer, perhaps it was the heat from the fire, or perhaps it was the years of stress draining out of my body, but I found my eyelids were becoming unbearably heavy and my arms were so tired, it seemed too much effort to reach for the remainder of my pint. I closed my eyes for a moment, took a slow, deep breath and allowed cotton wool to fill up my mind, trapping the few remaining wild thoughts and soaking up the last vestiges of fear.

I fell into such a deep sleep that it was all the waitress could do to wake me when she delivered my meal. She needed to wake me a second time twenty minutes later when she discovered I had fallen asleep over my uneaten food, and a third time after it was re-heated. In the end, with the help of some strong tea, I managed to remain awake long enough to do justice to the excellent pizza and even managed to eat a sweet. To compensate the bar staff, I forced myself to consume a second pint (it would have been rude not to) and, after leaving a generous tip, walked the hundred yards back to my cottage where I fell onto the bed, fully clothed, and slept like a dead man for 12 hours.

The following morning at 10 am, I was outside my solicitors' office waiting for them to open. The purchase of Glenmadrie was still looking doubtful. There were some genuine issues we needed to resolve and Daragh still considered any deviation from the norm to be an instant deal breaker. There were undoubtedly some problems with the property. I had spotted some considerable damp and wood rot in the exposed southern end, and some aspects of the building were not consistent with the plans on file. Although I was confident the structural damage could be fixed and had already renegotiated the price to take account of the cost, the planning issue could become a genuine obstruction to the purchase.

Ideally, plans would have been filed, approved and followed religiously. In practice, there is a more relaxed approach to planning in rural Ireland. At Daragh's suggestion, I went to inspect the 'filed plans' mentioned in our engineer's report. The Ennis planning office was housed in a drab old building on the outskirts of town. It was home to several council departments, conveniently grouped together opposite a large carpark. The interior of the building was painted institutional beige. Like any government building, it smelled of floor wax, dust, and old paper. The office was packed, so I joined the rear of what passed for a queueing system. Although 'civilians' like me were obliged to wait patiently to be seen by the harassed and overworked clerks, it seemed 'professionals' like architects, solicitors, and builders, simply elbowed their way to the window to be dealt with immediately.

After a short wait, I presented the clerk with my best smile and a yellow post-it note baring the file reference number. He disappeared into the bowels of the building and returned some time later, wearing a cobweb on his head and brandishing a dusty, brown cardboard file. Inside was a single sheet of paper, folded in two.

"Is that all there is?" I asked.

The clerk peered into the file and shrugged unenthusiastically. "I guess."

The 'filed plans' were actually just one grubby sheet of A3 tissue paper, showing a rough sketch of the property, along with some outlandish ideas of how the house was expected to be developed 20 years ago. I paid for a photocopy and returned to Daragh's office.

Both Aiden and the vendor's surveyors agreed Glenmadrie was broadly planning compliant, but Daragh was still refusing to condone the purchase. Call me a cynic, but I was starting to suspect he felt more allegiance to his liability insurance than he did to our best interests. Although the drawing was on file, and some aspects were consistent with what was actually there, much of the work had never been completed. This wasn't necessarily an issue because, according to Aiden, the sketch was not a formal plan and therefore compliance was only a matter of opinion. In any event, as we were cash buyers there was no requirement to seek the opinion of the planning office for parts of the house that did not exist. In the end, our saving grace was the statute barred rule allowing any non-compliant structure to remain, provided it had been in place and uncontested for more than eight years. After much conversation and consternation, Daragh gave a deep sigh and capitulated.

With the planning issue finally put to bed, Daragh and I piled all the documents on his desk and worked through each page, crossing off the completed issues as we went, until we were left with just the site clearance and payment to deal with. We arranged buildings insurance and agreed the sale could proceed, as soon as I had confirmed the pyramid and other rubbish had been removed. To lodge the funds into Daragh's client account ready for transfer, I wrote out the largest cheque of my life, clearing 70 percent of our bank account with a single signature.

After a delicious celebratory lunch of leek and potato soup at a nearby sandwich bar, I set course for Glenmadrie. As I had finally managed to navigate my way to the house without the repeated use of an ordinance survey map, I was feeling quite chipper when I pulled into the long curving driveway. I didn't get far. There was a brightly painted wooden caravan blocking the driveway. It was one of those old-fashioned horse-drawn gypsy caravans, like something a fortune-teller might use at a circus or carnival. There was an equally old dappled-grey horse, tied to a stake and eating grass on the front lawn.

The front door was unlocked and indoors I discovered a family of four, sitting on the couch and watching a small portable television with a bent wire coat hanger for an aerial. There was a fire in the grate and the room smelled strongly of something that was not tobacco. The two children were twin girls, no more than five years old. They were both wearing bunny rabbit pyjamas with ears, sucking their thumbs, and staring transfixed at the cartoon playing loudly on the television. The adults, a man and a woman, briefly glanced in my direction before swinging their eyes back to the television. I was reminded of insolent teenagers, which given their apparent age wasn't far from the truth.

"Hello there," I said brightly. "Who are you?"

The young mother ignored me completely. She wore filthy jeans, several sweaters and multi-coloured knitted fingerless gloves. Her long brown hair was arranged in a tumbling series of dreadlocks. The man sat up and spoke.

"We're only staying the night," he said defensively. The accent was unmistakably Somerset English. He wore an equally rag-tag selection of unwashed clothing. His long red hair was held in place by a black knitted bobble hat.

"How did you get in?" I asked as politely as I could.

"We knew where the keys was," he replied.

"The owner lets us stay like," the woman spoke for the first time. Her eyes never left the television. I figured her accent to be more west London.

"Which owner would that be?" I asked.

"Can't remember," the man shrugged, "we met him at a party."

"We're only staying the night," the woman reiterated, again without looking away from the cartoon.

I noticed they hadn't once asked who I was. "Excuse me, I need to make a phone call." I stepped outside and called Daragh.

"They sound like British New Age Travellers," he said.

"That's a new one on me."

"It's a catchall description for unwashed, unemployed and unemployable English tourists," he said. "No offence meant."

"None taken," I replied, trying not to take offence. "What should I do?"

"Chuck them out. You can't buy the house with squatters in it," he said curtly. "They've got no right to be there. You've signed the contracts and paid the deposit, so it's not unreasonable to ask them to vacate the premises."

"Okay. I'll give it a go," I replied, groaning inwardly.

I went back indoors and politely but firmly told the young couple why I needed them off the property. They seemed disappointed to be losing a source of free electricity and heating, but once they understood I was not going to back down, they grudgingly complied. With commendable efficiency, the mother bundled the children into the caravan and loaded their luggage, while the man hitched the horse. I had to move my car to allow the caravan to leave, and as they passed the children waved at me from the window. I waved back, feeling somewhat guilty and cruel. Raising two children in a tiny caravan not much larger than a car must have been hard going. Although the children looked fit, healthy and happy, it was hardly the idyllic lifestyle people would imagine, particularly during the cold and wet Irish winter.

Once the caravan was on its way, I spent an hour walking around the property, checking for any previously unnoticed problems and taking a few photographs. It was a pleasurable task since the pyramid had finally gone, as had the scrap cars and other items of rubbish. Once I was as convinced as I could be everything was in order, I sat on a rock above the quarry and phoned Lesley. As we chatted, she told me how her mother was moaning about Romany getting under her feet, although she suspected her mum was secretly happy for the company. She mentioned her back ached from sleeping in an unfamiliar bed, and complained about how busy and overcrowded things were in Essex. I described the awe-inspiring view before me looking across the moor towards the forest, where the mist was drifting silently through the tops of the mighty pine trees, like the ghosts of ancient smoke. I told her how the sun was setting in the west and turning the sky a glorious orange – a beautiful harbinger of an approaching storm. I said how much I loved and missed her, and how I hoped to see her soon. Finally, I reported the good news that everything was now ready for us to complete the sale.

"Last chance to change your mind," I joked.

"No way," she replied firmly.

I called our solicitor and gave him the go ahead to complete the sale without further delay. However, it seemed the legal profession would require a further couple of weeks to complete its black magic. Barring any last-minute disasters, Glenmadrie would be ours on April 4th, almost exactly six months since I had sat on the wall in Essex, looking at my doctor's car.

***

After such an intense period of activity, the next two weeks were like the calm after a storm, which was ironic, because the fine weather had deteriorated to wind, rain and some spectacular thunder storms. I had very little to do, other than read, listen to the radio and make the occasional trip to the house to check nobody else had decided to take up unauthorised residence. In retrospect, perhaps I should have squatted there myself – it would have saved me a bundle of money in rent and petrol.

Legally, everything required to complete the sale was in place and like any house buyer, we just had to wait patiently for the process to end. I managed to fritter away a few hours trying to change over the billing of the electricity and telephone, as both companies seemed flummoxed by the challenge of registering a foreigner who didn't already have three months of Irish utility bills as proof of identity. After a herculean effort to suppress my growing anger, I managed to convince both companies it could be to their long term financial advantage to exchange their electricity and telephone services for some of my money, as was traditional in other countries.

Apart from the prospect of seeing Lesley again and moving into the house, the only rays of sunshine in an otherwise dismal fortnight, were the enquiries I received for golf lessons from dozens of people responding to the posters and advertisements I had placed. It seemed I really was back in business.

On the first Sunday I was in Corofin we had yet another thunderstorm, an event which, although not entirely unusual for Ireland, was unexpected on such a frosty day in March. Sometimes, the warm, moist air flowing north-east from the mid-Atlantic hits the cold dry air sitting above the frosty ground in Ireland, leading to thunderstorms accompanied by torrential rain, hail, snow, and even the odd mini-tornado. The thunderstorms worsen when the mass of warm damp air encounters a line of hills. Although nowhere as spectacular as the thunderstorms seen in tropical countries, Irish thunderstorms excel at causing flash

169

flooding, and the accompanying lightning strikes are particularly adept at knocking bits from houses and trees.

As there was no rain falling in Corofin, I stood outside the cottage watching as a series of purple thunder clouds passed a mere five miles to the north and politely lined up, before marching on legs of lightning across the hills towards Loughrea. The ground at the base of each cloud was darkly obscured by a solid wall of falling rain and repeatedly illuminated by vivid flashes of lightning. I found it strangely captivating to stand in the dry, whilst watching a deluge of water and hail of almost biblical proportions falling on the poor villagers a few miles away.

In time-honoured tradition, I measured the distance to each storm by counting the seconds between the lightning flashes and the accompanying crash of thunder. Each wicked lightning flash was accompanied by an instant static crackle on my battery-operated radio and the frequent flickering of the lights as the lightning connected with the ground. I counted eleven separate storms that day and I knew many were passing close to the hills around Glenmadrie, which I could locate by spotting the distinctive radio mast near the house. At about 3 pm, I saw the radio mast take a direct hit, instantly silencing all the radio stations for the next three days. Mercifully, the electricity was spared on this occasion.

A few days after the thunderstorm, another quirk of Irish driving almost cost me dearly. I was driving from Ennis to Corofin, perhaps slightly faster than was entirely wise on a dark, wet road, but like most men, I live under the illusion I am an expert driver. As I rounded a slight bend in the road, I was irritated to discover I was facing a set of blindingly bright headlights on full beam. This is not an unusual occurrence in Ireland, as many rural drivers seem to be rather reluctant to dip their headlights until the last possible moment, if at all. Faced with such an impolite inconvenience, all one can do is flash your own lights repeatedly, while complaining loudly, and aim for a spot just to the left of the approaching car in the hope you'll miss each other.

However, on this night, although I had been aware of the headlights for the few seconds before I rounded the corner, I was still totally blinded as they were not only on full beam, but accompanied by some slightly misaligned fog lights as well. With barely two seconds to manoeuvre, I was instinctively aiming to the left of the lights when I realised the other car was actually parked on my side of the road and facing the oncoming traffic. With a screech of tires and a squeal like a schoolgirl, I hauled my car to the right, missing the other vehicle by mere millimetres. Had my heart not been so firmly lodged in my throat, I would have sworn like a drunken sailor all the way home. The next day, as I passed the same spot I could see that had I turned left to avoid the car, I would have driven directly into a very large tree, leaving everyone scratching their heads and speculating as to the cause of my fatal car crash.

Finally, the day arrived when we were to take ownership of Glenmadrie and officially become residents on the island of Ireland. To avoid unnecessarily paying another day's rent, I had to vacate the cottage at Corofin by 10 am that morning. Although I wouldn't have minded the additional expense, in truth I was as giddy as a child at Christmas and desperate to be in our new home. I packed up my car and headed for Ennis. By 11 am I was drinking my third cup of tea, in a café near to Daragh's office, and still waiting for confirmation the sale was finalised.

At half past 12, my phone rang. It was Daragh's secretary.

"Hi, Nick, it's Rose," she said. "Daragh asked me to call. The sale is complete. Congratulations!"

Punching the air, I gave an involuntary whoop of delight, startling the elderly lady at the next table. I pulled a face and mimed an apology.

"Thanks, Rose, that's the best news," I said, smiling like a village idiot. "I'm just across the road. Can I pop up and collect the keys?"

"Oh dear..." I could hear the rustling of papers. "We don't seem to have any keys."

"How am I supposed to get in?" I pleaded.

"I don't know."

"Hasn't Daragh got the keys?" I asked.

"I'm sure he hasn't, everything came directly to my desk," she explained. "There's no keys here. Anyway, Daragh has left for the weekend. He's off to France for the rugby or something. Perhaps you could call the vendor's solicitor. They must still have the keys over there."

I copied down the number and, after thanking Rose for her help, made the call. I only got as far as Jane, the office secretary.

"I'm afraid Julia is with a client at the moment," she explained. "I'll get her to call you back."

"There's no need. I've just bought Glenmadrie, but my solicitor didn't receive the keys from you. Can I come over to your office and collect them?"

"I'll have to ask Julia," Jane said. "Give me your number and I'll call you back."

While I waited, I called Alan, the estate agent, to check if he had the keys. He wasn't much help.

"Congratulations on the purchase, Nick, I'm sure you and Lesley will be very happy there," he said. "As far as I know, the house is all locked up now. But I have no idea what happened to the keys. Sorry!"

After an hour of waiting, my frustration was rising. I called the vendor's solicitor again.

"Didn't Julia call you back?" Jane asked.

"No, she didn't. Can I please speak with her now?"

"I'm sorry, Julia's out to lunch with a client. I'll get her to call you as soon as she gets back."

An hour later, I called again.

"Didn't she call you back?" Jane asked again.

"No, she didn't," I said through gritted teeth.

"Oh dear, that's most unusual. Well, I'm very sorry, but Julia is in court for the rest of the day."

"How do I get into my house?" I asked, my voice tight with desperation.

"I'll tell you what," Jane said, "let me have a hunt in her office for the keys. I'll call you back in a jiffy."

And so the frustrating cycle continued. I ordered lunch and waited. I called back, but there was no answer. My patience ran out at 4.30 pm, so I walked to the vendor's solicitor and presented myself at the reception desk.

"Hello," I said to the young receptionist, "you must be Jane."

"No, I'm Moira." She smiled. "Jane has gone home for the day."

I groaned. "I'm here to collect the keys for Glenmadrie. Is Julia here?"

"Oh no. Julia has gone for the day. She's away on holiday for a fortnight. If you give me your number, I'll get her to call you when she returns."

And that was that. For some reason, no one seemed to understand why actually having the keys to the house I had just bought might be nice. In the end, I decided to drive to Glenmadrie and take possession of the house, if necessary by breaking in. Fortunately, after an extensive search that lasted nearly 15 seconds, I found the keys hidden under a rock by the front door and, without any further ceremony, stepped across the threshold into our new home.

It was already getting dark and cold and I had a lot to do to get settled in for my first night in Glenmadrie. After calling Lesley to relate the good news, I unpacked from the car only the few things I would need before the morning and set about organising somewhere to sleep. The only furniture in the house was a large, cream couch in the sitting room, and although I had brought a collapsible camp bed and sleeping bag, I decided the couch would make for a more comfortable night's rest.

The cooking and central heating were via an oil-fired Rayburn range in the kitchen. There were no instructions but the operation seemed simple enough, so despite a disturbing smell of kerosene around the base and some loose wires sticking out at the side, I attempted to fire up the heating. Although the switches appeared to be in the correct position, nothing seemed to be happening so I tentatively wiggled the wires, and was rewarded with a big blue flash. I hid in the corner for a couple of minutes but nothing else happened and I was getting cold, so I daringly tried jiggling the wire again, and this time the boiler grudgingly came to life.

Newly inflated with false confidence in my manly abilities, I decided to try lighting a fire, in the hope of keeping warm overnight without running out of heating oil. There was a pile of hand-cut peat at the side of the house, loosely covered with an old blue builder's tarpaulin, but still reasonably dry despite the recent rain. The small fireplace was set into a massive chimney breast jutting four feet into the room and standing six feet wide. It was painted magnolia, the same as the rest of the room, but decorated with soot stains. I managed to start the fire without too much trouble, but the smoke was unwilling to take the arduous journey up the chimney, much preferring to stay in the room and keep me company.

I sat on the couch in front of the roaring fire and examined my new surroundings through the thin haze of smoke and red-rimmed, watery eyes. The sitting room was about 30 feet by 18, with a polished pine floor. Although the stone walls had a rough cement render decorated with exterior masonry paint, any protuberances carried highlights of dust, soot and cobwebs. On the end wall, beneath the staircase, someone, with a small amount of artistic talent and a large amount of mind-altering drugs, had painted a motif reminiscent of some Technicolor genetic experiment involving a dog, a sheep and a fire dragon.

Although slightly higher than the 70 inches in the kitchen, the ceiling was very low and covered in strange wooden slats that provided a safe haven for spiders, and delivered a light sprinkling of dust whenever the wind blew. The wood was red cedar and, according to Alan, probably recovered from old tobacco pallets and nailed to the rafters to provide a makeshift ceiling. It was a thriving source of woodworm and probably highly flammable.

Once settled in, I realised I was ravenously hungry, so I had to risk life and limb again to cook a meal on the Rayburn. I was delighted to discover the cooking side of this cast iron monster was in excellent order, apart from being caked in grease. Without a fridge, I was temporarily relying on tinned vegetables and eggs, which took me back to my student days, but nevertheless provided a decent meal when washed down with some warm Guinness.

Presumably to save some money on electricity, the previous owner had fitted low power incandescent light bulbs throughout the house. None of these bulbs were any stronger than a measly 40 watts, and a few were just 15 watt bulbs, intended to light the interior of fridges. After washing the dishes, I tried reading a book for a while, squinting in the gloom, but sensibly gave it up as a bad job before I ruined my eyesight. With nothing else to entertain me I pulled the couch in front of the fire, climbed into my sleeping bag and curled up for the night.

A few hours later, I was roused by my bursting bladder and took the shortest route to relief, by stepping into the courtyard. As I watered the shrubs, three things struck me. First, the total lack of light and dust pollution delivered a breath-taking view of the stars in the night sky. Above me I could easily identify Orion's belt, Venus, Mars, Saturn, and Jupiter, as well as the smoky band of the Milky Way. I first saw such a clear night sky in northern Nigeria, when a miscommunication over travel arrangements left me stranded in the bush overnight. Fortunately, a kind family let me share their mud hut for the night. This view was much the same, only with fewer lions and elephants. Whenever I see such a clear sky I always find myself saying the same thing – "Wow!"

The second thing I noticed was how quiet it was. The wind had dropped to a mere whisper, and all I could hear was the sound of a distant river, the squawk of an owl, and the whistle of my tinnitus, a legacy of too many loud discos during my long-lost youth. Finally, I was struck by how lucky I was to have such privacy. Peeing outside seemed an unlikely privilege. I recollected performing the same act outside the mud hut in Nigeria, and I found myself questioning if life hadn't just taken me full circle.

The next morning, I ate my breakfast in the conservatory while watching the wild birds squabble over some bread crusts I had thrown down. Afterwards there was little else I could do but read, explore our new house and clean. Lesley and our lorry load of belongings were not due to arrive for a couple of days, so I drove into Ennis and purchased a few essential items of cleaning equipment and a box of 100 watt light bulbs. I kept myself busy clearing the dust and cobwebs, and mopping throughout, including the bare floorboards upstairs. Frustratingly, each time I went upstairs, I triggered another shower of woodworm dust and dead spiders onto the floors below, so I had to clean the downstairs repeatedly – which kept me both occupied and dissatisfied.

As we were planning to put most of our belongings into storage in the so-called music studio, I spent some extra time preparing the area. Unlike the rest of the house, the studio had recently been renovated. It was freshly plastered and painted, and fitted with a new carpet in a mildly offensive purple colour. The room was empty apart from a desk, made from a thick slab of pine on rough blocks of wood, a few shelves and some loose skirting boards. Two large wooden gates were fitted into the west wall, creating a doorway to the front of the property which would provide easy access when we were unloading our belongings. Given how recently the studio had been constructed, I was concerned to see further signs of water damage above the exposed, south-facing window, and I suspected this would link up with the damp in the room above. However, the studio now appeared to be dry, suggesting the leak had been recently repaired. I was pleased at this development and mildly confident the damp would not prove to be a problem in the future.

After staying overnight in Wales, Lesley caught the early fast ferry to Dublin and made good time, arriving at the house shortly after lunch. She resisted my half-hearted request to carry her across the threshold, but we still took a moment to share a kiss and hug when she stepped into our new home.

"I can't believe it's ours," she said, doing a little twirl.

"I was starting to think it never would be," I replied. "With all the legal and planning problems, it was a close-run thing."

"It's ours now." She hugged me again. "I'll put the kettle on, you get Romany."

After such a long drive, Romany was happy to see me, and desperate to get out of the car and stretch her little legs. As a town dog, she was used to small gardens and walking on a lead. This new abode had acres of meadow and woodland for her to explore, almost an excess of new experiences for such an old dog. Fortunately, the garden and meadows are quite well defined, with fences and hedges providing a substantial enough barrier for a little lap dog, so we were confident she wouldn't get lost, and with little passing traffic, the road wasn't an immediate concern. Nevertheless, while I unloaded Lesley's car, I kept a close eye on Romany as she explored her new territory. After appropriately anointing the garden, she woofed at nothing in particular for a while before deciding to explore the house. We showed her where the water and food bowls were, and once Romany had sated her thirst and hunger, Lesley laid her dog blanket in a quiet corner of the sitting room. Romany proceeded to poke and prod at her bedding, as if attempting to sculpture an origami dinosaur. Finally, she circled the bed three times, let off a resounding fart and settled down to sleep for the rest of the day, evidently satisfied with her new home.

Our furniture had taken a slightly different route to the house, stopping overnight in Dublin, but conveniently arriving within an hour of Lesley. As would become normal practice for future deliveries, until we were familiar enough with the local landmarks to provide useful directions, I drove out to Feakle village, to help guide the lorry back to the house. The aging vehicle was overloaded and clearly struggling to climb the hills of County Clare, so I took them on a more circular approach to the house to avoid the steepest inclines. Once parked in the driveway, the doors opened and two men emerged.

The driver, red faced and breathless from the exertion of climbing down from the cab, introduced himself as Dave. Sweating profusely, he was a physically large man, although not in the vertical sense. His paint-splattered jeans hung well below the equatorial region of his enormous belly, and required constant pulling-up to maintain any contact with his hips. Above, several inches of exposed flesh, hair and belly-button, led to a Manchester United soccer shirt, which was several sizes too small and required regular downward tugs to bridge the gap with his jeans. Given that both of his hands seemed fully engaged in avoiding a wardrobe disaster, I wondered if he would manage to lift any furniture.

Conversely, his unbelievably skinny assistant, Wally, looked almost too frail to lift himself, let alone the behemothic weight of the boxes Lesley had packed. As we made our introductions, he leaned forward with his hand in his side, apparently winded by the effort of lighting a cigarette.

"Blimey," he wheezed, "the air's a bit thin up here. I might have to sit down for a bit."

Dave rolled his eyes at this comment, suggesting Wally's breathlessness was not a new malaise.

"Are you unwell?" I asked.

He shook his head and puffed furiously on his cigarette. "Just a bit windy. I'll be alright if I take it easy."

Lesley and I shared a worried look. We were conscious of how much furniture there was to shift. It had taken a team of six strapping lads almost four hours to empty our Essex house.

"Don't worry, Wally," Dave said, giving the thinner man a mighty thump on the shoulder, "you ain't dead yet."

Wally staggered and smiled shyly. "Put the kettle on, love," he said to Lesley.

My wife is a strong and independent woman who has never been a fan of slavery or misogyny, so I inadvertently flinched at the prospect of Wally receiving a second and somewhat larger blow. But after a moment of internal conflict, Lesley wisely decided to postpone her response until after the lorry had been unloaded. She silently spun on her heel and marched stiffly toward the kitchen, I followed at a trot.

"How the hell are they going to unload our stuff?" she whispered. "That skinny fellow can hardly walk, and the other has to hold his trousers up all the time."

"How's your back feeling?" I asked.

Lesley had several bulged discs in her lower back. "Don't ask."

"Well, take it easy. Particularly if we get roped into helping."

"You too," she replied. I was recovering from a slipped disc myself.

"I'll do my best," I said, with a tight smile.

In any event, we were delighted our furniture had arrived, and excited to move it into our new home. Once the tea and biscuits had been consumed, I opened the double doors into the music studio and showed Sweaty Dave and Wheezy Wally where the things we didn't immediately require were to be stored.

"Oh! This'll be a breeze," Dave said.

"That's a lot of walking we have to do," Wally wheezed.

"Right!" Dave clapped his hands together, sending out a fine mist of sweat. "Let's get started."

He cautiously opened the back of the lorry and we were presented with a nightmarish three-dimensional jigsaw puzzle, constructed from our most precious possessions jammed in at all kinds of unbelievable angles.

"The big truck broke down, so we had to fit it all into this one," Dave explained.

"Oh my goodness!" Lesley exclaimed.

There was nothing for it. With darkness less than five hours away, the only way everything would be unloaded in time was if Lesley and I chipped in. We decided I would work with Big Dave, moving the heavier items, while Lesley, with the help of Wheezy Wally, would oversee operations, making sure most things found their correct place within the house. When needed, everyone would run up and down the path to the studio with items for long-term storage.

Dave and I cautiously approached the gridlock of furniture in the back of the truck and, like a giant game of KerPlunk, tried to identify which pieces we could remove without setting off an avalanche. With generous applications of care, swear, and prayer, we managed to extract a few of the larger pieces without causing

179

havoc. After that things progressed swimmingly. The bigger pieces, like beds, wardrobes and dining tables, were located to the rooms they would be used in, along with various boxes of kitchen implements, clothing, and tools.

Next began the process of laboriously carrying almost a hundred boxes, bags, and ancillary items along the path and into the studio. However, as I returned along the path after stacking another box of books, I saw Dave struggling and sweating under the weight of a chest of draws, my wife carrying three bags of winter clothes, and a smiling Wally, jauntily strolling along with a pillow under his arm. A minute later, Lesley pulled me to one side.

"That pillow is the heaviest thing I've seen him lift all afternoon," she hissed. "You should do something!"

"I'll speak to Dave," I replied.

"That won't help, he's a..." she stamped her foot in anger. I bravely put my hand on her arm.

"Here's an idea," I whispered calmly. "Rather than risking your back carrying stuff, you should become director of operations. I'll help you climb into the van. You can stay in there and tell the lazy so-and-so which boxes to take."

"Brilliant!" She beamed a smile. "Come on."

Amazingly, my plan worked. Between us, we managed to unpack our entire lives in just four hours, collecting only two minor dinks on the freezer and a scratch on an old chest of drawers. We even had time to stop for tea and sandwiches. We thanked Sweaty Dave and the newly-named Lazy Wally for their assistance, settled our bill and sent them on their way with a bottle of whisky for their troubles.

An hour later, Lesley was in the kitchen, unpacking boxes into the larder (called a press in Ireland) and I was in the room above, which I was going to use as a temporary workshop and shed. Thinking it was starting to get dark, I foolishly turned on the light.

"Hey! The lights have just gone off down here," Lesley shouted up the rickety spiral staircase connecting the kitchen with the two floors above.

"Try the switch, perhaps it's loose," I shouted back obligingly.

"Okay. That worked, the light is back on," she replied.

"Now the light has gone off up here!" I complained and flicked the switch again.

"Hey! Quit it will you, the light in the kitchen is off again."

I went up to the next floor and tried the light switch up there to see what happened, the light in the workshop went off and the light in the conservatory came on. In the end, we figured out the sequence necessary to illuminate the rooms we were in, and I added 'fix the electrics' to my already extensive to-do list. Back in the middle bedroom, above the sitting room, I had finished assembling the wardrobes. As the floor sloped so severely, they leaned forward fully ten degrees and needed propping up to stop the doors swinging open. I sat on the bed to consider the options, only to hear a loud crack and the sound of falling debris below.

"Nick, did you know the leg of a bed is sticking through the ceiling down here?" Lesley asked helpfully.

"Yes, thanks," I replied with a stiff smile, adding another job to my list.

Later that night, fed and watered, we sat together on the couch and enjoyed the peace and quiet of our first night living the dream.

"You're going to have to get this chimney sorted out," Lesley said as smoke billowed into the sitting room for the third time in less than an hour.

"Yes, dear, I've already put it on the list," I replied sleepily.

"So, now what?" Lesley asked, as our first day together in Ireland began.

"I suppose we'd better make a list. Or several." I smiled, delighted at the prospect.

"There's so much to do, I don't even know where to begin."

"That's why we need a list," I explained. "So we can prioritise things."

"You and your lists!" Lesley rolled her eyes.

"Like you said, there's a lot to do. If we don't have a plan, we're going to end up wasting a lot of time, or money, or both."

My wife gave a deep sigh. "*Alright!*"

I smiled and pulled a sheaf of papers from my briefcase. "As luck would have it, here's one I prepared earlier."

"Well, there's a shock," she said with mock sarcasm.

"There was no telly. I got bored." I held up a hand in defence. "Come on, I'll make a drink while you read this."

With the tea made, we sat at the table in the conservatory and discussed our plans.

"There's no mention of the garden," Lesley said, flicking through my list.

"I was more concerned with the house. There's such a lot to do. Anyway, I figured you would want to plan the garden. Or would you prefer I do it? We could have a lovely putting green and a couple of bunkers!" I joked.

Lesley didn't look amused. "Leave the garden to me for now."

"Of course, that's your department," I quickly agreed, knowing there was no point in arguing otherwise.

"I want another dog," Lesley said.

I smiled and nodded. "And I want another car. That Ford is uncomfortable, expensive to run, and the boot's too small."

"Okay."

And so the conversation continued. Even before the purchase was finalised, we had started drawing up plans for how we would like to renovate the house. The options were to repair, rebuild or replace, and it was important to choose correctly at each stage if we were to keep the feel of Glenmadrie as original as possible, while transforming it to a warm and pleasant home. On closer inspection, it was clear much of the existing structure had either been built poorly in the wrong place, or built quite well but on top of something else that was about to fall down. Many of the floors were uneven, or damaged by rot and some of the rafters were so infested with woodworm they could hardly support their own weight. This problematic theme continued throughout the house, so we decided to save and repair the things we liked, like the stone walls, windows, conservatory and roof – almost all the external structure. Internally though, pretty much everything would have to go.

During my short stay, I had already realised that although the house was generally watertight, it was in desperate need of insulation. The wind blew unimpeded from the loft into the bedrooms, and the stone walls, although over two feet thick, were constantly cold to the touch, sucking away any attempt to heat the house. The ceiling heights were less than six feet throughout the ground floor, and on the top floor, over the kitchen, the clearance was just over five feet. We decided the first-floor levels would have to be changed throughout the house, with the walls dry-lined and insulated. At the same time, we would move or replace the electrics and plumbing. Put simply, we were planning to gut our house and rebuild another, inside the stone shell of the existing building.

"It might be easier and cheaper to knock it down and build another house," I joked.

"If we wanted a jelly mould, we'd have bought one," Lesley snapped.

I held up the calming hand again. "I know, I know."

"At least we've got enough cash to get a builder to do the bulk of the work. Except for decorating, we can do that."

"Assuming we can get one, Aiden thinks we'll struggle to find someone."

"In that case, we'll do it ourselves," Lesley said, with firm finality.

I linked my fingers behind my head and blew a sigh. "That's a big job. Way more than we've ever attempted."

"Do you think we could do it?"

I ran my fingers through my hair – it didn't take long. Before moving to Ireland, and with the aid of a large and very comprehensive DIY manual, I had spent several days drawing up plans for how we wanted the interior of the house to look. While we still had easy access to the internet and several large builders' merchants, I had also priced most of the materials we would need. My research had given me a good insight into how big the job was, what it would cost, and the sequence in which things would need to happen. Although it was a dauntingly huge job, when broken down into a series of smaller projects, it became marginally less intimidating – but only just.

"It wouldn't be my first choice, particularly as I'm already pretty busy giving golf lessons. But…if we must, and you can help a bit, I think I can do it."

"Great!" She smiled. "That's settled then."

"Woah!" I put a restraining hand on her arm. "At least let's exhaust the possibility of getting a builder first."

"It's a shame we can't get Wally Sidebottom to come over for a few weeks."

"He's retired and living in Spain," I said. "Bitch of a commute to Ireland."

My wife pulled a disappointed face. "Shame."

We decided the immediate priorities were heat and water.

As the house was many miles from the mains, our only source of water was pumped from a shallow well in the wood below the house. The well head was only the size of a kitchen sink and dangerously close to the septic tank, although the presence of frogs and water nymphs suggested it was currently unpolluted. However, apart from the risk of sewage seeping into our drinking water, such a shallow well would also be inclined to dry up without warning. We decided we would get a deep-bore well drilled. This was definitely a job for the professionals.

The huge stone fireplace was another problem. It was an eyesore. Poorly constructed and inefficient, it intruded substantially into the lounge. Our surveyor had recommended removing the external chimney, but we weren't sold on the idea as it would ruin the external appearance of the house. We opted instead to remove the internal fireplace and install a wood burning stove, but first we sought the advice of a chimney expert to help sort out the smoke problem.

He was either efficient, or underemployed, as he was available to visit the next day. Despite our remote location, he found Glenmadrie without a hint of drama. After parking his unmarked white van in our driveway, he borrowed a ladder and a torch, and spent almost three minutes inspecting the chimney before delivering his verdict.

"That's fecked," he said.

In polite Irish society, the 'f' word can be used as a noun, a verb, or as an adjective – but not for swearing, that is reserved for the word 'feck' which is acceptable in multitudinous applications, from a builder's skinned knuckles to a priest banging his knee on the pulpit.

"Oh dear," I replied. "Can you fix it?"

"Ah sure."

"Do you have any idea how much it would cost?"

He looked up at the chimney and loudly sucked his teeth.

"Scaffolding…demolition…clearance," he mumbled, "couple of lads…block layers…"

He counted on his fingers for a moment and whispered a builders' incantation, before turning to face me.

"Ten thousand, three hundred," he said.

"Euros?" I asked in horror.

He pulled a face, suggesting he felt my pain and understood.

"Tell you what." He held up a finger. "Let's call it an even ten thousand."

"Let's not," I said, gently edging him towards his van.

"Are you sure? Builders are hard to find in this economy."

"I'll call you," I said, using the Irish phrase for 'no thank you' and sending him back to Limerick.

***

The next morning, Lesley went out to register with the local doctor, dentist and vet. Along the way, she stopped at the post office to tell the postmaster who we were and which house we were living in.

"I've got some good news," Lesley said, as she bustled into the house, smiling like a lottery winner.

"Obviously," I said.

185

She waved a small slip of paper with a phone number. "I've found us a builder. He's highly recommended."

"Oh good."

"And a dog!" She flashed her eyes, challenging me to object. I didn't.

After visiting the post office, Lesley had looked over a nearby fence and spotted what resembled an escaped herd of gerbils, chasing a small dog around a garden. On closer inspection, she realised they were several delightfully small and energetic puppies, resolutely chasing their mother. Some further investigation revealed they were the result of a late-night mating between a Pomeranian bitch and a somewhat determined Wire Fox Terrier dog. All the puppies were available for rehoming.

"I've picked one," she announced, her face alive with delight. "It's a girl."

"Oh…err…okay then." Caught off guard, I stumbled for an appropriate reply. "When do we get it?"

"The end of the month. She should be weaned by then." Lesley beamed a huge smile. "You should see them. They're *sooo* cute!"

"I can't wait." I was genuinely pleased and excited. "Now. Tell me about this builder."

***

Peadar, the builder, was a local lad. Tall, muscular, and as honest as the day is long, he could easily have been an Irish relation of the wonderful Wally Sidebottom. On Friday afternoon he came to inspect the house and discuss my plans. Despite his impeccable credentials, he did not have good news.

"I love your ideas, Nick, but I have to be honest with you. Much as I would love to do a renovation like this, I just haven't got the time."

My heart fell. "I'm starting to believe we'll never get a builder," I said, shaking my head. "Everyone's telling us the same thing, except for the guy who wanted ten thousand euros to fix the chimney."

"*Ten thousand!*" he exclaimed.

I nodded.

"Sorry." Peadar scratched his head in obvious frustration. "That's called an 'English Price', some people try it on with foreigners. You'll find the same with some big-ticket items like cars and televisions."

"That would explain why he didn't seem very upset when I refused his quotation," I said.

He shrugged. "What can I say? There's just too much work around."

"It's a good complaint to have."

"It is, but…" He cast his eyes around. "It's all new build. I miss doing projects like this." He shrugged again. "Things are just mad right now. If you knocked this place down and cleared the site, ready to build a new property, it would still be two years before I could get one of my lads up here to start work."

"It's ironic," Lesley said. "Now we can afford a builder, we can't get one."

"It doesn't matter how much money you have, nobody wants to do renovation work these days – it's too hard and too dirty," he said. "Why don't you just do it yourself? You English are supposed to be keen on DIY, aren't you?"

"That's that then," I said, resigned to my fate. "It looks like I'll be doing it myself. I just hope I'm up to it."

"Don't worry, you'll manage. And just think of the money you'll save." He patted me on the shoulder. "If it's any help, I can pop up tomorrow with one of my lads and remove this fireplace."

"That would be great! What about the chimney?"

"I think the chimney will be fine once this huge fireplace is out. Particularly if you're getting a stove."

"That's the plan," Lesley said.

"Okay then." Peadar stood. "I'll see you in the morning."

It took Peadar and two young apprentices all day on Saturday to remove the fireplace, and most of Sunday to build a plinth for the stove and repair the wall with cement render. All we had to do was tile the base and purchase a nice wood burning stove.

***

The next few weeks revolved around settling in to our new home, cleaning almost constantly to keep ahead of the dust, unpacking only the things we needed for daily use, and getting out and about to discover the local area. We visited Galway, Ennis and Limerick to get a feel for the kind of shops we had access to, not only for food shopping, but for our gardening and building needs as well. Living in England, we were used to a wide range of shops, with local competition helping to drive down the prices. British towns and cities tend to follow a similar layout – major retailers in the high street, smaller shops in the side streets, and perhaps a supermarket or two in a development out of town, with large computer, electrical, DIY and garden centres in dedicated retail parks. The commonality and logic of this retail geography made finding places to shop quick and easy, even for a stranger to the area.

We found shopping in Ireland to be very different. Although many of the retailers we were familiar with had yet to become established in the west, there was a commendable generational tradition of shopping locally. However, with so many loyal customers, many stores did not need to advertise their presence or whereabouts, making shopping more difficult for Irish newbies like us. A few afternoon scouting trips identified where we could buy groceries, but given the distances involved, we soon decided to keep a stock of milk and bread in the freezer. But building materials and other hardware items proved to be more problematic. I was rendered almost speechless with confusion and anger when I was told my money was no good, as many of the hardware suppliers were for trade only, something I hadn't encountered in England since the mid-1980s. Luckily, in a throwback to the 1950s, we found a tiny local hardware shop capable of supplying everything I needed, from cement mixers, through concrete blocks to tap washers, and everything in between, including single screws. And all with free delivery.

Most Irish retailers were not listed on the internet (a moot point as our internet access was too slow anyway) or in the Golden Pages business directory, and the phone book was of little use unless we knew the exact name of the business. The only hope was to ask someone. We ran into our first cultural problem when I enquired if our grocery checkout assistant knew where I could buy a sack of wild bird seed. She thought for a moment and checked with a colleague before delivering her opinion.

"Try Mack and Ernies," she said, in a brisk Irish accent.

"Is that in Ennis?" I asked.

"For sure."

I waited politely for further information and directions, but none were forthcoming.

"Could you please tell me where it is?" I asked politely.

"By the river," she replied. "Near Ashford Court."

"Thank you very much."

"You're welcome." She smiled.

There was no A to Z of Ennis, or any online map, so we were relying on the tourist town map we got during our first trip. I could see no mention of Ashford Court, or Ashford Court Road, or Ashford Court Lane, or any other combination of those words. In the grocery store carpark, I asked a passer-by for directions.

"Excuse me. We're looking for a road called Ashford Court."

The man squinted in thought, before shaking his head. "Ain't never heard of it."

"What about Mack and Ernies?" Lesley asked. "We're trying to buy some wild bird seed."

"Sorry." He shook his head again.

"Okay, thank you anyway." We started to walk on when the man shouted after us.

"If it's bird seed you're after, why don't you try the farm supplies shop on Cornmarket Street?"

"Thank you. You're most kind."

Cornmarket Street was on our little map. When we got to the farm supplies shop, Lesley pointed to the big sign.

"Oh look. Dan McInerney Farm Supplies." We both laughed at the misunderstanding and a moment later we laughed again. I pointed to another sign on the building next-door.

"Ashford Court Hotel!" I read, "I never thought..."

***

The countryside around Glenmadrie is stunning, truly breath-taking, but oh so easy to take for granted. With so much to do at home, along with my fast-expanding golf coaching business, it would have been easy to fall into a routine of working from dawn to dusk. We moved to Ireland in search of a better life, and now we were here it was important to make sure we found it. So, one day at a time, we started to explore and experience our surroundings.

We thoroughly enjoyed discovering new walks we could take with Romany. Opposite the house, there is a rough hiking trail with marker posts every hundred yards or so, sufficient to keep even the most hapless ramblers on course. The path snakes across the rolling moorland, rising and falling for several miles, until it links up with a rough forest track alongside a glacial lake. It is a beautiful walk, with spectacular views down the valley towards Lough Graney in the far distance.

Perhaps it's my naturally rebellious character, but I prefer to go off-piste, striking out across the heather-dotted wild grass in whatever direction I chose. There is a tremendous sense of freedom and isolation when walking in an area so remote that I may be the first human to pass this way in a hundred years, or perhaps ever. However, some caution is required, as the ground is rough, uneven, and laced with deep holes and fissures where rainwater has undercut the peatbog. Some of these clefts are filled with a porridge-like mixture of water, peat and sphagnum moss, creating moorland quicksand easily capable of swallowing a cow.

Immediately behind the house, there is a large forest with a logging trail, looping clockwise around the hillside and back to the road where it started. Once on the far side of the hill, we have an unobstructed view across the green valley, as far as Shannon and Lough Derg. Often in the early mornings the valley floor below will be shrouded in fog and stained light pink by the rising sun.

Sometimes, on a Sunday morning, we will jump in the car and drive through Flagmount to the north end of Lough Graney, where a forest path leads down to a beautiful, secluded beach, known locally as Silver Sands. There we can walk for hours without sight or sound of another person. The water is crystal clear and shallow for up to fifty yards out. If it isn't too cold, I will remove my shoes and socks, wade in knee-deep, and walk around Black Island, which sits at the head of the lake. Alternatively, there is a picturesque, looped walk along a decent footpath leading to the unfortunately named River Bleach, which flows down from Lough Atorick, high in the hills towards the Slieve Aughty Mountains. I am always amazed and grateful to discover this idyllic beach is still completely deserted, when in most other countries, dogs would have to be kept on a leash, the beach would be covered in tourists and their discarded rubbish, and the water would be churned to foam by hundreds of speedboats and wakeboarders. God bless you, undiscovered County Clare.

23. Stoves and Midgets

No sooner had we arrived in Ireland, then my wife was heading back to England. Due to several bulging discs in her spine, Lesley had previously been receiving a course of treatment from a back specialist at a hospital in Colchester. She still needed to have the last three rounds of steroid injections, and although we were now under the care of our local doctor, my wife had wisely decided to complete the course of treatment in the UK. A few days before her flight, we decided to take a day off so we could buy our stove. On the advice of Peadar, we were heading for a stove and tile shop in Ennis. It was a dry and sunny day and, emboldened with the spirit of adventure, I had used my trusty number 58 Ordinance Survey map to find a shorter route from Glenmadrie to Ennis.

"You'll get us lost," Lesley warned.

"No I won't."

"Remember what happened the last time you took a shortcut?"

"That was *thirty years* ago," I sighed. "Why do you keep bringing it up?"

"I'm just saying…"

"I've got a map, we won't get lost."

"Why can't we go the usual way?" my wife asked.

"This is a much shorter route, it'll save time."

"If you say so." she mumbled.

Fortunately for me, we didn't get lost, and we both enjoyed the drive. Although our journey along the narrow back-roads was a shorter route, this being rural Ireland, the trip took a good bit longer. Along the way we encountered several delays, but we didn't mind. It was all part of our new lifestyle. First, we met a herd of cows coming toward us along the narrow road. We could only stop and wait while the farmer encouraged them to pass our car with several energetic whacks from his walking stick. This proved to be rather an impressive feat of dexterity and balance, as he was on an ancient and very rusty bicycle, and unwilling to take his feet off the pedals. For their part, the cows obviously considered us to be an interesting diversion from their usual routine. It was indeed a strange sensation to sit in our car, like exhibits in a zoo, while each of the 40 or so cows stopped momentarily to press an inquisitive eye against the side window. I imagined they were thinking, *"Oh look, this species is from England!"*

A mile further and we were delayed again. This time the road was blocked by two cars, facing in opposite directions. With their side windows lowered, both drivers were having an animated conversation, aided by a lone farmer leaning on his walking stick. Alan Sykes had warned us about this phenomenon.

"The best thing to do is wait patiently," he had said. "Read a book, enjoy the view, but never toot your horn."

We took his sage advice to heart, and waited. I do patient better than my wife.

"What the hell are they playing at?" she hissed.

I considered the question to be rhetorical, so I kept my eyes trained on the field opposite.

"They know we're here." Lesley whispered. "Why aren't they moving?"

"It's the English number plates," I explained. "Alan said they sometimes add a couple of minutes. They probably think we're tourists."

Lesley's fingers tapped out her frustration on the dashboard. I leaned away in case her airbag deployed from the violent pounding. A couple of minutes later, the farmer whispered something into the cars. It may have been, *"That's it lads, they've had enough,"* because the cars suddenly drove on. The farmer smiled and gave a friendly wave as we passed. I responded in kind.

A little further up the lane, our journey was appreciably slowed as we encountered a tractor pulling a horsebox. The road was narrow, so there was nothing I could do but creep along behind this mobile obstruction until one of us was able to turn off.

"Good grief," Lesley exclaimed, "one of those horses is waving."

Sure enough, someone was waving, but it wasn't a horse. It was children. By my count, there were at least six children in the back of the horsebox, waving their arms through the ventilation gaps. Three faces were peering above the rear door, displaying tufts of ginger hair and toothy smiles. We both waved back as the tractor turned into a field.

"They seemed to be having fun," Lesley observed.

"I guess it's a convenient way to transport a large family."

Buying the stove was about as interesting as I had feared. When shopping, Lesley likes to drift almost aimlessly from item to item, like a feather at the whim of the wind. I prefer to take a more direct approach, focusing on quality, product efficiency, value for money, and whatever will get me out of the shop with alacrity. On this day, I hoped to get the deed done in record time, but it was not to be. However, when we were accosted by a sales assistant within yards of entering the shop, I still had high hopes of a speedy purchase.

"How can I help you?" he asked.

I squinted at his name badge before consulting my list.

"Hello, Adam," I said. "We would like to buy a cast-iron stove please. It should be multi-fuel for burning wood, peat, or coal, and capable of producing more than 60,000 BTUs."

Adam's mouth opened and closed like a goldfish.

"Also, we would like it to have a glass front, a top exit for the chimney and the option to add a back boiler later." I smiled and handed over my list.

"*Riiight!*" Adam said. He looked at a couple of the larger stoves on the display stands and carefully checked their specifications before patting a shiny black behemoth. "I think this one will do everything you asked for." Adam held out the product details for me to see. He was right. I checked the price, it was more than I had paid for my car. I mentally pulled a face.

"I think this will do. What do you think, dear?" I turned to consult with Lesley, but she was a distant figure at the other side of the shop. She heard my call and waved for me to follow.

"This one's pretty," she said, pointing to a bright red model, not much larger than a laundry basket.

"It's too small," I explained, "and it's oil-fuelled. We need a multi-fuel wood burner. There's one over there."

"Yes, I know." Lesley pointed again. "What about this white one?"

"That's the same as the red stove, only in white," I said. "Come and see the one we were looking at over there."

We didn't get far. My dear wife was determined to look at, and in, every stove in the shop, before turning her attention to the one I had found with Adam.

"Oh I don't like that," she said, waving her hand dismissively. "It's too shiny."

"Oh for God–"

Adam cut me off. "I'll check the catalogue to see if they have it in another shade."

Lesley raised her eyebrows. "You have a catalogue?"

"We have three," Adam replied.

I groaned and closed my eyes. The next 90 minutes passed with glacial slowness as Lesley and Adam flicked between the pages of three catalogues. I sat and waited.

"What about this one?" she asked.

"Perfect!" I replied.

"Or this one?"

"That'll do just fine."

"Or would you prefer that one?"

"If you like it, I'm happy," I said.

Lesley glared at me. "Nick, this is a very important decision. I don't think you're taking it very seriously."

"Of course I am," I complained. "As long as it does all the things we want, I'm happy with whatever model you choose."

Lesley humphed loudly. She flicked violently through several pages before pointing to a stove. "What about this one?"

"That will do nicely." I smiled. It was after all the same model stove I had chosen at the beginning, only in a dark matt grey finish.

Our journey home was no less interesting than the trip out. On the main road, a few miles out of Ennis, we saw a very large tractor travelling towards us at considerable speed and towing a long trailer stacked high with black plastic-wrapped bails of silage. Unlike the common green-painted farm tractors, this yellow monster stood as high as a bus on four huge tyres, each taller than a man. Accessed by an integral ladder, the cab was an all-glass affair, slung low between the front wheels, giving the vehicle a sinister, robotic insect appearance. It was the second time we had seen this vehicle, so we were prepared to confirm our earlier suspicion. The driver was indeed a person of very short stature. However, the attention-grabbing point was not his lack of height, but that he was standing to drive. As the tractor passed, we could clearly see how this unusual driving position allowed him to operate the foot pedals and still reach the steering wheel, which was above his head. This remarkable demonstration of equilibrium and legerdemain was even more impressive, given the uneven ride and his simultaneous use of a mobile phone.

Two miles later, we turned off the main road and began the gradual climb towards our house. We hadn't gone far when we encountered another obstruction.

"Well, there's something you don't see every day," I commented.

Ahead was a man on a bicycle. He was skinny and of an indeterminate age, wearing jeans, a red baseball cap and a black jacket. It was all very mundane, and if it wasn't for the sofa strapped on his back like a rucksack, we wouldn't have noticed him at all. How he had managed to lift the sofa, let alone ride a bike with it, was a mystery.

"Perhaps he's practicing for an Iron Man event," I speculated.

"Or a talent show," Lesley suggested.

"I've got it!" I snapped my fingers. "It's Ryanair's new business venture. Low cost removals!"

Lesley laughed.

As we neared Glenmadrie, a dark blue car passed in the opposite direction. The driver, an elderly grey-haired man waved in acknowledgment and I reciprocated. Running behind the car was a gangly-looking young dog. It was hard to tell if he was chasing the car, or just following, but either way his expression suggested he was having fun. Lesley turned in her seat and watched the dog go by.

"How extraordinary!" she said.

"I've seen that car a few times now, I think the owner's one of our neighbours," I said.

"If we see him again, we should stop and say hello."

"I'm not sure about that dog though, it looks like a bit of a nutter."

"You'll be in good company then," Lesley said, patting my arm.

***

While Lesley was away in England for her back injections, I got on with some jobs around the house. The first two tasks on my list took little of my time and money, but saved us thousands. Ever since we moved in there had been a strong smell of kerosene in the kitchen. I was able to trace it to a leaking valve on the Rayburn that took just seconds with a spanner to rectify. As a precaution, I also cleaned the filter on the oil tank outside where I discovered a steady drip of oil from another loose valve, again easily tightened. Secondly, with just two telephone calls, I had acquired ten gallons of commercial woodworm treatment and, using the same equipment saved from our previous house, I spent two happy days crawling through hundred-year-old cobwebs in the loft, protecting our biggest asset.

As Ireland had only three TV channels, I'd arranged for the installation of a satellite television system. The engineer telephoned to report he was lost, so I drove down to the local village and guided the young lad back to the house. I suspected he was quite new to the job because, although he was equipped with a shiny new ladder and a van full of satellite dishes, cables and connectors, his rechargeable drill was no match for our granite walls. He did his best to fit the new dish, but I had to replace the fixing bolts the next day for fear of losing the signal with the first light puff of wind.

The next task was a two-handed affair, so I waited until Lesley returned. We'd realised there was a problem with our drains. The water flowed slowly from the bath and sinks, and there was a pervading smell of bad eggs whenever we ran a tap. I soon figured out there was a blockage somewhere in the confusion of old drainpipes that took the wastewater from the bathroom, via the kitchen sink, and out through the wall towards the cesspit.

Even though I had plans to replace the pipework as a part of the renovations, that task was still many months away and, in the meantime, we needed to get rid of the blockage. A drain auger would not work as the pipe was 40 feet long with several branches. We had tried using a toilet plunger without success, and even the strongest drain cleaning chemicals had done nothing more than add to the smell. However, a little research and a trip to the hardware superstore in Limerick resulted in me purchasing an air-bust drain cleaner. This handy toy is a can of compressed air, with an attachment rather like a sink plunger, which sends a rapid blast of carbon dioxide gas down the drain, instantly clearing any obstruction. To ensure the gas drives the blockage safely outside, and not back up the nearest sink, all intermediate plugholes and overflows must be firmly sealed before letting fly with the explosive blast.

Lesley and I began preparations for our drain clearing extravaganza. It was a lovely morning, warm and sunny, so Romany soon lost interest in what we were doing. To keep out from under our feet, she wandered off into the garden to do some sunbathing.

With a little twisting, a skinned knuckle, and the careful application of some swear words, I removed the downwards section of the outside drainpipe, to permit the blockage an unrestricted path to freedom. Indoors, I had used duct tape to cover the overflows and all but two of the plugholes. Lesley would block one with half a tennis ball and the other would be the recipient for the air-blast. Hopefully, the violent rush of gas would follow the path of least resistance, along the 40 feet of drainpipe and out through the wall, taking with it the foul crud that had accumulated during the previous 50 years.

After a final check to ensure everything was sealed, we moved to our allotted stations. I was in the upstairs bathroom ready to fire the gas down the bathtub plughole and Lesley was blocking the kitchen sink plughole, by leaning as hard as possible on her half-tennis ball. I shouted down to check she was ready, and, after an overly dramatic countdown, I braced myself and released the gas.

At my end the results were disappointingly anticlimactic. In the space of two seconds, the gas went down the plughole with a sound like a geriatric steam engine whispering *chew*. Further along the pipe, Lesley heard something that sounded like a subway train rushing by. She was delighted when it continued along the drainpipe, rather than attempting to escape around her half-tennis ball. A moment later, we heard what sounded like an overfed elephant with dysentery. I ran some water into the sink and was delighted to see it disappear down the plughole without the usual smell or sluggishness. Downstairs, I proudly gave Lesley a high-five. Result! Or so we thought.

A few moments later, as I stepped outside ready to sweep up the mess, I was mortified to discover our once-white dog, sitting miserably in a pool of foul water and covered in the most obnoxious grey filth one can imagine. Unfortunately, Romany had heard the approaching commotion and decided to investigate the source of the noise by sticking her nose into the open drainpipe, which was conveniently situated at exactly the right height for our little dog. A moment later, her curiosity was rewarded when she was hit by the full contents of the blocked drain, containing a combination of 50 years of toothpaste, lost hair, toenail clippings, kitchen grease, and God knows what else. The dirt and smell was almost unbearable, but it soon washed away. However, for many weeks Romany continued to glower at me in the unwavering certainty I had deliberately showered her in filth.

**

Although we had seen and waved at the elderly man in the dark blue car several times, he had yet to stop or even slow down. Each time he flashed by, giving a jolly wave, he was pursued by the same gangly black and white dog. Curiously, this tenacious automobile chaser had started to wear some unusual canine accessories. On Monday, I noticed he had a long dog lead attached to a tennis ball, which bounced along behind as he ran. On Tuesday this had been replaced by a stout rope and what looked like a soccer ball. By Wednesday he was wearing a long chain, and the next day this acquired a lump of concrete the size of a briefcase. We wondered if these strange contraptions were part of some unusual Irish tradition, or just an attempt to stop the dog from chasing cars. Whatever the case, it clearly wasn't working. I resolved to ask the elusive man in the blue car at the earliest opportunity.

A few days later we spotted someone walking along the lane at the rear of our house. I called out and he stopped to have a chat. Jim is a local farmer who lives around five miles away. He is a delightful man, with a ready smile, twinkling blue eyes and a tendency to call everyone 'sir'. Today, he was wearing boots, jeans, and a mud-smeared jacket that may once have been green. A faded baseball cap partially covered his tousled dark hair and like an eight-year-old boy, his pockets overflowed with bits of twine, pocket-knives, apples and cattle feed. Next to him was an actual eight-year-old boy. He was immaculately dressed, standing politely to attention and shyly watching us from under the brim of his Munster rugby baseball cap.

After introducing ourselves, Jim welcomed us to the area and explained he was in the habit of grazing his cows on the pasture attached to our property. Apparently his relatives once owned much of the land in the area, and his great uncle used to live in our house. I promised to take great care of the property and asked his opinion of what it would be like to live here.

"Well, sir," he said. "You will find it's grand – apart from the midgets."

"Midgets?" I queried, thinking of the dwarf we had seen twice, driving a tractor while standing up. "What about them?"

"I fecking hate them. They're BASTARDS, sir!" he replied.

I knew some people had a prejudice against those they considered outside of the norm, and while everybody is entitled to their own opinion, I felt very uncomfortable with Jim's venom. However, I was conscious this man was my distant neighbour and I didn't want to get off on the wrong foot.

"Really? That seems a little harsh," I offered in pacification.

"Harsh?" He seemed genuinely shocked. "Harsh is it, sir? Them little bastards cum up here in their 'undreds. They's after me cows they is. Well, you ask my opinion, they should feck off to Scotland, where they come from." He turned his head and spat.

I looked out over the hills and pictured a missing scene from the movie *Braveheart*, with hundreds of kilted dwarfs, belonging to some secret cattle rustling clan, charging across the moor like slightly taller versions of Mel Gibson. It seemed a little far-fetched, but I was new to the area.

"I'll have to try and keep out of their way, I suppose," I offered.

"You can try, sir, but it won't work. The girl midgets are the worst. When it's time for them to breed, they can smell you out for miles. So I've heard."

"Good gracious – how extraordinary! You learn something new every day." I was picturing a miniature version of an Essex girl's hen night. "Perhaps they're attracted to the smell of Guinness."

"Oy don't know about that," he said. Suddenly, he changed tack like a drunken sailor. "Can I still graze me cows on yer field, sir?" he asked.

"Yes, Jim, I don't see why not."

Jim's hatred of little people remained a perplexing mystery until the first muggy day in late April. I was trying to wash the mud from my car, when I became aware of tiny hot pinpricks of pain on my neck and face. I noticed several small lumps were already growing on the backs of my hands. In the sunlight, I could see a cloud of dancing dust that seemed to follow my every move.

"Oh! MIDGES!" I said slapping my forehead, physically and figuratively. I quickly made my escape indoors in search of the antihistamine cream, and told Lesley the puzzle of the midgets was now solved.

24. Amber Arrives

During the three weeks we waited for the arrival of our new puppy, our excitement had been building, and now the big day had come. Being so busy at work, and not wanting to impose on the breeder, I hadn't had the opportunity to see the litter, so I had no idea what to expect, other than Lesley's description. However, we had still found the time to visit an Ennis pet shop to purchase puppy food and bowls, a dog lead, a bed, and several toys of varying size and style. Had the wait for our new pet been any longer, I suspect we would have ended up with a hole in our bank account the size of the Grand Canyon and enough canine paraphernalia to open our own store.

On the day in question, I arrived back from work just as Lesley was setting off to collect our new dog. It was a ten mile round-trip, so I had enough time to take a shower, put the kettle on, and give Romany a fuss, before I heard a car pulling into the driveway. Full of excitement, I dashed through the kitchen and met my wife at the door. She was carefully carrying the puppy in her arms. Amber, as we had already decided to call our new charge, was wrapped in a towel and fast asleep.

"Here, have a look," Lesley whispered, peeling away the towel. Sleepyhead opened her eyes, gave a huge yawn and blinked at the world.

"Hello, little one," I said, reaching out to give her a gentle stroke.

Amber snuggled against my fingers and gave my hand an experimental lick. I gently took her from Lesley and cuddled her in the crook of my arm, like a new-born baby. Our new puppy was just nine inches long. She had short, soft fur, dark beige in colour, with a pointy face, black button eyes, huge ears and a curly tail.

I tickled the soft fur on Amber's tummy. "She's beautiful."

Romany had noticed we were giving someone other than her attention, so she waddled over and began her bum-balancing act. Sitting upright on her bottom with her paws up and balancing precariously until she got what she wanted, or fell over.

"Time for some introductions," I said, crouching down and allowing Romany to see Amber for the first time.

Romany leaned forward and gave the tiny puppy an experimental sniff, and Amber responded by enthusiastically licking the larger dog's nose. Backing away in surprise and a little disgust, Romany plodded away and plopped back onto her bed with a huff, as if to say, *"I'll let it live here, but don't expect me to play with it."*

Amber had a different opinion. Squirming out of my arms, she jumped onto the floor and ran over to investigate Romany and her bed.

"Well, she seems pretty fearless," I remarked, laughing.

"It must be the terrier in her," Lesley responded, her eyes twinkling with humour.

Realising the little rat-like puppy was about to invade her space, Romany jumped up and moved away, closely followed by Amber, who was now wide-awake and keen to play chase. Doing her best to look casually brave, Romany trotted behind the couch, circumnavigated the nest of tables and ran to Lesley in the hope of some protection, all the time being followed by the determined puppy. With nowhere else to go, she looked around in desperation, backed into Lesley's feet and gave a single warning bark. It was unlikely Romany would make an aggressive move toward another dog, it just wasn't in her nature, but Amber had yet to learn the importance of good manners, so I scooped her into my arms before her determination to lick the other dog's face caused an international incident.

"Come here, little one." I tickled her tummy as an aid to distraction, and this immediately turned into a game of tickle and bite. "Let's get you a toy to play with."

Lesley opened the large bag containing our pet shop purchases and selected a toy. It was a furry, foam-filled red pyramid, perfect for throwing and tugging. Although it was the smallest toy we had bought, it was still much larger than the puppy. My wife looked at it in consternation.

"I guess she'll grow into it," she said.

I sat Amber on the ground and, as soon as Lesley had thrown the toy, the little dog enthusiastically raced after it with her claws scrabbling for grip on the polished wood floor. Clearly, she was no respecter of size. Immediately understanding the purpose of the game, she grabbed the pyramid and dragged it back to Lesley, where she woofed excitedly until it was thrown again. The game repeated three times, but on the fourth throw, Amber dropped the toy at my feet. She looked up, smiling expectantly with her tail wagging furiously and woofed twice, as if to say, "*Your turn*".

I obliged, but perhaps a little too enthusiastically, because her toy bounced through the door and into the kitchen. Unperturbed, Amber chased the toy across the sitting room floor and, like a beige ninja, threw herself down the steps and into the kitchen before pouncing just as it slid under the table. I watched helplessly and winced as she collided with the chair legs with a sickening crash, but I need not have worried. The little dog just shook her head and raced back to my feet as if it was all part of the fun. And so the game continued.

Despite our enthusiasm, after an hour we were tired and a little bored. Now we were watching television and taking turns to casually throw the toy as Amber raced up and down the lounge, all scrabbling feet and panting in excitement. We had tried to stop the game, but Amber had other ideas, woofing loudly until someone threw her toy again. Aware that a terrier puppy would need lots of play and attention, we'd bought the multiple dog toys hoping to provide a distraction, but it was not to be. They were piled in a corner and ignored. The furry pyramid was her toy of choice, even though it was now wet and sticky with saliva.

"She obviously considers us her main source of entertainment," I remarked.

"Don't worry," Lesley said, "she'll get tired soon."

"That's what you said half-an-hour ago," I complained, throwing the toy for the umpteenth time.

"We can't do this for the rest of our lives," Lesley said wincing. "My shoulder is getting sore."

"I told you to use more wrist. Anyway, she'll have to learn that playtime is over when we say–" I was interrupted by Amber's impatient barking. Lesley laughed. Apparently, it was my turn to throw.

"Tell you what," Lesley said, "I'll dish up their food. Perhaps that'll distract her."

Luckily it did, but not without incident. Accustomed to competing with her siblings at meal times, Amber devoured her bowl of puppy food in six mighty gulps, before searching for seconds. Romany was an old lady and laid back about everything in life, including her food, which she liked to savour slowly and over several visits. Nevertheless, she was somewhat taken aback when the highly-strung terrier's head appeared directly under her chin and began to devour her dinner. I saw the old girl do a comical double-take before stepping back in surprise at the puppy's bad manners. Although I was quick to scoop the tiny kleptomaniac away, by that time half of Romany's food was gone. With our squiggling puppy safely locked out of the room and the missing food replaced, we managed to avoid an incident, but only just.

After her initial ambivalence, Romany took a motherly interest in the new arrival. This may have been through some in-built maternal instinct, or perhaps in the hope of garnering some attention for herself. In any event, at least we were reasonably confident Amber wasn't going to be murdered in the night. Maintaining our usual routine, at 10 pm we moved Romany's bed out to the conservatory where she settled immediately and went to sleep. Then we set about trying to get Amber into her bed.

"I hadn't realised this was so large," I said, laying out Amber's new bed alongside Romany's spot in the conservatory.

Lesley pulled a face. "I remembered the puppy being bigger."

"Amber will get lost in this."

"She'll be fine. Don't worry."

"The poor thing has been used to sleeping with her mum and a pile of puppies," I said.

"She'll probably appreciate the extra space," Lesley replied.

"Here goes." I picked up the little puppy, gently placed her in the centre of the bed, gave her a stroke and stepped back. She set there looking around and blinking at the new surroundings.

Lesley leaned in and added her own affectionate stroke. "Nighty night, Amber."

We headed back to the kitchen, pausing only to give Romany a stroke. As we reached the door, we turned to check on the dogs, only to discover Amber sitting patiently at our feet. I scooped her into my arms.

"No you don't!" I said. "You have to sleep in here with Romany."

I returned her to the bed and headed back to the kitchen, a little quicker than before. But not quick enough. Amber beat me to the door. Lesley grabbed the rat-sized fur ball and marched her back to the bed. Amber was back at my feet before Lesley had turned around. I was starting to suspect the little dog considered this to be a new game. By the fourth attempt, it was clear Amber wasn't going to stay in her bed, so I resorted to pushing her into the conservatory with my foot and quickly shutting the door.

"We'd better wait down here until she settles down," Lesley said, raising her voice to be heard over the pathetic whining from the other side of the door.

"We'll see who gives in first," I thought.

It was Lesley.

"Oh, you poor baby!" she said, as Amber licked her face, desperately scrabbling in her arms. "Perhaps I could have her on the bed – just for tonight."

"No!" I said, rather more firmly than I had intended. "If she comes on the bed once, there'll be no end to it."

Lesley gave me her little-girl-lost pout.

"And what about Romany?" I added.

"Oh, *all right!*" Amber went back into her bed, and we returned to the process of outwaiting a whining puppy.

The second time we survived almost ten minutes, the third was a record at twelve. By the fourth, we were upstairs, trying to get to sleep. An hour later, things hadn't improved.

"She's certainly tenacious," I observed.

"She'll get tired and go to sleep eventually," Lesley said, with rather less conviction than she had intended.

A new voice joined in. "Now what?" I asked, rolling my red-rimmed eyes in frustration.

"That's Romany," Lesley groaned.

"Perhaps she's tired as well," I said. "Her harmony's certainly a little off key."

"I'll go down." She sat up in bed, but stopped when I put my hand on her arm.

"Leave them," I replied. "They've got to learn."

Lesley buried her face into her pillow and growled in frustration and exhaustion.

"Leave them," I repeated. "They'll settle down."

"Eventually..." Lesley mumbled into her pillow.

And eventually they did settle down, but it was a close-run thing, lasting well into the early hours. In the morning, while Lesley and I were both bleary-eyed and tousled-haired, Amber was wide awake and full of playful energy and demanding to be entertained. After her breakfast, Romany glared accusingly at me and returned to her bed until lunchtime, whereas the little puppy played with her toys – and her new slaves – until she had used up all her excess energy.

To minimise the risk of our new puppy catching any infections from stray dogs, Amber's outdoor activities were limited to the courtyard for the first three weeks, until her course of inoculations was completed. As Ireland was enjoying an unusually warm and dry spring, we could leave the doors to the courtyard open for most of the day, which helped tremendously with the housetraining. Although she wasn't domesticated when she arrived, being an intelligent puppy, Amber copied Romany and quickly learned to use the outdoor facilities for her toilet. Within a week, Amber was housetrained and sleeping through the night without complaint, she had also become firm friends with Romany, doubled in size, and taught her slaves how to tend to her every need.

Unlike Romany, our new puppy had a high capacity for play, so we had to ensure our attention was evenly spread between the two dogs, even if this meant ignoring Amber for a while, or fussing Romany when she would rather be left alone. Irrespective of what her slaves were doing, whenever she wanted to play, Amber would unceremoniously drop her favourite toy at our feet and deliver a series of high-pitched barks until we complied. If we were unavailable, she would resort to giving Romany the same instructions but without any success, as the older dog was half-deaf and as obstinate as a mule. Fortunately, Amber's energetic enthusiasm was equally balanced with a need for regular naps, so despite many happy hours of play and cuddles with the fluffy rat, we still managed to get some household chores done.

Those first three weeks flew by, aided by the glorious sunshine and my increasingly busy schedule at work. When it was time for Amber's inoculations, we doubled-up the appointment so Romany could get a check-up as well. Although she was still quite sprightly for an old dog, Romany was showing some worrying signs of age, sleeping for most of the day and suffering from recurring bouts of colitis. Although she was bathed and groomed frequently, she also suffered from infected eyes, caused by irritation from the thick hair on her face – a common problem with the breed. Before she died, Brandy, had taken on the job of keeping Romany's eyes clean. For an hour every day, Romany would stand quite still, patiently waiting as Brandy licked at each eye, until every sign of crud had gone. The combination of Brandy's obvious affection, and the natural antiseptic properties of high-quality dog slob, did a wonderful job of keeping Romany's eyes clean and infection-free. However, Brandy was long gone, and despite our best efforts with a warm flannel and baby shampoo, Romany's eyes had become crusty and sore.

Our local veterinary practice is housed in a converted two-bedroom cottage, in a small village around 12 miles from our house. Although the vets probably spend most of their days treating cattle, sheep and horses – as you would expect in a rural practice – they were also skilled at tending to small animals. On this particular day, I was keen to get out of the house and enjoy the sunshine and so, on the pretext of being a helpful husband, I drove the car while Lesley sat in the back with Romany and Amber on her lap. The journey to the veterinary surgery was uneventful, which is code for neither dog threw-up in the car. There was a short wait to be seen, but it was plenty of time for the other customers and staff to lavish attention on our delightfully cute puppy, something she was happy to receive. Not to be left out, Romany filled the time by balancing precariously on her bottom and demanding a fuss from each person in the waiting room, until Katy, the vet, called us through.

She was a tall and elegant young woman, with soft skin that spoke of clean living and country air, and tired eyes from too many late-night callouts. Katy examined Amber with professional efficiency and delivered the inoculation without raising a squeak of disapproval. But being a dog lover, she couldn't resist giving the little fur-ball a cuddle.

"She's *sooo* cute. But it looks like someone is getting jealous," Katy said, looking down at Romany trying to climb up her leg.

"We have to make sure we lavish them with equal quantities of affection," Lesley explained.

"That's a good idea."

Katy handed Amber to Lesley and carefully lifted Romany onto the examination table. The little dog accepted the medical palpations, the vitamin injection into the scruff of her neck, and even the thermometer up the bum without complaint, but she firmly drew the line when Katy tried to examine her eyes.

"Oh dear! Her eyes are very sore, aren't they?" Katy said, as Romany squirmed to avoid the examination.

"Yes, we've been worried they're infected," Lesley commented.

Katy gently held Romany's head still, while she leaned in, almost nose-to-nose with the little dog, to examine her eyes.

"There's definitely some infection there and a good bit of crispy mucus as well. That can't be very comfortable," Katy said, wrinkling her nose. "It doesn't smell too nice either. I'll give her an antibiotic injection for the infection and I'll give you some eye drops which should help."

"Thanks," Lesley said. "It's a shame, but Romany won't let any other dog lick her eyes at all. Amber tries, but for some reason Romany won't have it."

"It's probably something to do with which dog is dominant." Katy shrugged. "Anyway, from now on you'll have to keep her eyes clean yourself."

"I've tried," I said, adding my brightest smile, "but I don't like the taste!"

Katy gave me a look that would have silenced a classroom of rowdy children. Then her eyes flicked back towards Lesley.

"Is he always like this?"

"I'm afraid so," Lesley replied, "it must be his hormones or something."

Katy nodded sagely.

"Perhaps he needs to be *done*, I could see to it while he's here."

"No need," I said, "she had *them* removed the day after we got married!"

This time both women gave me the 'evil-eye stare', but it was wasted on my Teflon sensibilities.

I was flushed with excitement and grinning like a lottery winner as I waited for our daughter at Shannon airport. This was Joanne's first visit to Ireland, and although she was only staying for a long weekend, Lesley and I were keen to make her visit memorable and enjoyable. As I stood in the spacious and uncluttered arrivals hall, watching a steady stream of people pass through the sliding doors, each pausing momentarily to find their bearings, or search for loved ones, I contemplated how our lives had changed and separated.

Joanne, the pretty little girl who once told me she would never leave our side, was now a beautiful and successful career woman, sharing a house with her boyfriend, working in London, and quickly developing a new circle of friends. Conversely, Lesley and I had traded our membership of the rat race, for the tranquillity of a derelict farmhouse atop a mountain, far from what most people considered civilisation. Our single regret was separation from family, but that was only a perception. Perhaps the only difference brought about by our move to Ireland was the need to plan visits which otherwise could have been more spontaneous. As our first house guest, Joanne's visit was proof of concept, and therefore even more important.

And there she was, taking her turn to stop and look around in mild confusion as she came through the doors. I waved my arms energetically and attracted her attention. Even after such a short separation, our embrace was emotional.

"Hi, Dad!" she looked around the arrivals hall. "Where are all the people?"

"This *is* all the people." I swept my arm around and smiled. "England used to look like this."

"Wow! It's certainly quieter here than Stansted, it was heaving with people. Huge queues at security."

I took her bag and led the way to the exit. "How was your flight?"

"Smooth and quick," she said. "Lovely views on the way in. Everything was so green."

"Welcome to Ireland." I pointed to my car. "Here we are."

"You're parked right outside the doors," Joanne gave me a sideways look. "Are you a VIP now?"

"Nah," I pointed to the large carpark opposite. "That's the long-stay parking over there, but if you're picking up or dropping off you can leave your car on the street."

"Awesome!" she laughed. "At Stansted, I'm parked a couple of miles away. I had to get a bus, it took ages."

"Welcome to the dark ages," I joked.

Taking my usual route from Shannon to Glenmadrie, I paused the journey for a moment at the village of Sixmilebridge so Joanne could take a picture of the pink pub with its identical duck house floating alongside. Along the way, I pointed out our dentist and doctor's surgery, and a couple of the shops we frequented. Nearing the house, I pulled over at a spot where we had an unobstructed view of the valley far below.

"Oh, wow, Dad. What a view."

"Isn't it just?"

"Is that cloud down there?" Joanne pointed.

"Sometimes there is, but I think it's just a little early morning fog."

"It's a really beautiful view. How high up are we?"

"A thousand feet," I replied. "Over there to the left you can see Mountshannon and Lough Derg."

"I think we flew over it on the way in. It's a really big lake."

"That's right. Look, there's a plane flying in now. The airport is way over there to the right. And beyond is Limerick."

"What are those mountains called?" she asked.

"The ones in the foreground are the Slieve Bloom Mountains, the distant peaks are part of the Killarney national park. You know it's a clear day when they are in view."

"The air is so fresh."

"It's not surprising really." I pointed to my right. "If you head east, there's nothing but water for thousands of miles. For planes crossing the Atlantic Ocean, Shannon airport is the first landfall. Before modern jets, they used to land flying boats in the Shannon estuary. There's an aviation museum at Foynes near Limerick."

Joanne gave a mighty yawn.

I laughed. "We should move on, you had an early start."

"I'm fine," she said, smiling. "I was just getting bored."

211

"Don't worry, we'll give the museum a miss on this trip."

When we arrived at the house, there was lots of hugging and kissing. Joanne scooped Amber into her arms and cuddled her like a new-born baby. Romany did a little dance to win her fair share of the attention. It was lovely to see my wife and daughter together again, looking so happy, so healthy, and so much alike. While Lesley cooked up some brunch, I showed our daughter around the house and land.

"I love the house, Mum," Joanne said, piercing an egg with the corner of her toast.

"So do we."

"Lots to do though."

"There is."

"Daddy said you can't get a builder, so you're doing it yourself."

"That's his plan," Lesley said.

Joanne leaned in close to her mother and whispered, "Do you think that's wise?"

"Hey! I heard that," I tapped the handle of my knife on the table. It slipped through my buttery fingers and fell to the floor. Two furry hoovers ran forward to lick up the egg. The girls both laughed.

"Anyway, your mum bought me a proper DIY book. It tells you how to hit your thumb with a hammer and everything."

"Now there's something you don't need help with!" Joanne was aware of my talent for accidents and self-inflicted injuries. "You'd better get a hard hat – and a fire extinguisher."

"I'm way ahead of you. I've got some fireproof overalls." I smiled proudly.

"Are you *really* going to do all the work yourself?"

"We don't *really* have much choice," Lesley replied. "The builders here are just not interested in doing renovations."

"We'll see how it goes," I added. "It'll be okay if we take it one step at a time. The first thing I've got to do is build a pump house for the well head. If that doesn't fall down, next I'll convert the cowsheds into a granny annex-come-apartment. It'll have a double bedroom, an ensuite, a sitting room and a small kitchen. And if *that* doesn't fall down, we can live in it while we renovate the rest of the house."

"Sounds great – if it doesn't fall down," Joanne joked.

"Daddy thinks building the apartment will help us to learn most of the basic skills we'll need to renovate the rest of the house."

"So, when are you going to build this pump house?" Joanne asked.

"I can't start building until the well is drilled. Next week, there are two different contractors coming in to do site surveys and quotes. Once the drilling is over, we have to cut trenches for the pipes–"

"And we're moving the electricity pole, so we'll need a trench for the cables as well," Lesley interjected.

"*You're* moving the electricity?" Joanne exclaimed.

"Well, the electric board move the pole and the cables," I explained. "But we have to dig the trenches for the underground cable. I guess I'll have to hire a digger."

"Boys toys!" Joanne held up a hand for a high five. I obliged.

Lesley tapped her watch. "If we're going to go out, we'd better get a move on. Can you two children walk the dogs while I wash the dishes?"

"Sure," Joanne said, standing up. "Where are we going when we go out?"

"We thought we'd take you to the Cliffs of Moher and then loop back through the Burren to Corofin," I said. "There's a good restaurant there where we can eat before heading back here."

"That sounds lovely." Joanne smiled.

"Don't be too long walking the dogs," Lesley warned.

"We'll go up on the moor," I said to Joanne, and turning to my wife, "half-an-hour, okay?"

She nodded her approval. Even though the chances of encountering any traffic were unlikely, we put both dogs on their leads to safely cross the road. After 200 yards, we climbed over a sty and followed a rough path leading steeply uphill to where some cliffs overlooked the moor. There we could give the dogs a good run and allow them to do the other things dogs need to do before they're locked indoors for the afternoon.

"You look a lot better – more relaxed," Joanne said, as she took photographs of the dogs, the moor, and the valley below. "Mummy too."

"Yes." I nodded. "Life is good."

"I'm pleased for you both."

"Thanks." We hugged and kissed. Father and daughter together again. My heart sang.

By the time we reached the Cliffs of Moher, the weather had become somewhat more Irish. The sun was hidden by heavy cloud and a stiff wind chilled our bones and slapped our faces with salty drizzle. Lesley and I enjoyed our second visit to the cliffs and the Burren and, despite the conditions, Joanne was suitably impressed, making lots of oohs and aahs as she put her new digital camera to good use. Nevertheless, we were pleased when we reached the sanctuary of the restaurant, where we could relax in the warmth and enjoy some fine food and a friendly chat. After we had eaten, our daughter shared her own bit of good news.

"I've been headhunted!" Joanne said, proudly.

"A new job?" Lesley asked.

"Yep. It's an American company. They do text message advertising. I start next month."

"Oh, that's wonderful!" Suddenly my wife's eyes went wide. "You're not moving to America, are you?"

Joanne laughed. "No. They have a London office. But I am moving to Chelmsford. I'm renting a house with Becky."

"What about…"

"He and I have decided to go our separate ways," Joanne said. "Well, I have, anyway."

"Oh! I'm so sorry." Lesley reached out to hold Joanne's hand, but she waved it away with a smile.

"I'm not. I should have kicked him out a while ago." She toasted herself with a large sip of Guinness and then pulled a face. "I know I'm supposed to like this stuff, but…"

"Can I get you something else?" I asked.

She nodded and I gently took the glass from her hand. I narrowed my eyes.

"So…sharing a house with Becky…rather like out of the frying pan and into the fire?"

Joanne rolled her eyes dramatically. "I *know!*"

Rebecca was one of Joanne's childhood friends, and our honorary second daughter. However, in our household she had a fearsome reputation as a hard-core party animal, with the stamina of a prairie dog and the drinking capacity of a camel. I wondered if a house-share with Genghis Khan would be less disruptive to someone about to begin a new career. Joanne held up a calming hand, and then another.

"Don't worry. I won't get distracted."

"Well, we're both delighted for you," Lesley said.

I nodded in agreement. "And very proud."

***

On Monday, Joanne's final day in Ireland, we would visit Bunratty Castle Folk Park, which was on the way to the airport, but Sunday was to be a family day, spending time together at the house. After breakfast, Joanne and I drove to Silver Sands, a deserted beach at the north end of Lough Graney. We walked the dogs along the forest path alongside the river before taking a second path leading down to the beach.

This was the first time Amber had experienced such a large expanse of sand and water, so she made the most of the opportunity, madly charging around on the beach, kicking up the sand and digging dozens of holes with frantic energy. Romany, being a more laidback dog, found a slight depression in the sand and settled down to do some serious sunbathing, until it was time to go home. Amber eventually worked up enough courage to venture into the water, partly encouraged by a game of fetch that gradually extended further and further into the shallow lake.

At first, she stopped at the water's edge and woofed angrily at the stick, floating frustratingly just out of reach. But after running back and forth along the shoreline in a futile search for an alternative strategy, she realised she would have to venture into the lake, or her stick would be lost forever. Cautiously, Amber dipped a toe into the water, and as she quite liked the feeling, she splashed forward and retrieved her beloved stick. After her initial scepticism, and helped by several throws where the stick landed in deeper water, Amber even learned to paddle a little, an essential skill for such a short dog in a wet country.

Although the little puppy was happy to continue this watery game for several more hours, we were not, so I called time with a stern warning of *Game Over*. When her stick is removed or lost, Amber will often look for a suitable substitute in the hope of prolonging the game. On this occasion she spotted a shiny pebble of exactly the right size and shape. Unfortunately it was under four inches of water, and Amber was unaware she needed to hold her breath. There was an explosion of water and bubbles along with a fit of coughing. Amber looked at me with an expression that spoke of both surprise and shock.

"You silly dog," I shouted, "you're supposed to hold your breath. Look." I mimed holding my nose.

Joanne looked at me as if I had just been elected village idiot.

"You should rescue her. You've got wellies on."

I was about to, but Amber had other ideas. She is a terrier – small of brain, but big in heart and not one to be put off by a near-drowning. In any event, her favourite pebble still lay on the floor of the lake. With a pounce like a kitten capturing a mouse, she dived in again, only to reappear in a similar explosion of water, coughing, consternation and confusion.

"Hold your breath, you silly dog," Joanne shouted, almost doubled over with laughter.

Ignoring our sage advice, the little dog dived in two more times, with the same result. Just as I began to wade in, she suddenly hit on a solution. Not by holding her breath, as we had advised, but by breathing out. Looking like a beige scuba diver streaming a line of tiny bubbles, she plunged her face under water and hunted about for a moment, before emerging triumphantly with her pebble clutched proudly in her mouth, which she unceremoniously dropped at my feet. In the face of such determination, who was I to refuse? This new game continued for several minutes, with Amber looking increasingly more like a strangely coloured gannet than a puppy.

"Oh, I love her!" Joanne said, laughing. "But she is rather a silly dog."

"You don't know the half of it," I commented, throwing the stone again. "Her antics at the house have been endlessly entertaining."

"How so?"

"Well, as far as Amber's concerned, her principal responsibility is to defend the house against all and sundry. Friend or foe, stranger or long-term acquaintance, it doesn't matter. The terrier in her demands every new arrival, or passing shadow, be challenged with a cacophony of intense barking."

"Is she that bad?" Joanne asked.

I nodded and smiled. "She's particularly adept at repelling aircraft. Whenever one appears in the sky, Amber sits on her haunches and barks incessantly until the pilot has been gripped with fear and flown his plane to a more welcoming part of the sky."

Joanne laughed.

"Regardless of how high the jet is," I continued, "or how far away the helicopter, for Amber, she drives them away. The other night, she even managed to ward off the Space Station as it silently passed over Ireland."

"You can see the ISS?"

"Oh yes, it's quite large and very bright. There's a bit on the NASA website that tells you when the overflights are."

"That must be great," she said, "apart from the nutty puppy kicking off."

"I suppose it's reassuring to know we're so well defended should some future enemy send a fleet of aircraft to drop bombs on Ireland, but I guess things may get a little awkward if we ever needed the services of the air ambulance."

Joanne laughed again. "I told you...*wear a hard hat*."

"But Amber doesn't restrict her barking to passing aircraft. Being so low to the ground, and perhaps lacking an understanding of the finer points of visual perspective, she also gives birds, bees, bluebottles and even butterflies the full treatment. And, she'll kick off at the sight of any ground-based means of transportation which appears to be acting in a suspicious manner. With the obvious exception of any vehicle actually acting in a suspicious manner."

"Robbers and vagabonds are ignored by all dogs," Joanne added helpfully. "It must be a law or something."

"Anyone approaching the house, or casually walking by, is treated as if they're potential axe murderers, and woofed at accordingly. But, once she's satisfied they're not a threat, they immediately become her best friend and new plaything."

"Whether they like it or not," Joanne added, smiling.

"Absolutely!" I looked at my watch and grimaced. "It's lunch time. We'd better go, or Mummy will lock us out."

Back at the house, I had one more dog tale to share with my daughter. Stealthily, I guided her into the sitting room. Knowing what was about to happen, Lesley joined us.

"What's going on?" Joanne asked.

I held a finger to my lips to ask for silence. Picking up my mobile phone, I dialled our landline number.

"Watch," Lesley whispered.

As soon as the phone began to ring, Amber bounced up on the couch and joined the ringtone with her own attempt at a perfectly harmonised howl. It was endearing, and incredibly funny. Joanne covered her mouth with her hand to stifle her giggles, but her eyes were alive with laughter.

"Sometimes it's difficult to answer the phone with anything approaching decorum," I complained, cutting off the call. "Several times my opening words have been, '*Sorry I'm laughing, but my dog was singing off-key again.*' I'm sure our solicitor thinks we're a bit nutty."

"Nothing new there then," Lesley joked.

As we ate dinner, Joanne was looking out of the window watching the wild birds feeding.

"I like your bird table," she said. "Did you build it?"

"Yes. I only installed it last week."

"It's quite *big*..." my daughter commented.

"Daddy likes his constructions to be *robust*," My wife added, referring to my propensity for over engineering things.

"I'll say," Joanne laughed. "It's bigger than my first apartment. You could land an aeroplane on that thing."

"He wanted plenty of room for the birds."

"At least it's not going to blow away," I replied, somewhat defensively. Lesley patted my arm.

"When we first got here, there were hardly any wild birds," she said, "but now there are loads. And there seem to be more every day."

"Free food! The word must be out." Joanne smiled. "I think it's great. By the way, what's that big triangular thing on the front lawn?"

"It's a combination coop and chicken run," I explained, full of excitement. "We're getting some chickens on Saturday."

"That'll be nice," she said. "It's an interesting shape, how does it work?"

"The chickens sleep in the bit at the top and scrap and feed in the fenced off area below."

Joanne nodded. "How do they get up and down?"

"There's a ladder on a bit of string. At night, it pulls up like a drawbridge," Lesley said. "It's really quite clever."

"Indeed. It's very clever," Joanne said, with a devilish twinkle in her eye, "and rather *robust* as well."

She had a point, it was a typically stout construction. Working from plans I had found on the internet, I used some scrap wood, roofing felt and chicken wire to make an eight by six foot cage, with sloping sides that rose to a five foot apex housing the nesting boxes. This nesting area was accessed from below by the chickens climbing a drawbridge ladder and by a door at the top so we could collect the eggs and refresh the straw. I had seen similar arrangements on sale in Ennis for about €300, but they were so lightweight they would have blown away during the first winter storms. My manly construction may not have looked as twee, but it was almost free to make and would not resemble a wooden kite by the first week of November.

"Well, it's not going to blow away," I said, defensively.

Joanne sat back and crossed her arms.

"Well, Mum, I'm confident Dad will be able to renovate the house," she said, smiling wickedly, "and when it's done, we can be sure of one thing…"

My wife and daughter delivered the punchline together.

"It's not going to blow away!"

26. The Chicken Lady

After breakfast Joanne and I took the dogs for a walk on the moor. Our schedule was for a day out at Bunratty Castle before taking our daughter to the airport for her flight home. The dogs were going to be locked up for a few hours, so a long walk was in order. Following the signposts for the East Clare Way, we walked out across the moor for 30 minutes, before heading back towards the house.

"I can certainly see why you two chose to move to Ireland," Joanne said. "It's so beautiful and peaceful."

"I'm glad you like it."

"Oh, don't get me wrong, it would do my head in to live somewhere this quiet. But it's perfect for you old guys."

"You'd get used to it," I laughed.

"I doubt it. I woke up last night. It was so dark and quiet, I thought it was pretty eerie." She gave an involuntary shudder. "I had trouble getting back to sleep."

"Really? I love the silence."

Joanne shook her head. "I didn't feel safe."

"But in the city, you do?"

"Sure."

I was confused. "So, in the city, alongside drunks and drug dealers and axe murderers, you feel safe. But up here you don't?"

"I know it sounds silly, but when I'm in a crowd, I always feel there is someone to help me."

"To help you not be attacked by the drunks and drug dealers and axe murderers?" I joked.

Joanne waved my objection away as if it were an annoying fly.

"I get what you're saying, Dad, but you have to admit, this place is a long way from civilisation. What would happen if one of you got ill, or had an accident?"

"We'd call for help, just like you," I said. "We're closer to the hospital and ambulance station than you are. And there's no traffic here to slow the ambulance down."

"I suppose you're right," she conceded reluctantly.

"And if I cut a big H out of the grass on the meadow, we'll have our own landing pad for the air ambulance."

Joanne shook her head. "Nah ha, Amber would chase them off."

"Talking of Amber, where is she?"

We shouted for a full minute before the little beige head popped up from behind some heather. Like a rat escaping a sinking ship, she bounded over and bounced into Joanne's waiting arms. As we walked, Romany did her 'jealous dance' and Amber nuzzled my daughter's face. Joanne wrinkled her nose and grimaced.

"Phew! What *is* that smell?"

I sniffed the air and cautiously leaned a little closer to the puppy.

"Ugh!" I dry-heaved involuntarily. "You might want to put her down. I think she's been rolling in something."

"Oh yuck!" Joanne went to wipe her hands on her jeans, but wisely opted to use some grass as an alternative.

"Come on. She'll need a bath before we go out."

Two washes with baby shampoo, and some vigorous scrubbing with a towel, shifted the visible signs of contamination, but had only a marginal impact on the smell. Notwithstanding the lingering fragrance, we gave the dogs a biscuit and set off for Bunratty and the airport.

This was our second visit to Bunratty Castle, the first being a somewhat hurried affair when Lesley and I were house hunting, so we wanted to give our full attention to every detail of the castle and Folk Park. The castle is actually more of a tower house, with a long history of being repaired and renovated, not unlike Glenmadrie. Once we had paid and negotiated our way through the gift shop, we began our unguided tour by climbing the uneven steps to the top of the tower.

Lesley read from the guidebook. "The name Bunratty means castle at the mouth of the river Ratty, which one can see from the top of the castle. Built in 1425, it was restored in 1954 to its former medieval splendour and now contains fifteenth and sixteenth century furnishings, tapestries, and works of art, which capture the mood of those times."

Below we could see the Shannon estuary, the carpark, and the motorway.

"It's great, but this probably isn't the best view in Ireland," Joanne mumbled, looking at the vast expanse of grey mud below.

I nodded. "Despite the abundance of wildlife, I've always found tidal estuary mudflats to be rather dull and depressing places."

Looking down at the motorway that would soon take my daughter to the airport, I felt a pang of sadness. I gave her hand a squeeze. Behind me I could hear the distinctive twang of a west coast American accent.

"Gee, honey, this is so cool," the woman said. "But why did they build it so close to the freeway?"

"Probably so the tourist coaches have better access," came the reply.

Joanne looked at me and rolled her eyes. I suppressed a grin.

"Come on, let's explore," Joanne said, leading the way down.

In common with most castles in Ireland, Bunratty has an interesting history, as well as fascinating architecture, with many narrow corridors, passages and winding stairways providing various ways to access or defend each floor.

"Some of the stairways are deliberately constructed with risers of various heights and sizes," Lesley read. "These 'stumble steps' will force a sword wielding attacker to look down to ensure better footing, or risk a trip and fall."

"At a time when any distraction could make you bleed all over your opponent's sword," I added.

"Thanks, Dad. That's a delightful image."

The stumble steps were having the desired effect on the two American tourists, making them stagger and giggle like drunken teenagers. At the bottom, they unwisely attempted to squeeze through a second narrow doorway with steps leading down to the dungeons. With commendable determination, they pushed forwards for a few yards, but gave up when the width of their *derrières* threatened to exceed the dimensions of the tunnel. Unfortunately, by that time, several other visitors had entered the passageway. Unable to go forward or turn around, the hapless couple were attempting to reverse blindly back up the stairs, whilst pushing against a tide of inquisitive Japanese tourists. As the two cultures collided, there was much shouting – most of it in a language we didn't understand. Along with their experience of

222

squeezing into overcrowded Tokyo subway trains, the Japanese had the benefit of numbers and the assistance of gravity, and should have won the shoving match. However, the Americans were desperate claustrophobics who used their bulk and incredible leg strength to win the battle, bursting from the doorway like a champagne cork, and upending several of the Japanese in their wake.

As is often the way in such situations, there was some merriment, a few formal bows, and a little hair-straightening before everyone went on their way. However, for the rotund tourists such embarrassment could not be allowed to pass without complaint. Spotting a castle employee, the man strode over.

"Why do you idiots build these passageways so narrow?" he shouted angrily, his nose just inches from the employee's face.

The poor man leaned back on his heel in shock, his face splattered with a shower of spittle. "I'm sorry, sir, what seems to be the problem?"

"I'll tell you what the problem is," the tourist bellowed. "My wife and I almost got stuck in that doorway!"

The tour guide blinked as slowly as a sloth, before leaning his head to one side. After a moment's contemplation, he returned his gaze to the angry tourist.

"I can see why that passage would cause a problem," he said, diplomatically.

"You should change it," the man snapped. "Make it wider."

The employee blinked again and looked around at the gathering audience. "Well, it's been like that since 1425, so I guess it's time for a change," he smiled benevolently and gave the tourist a conspiratorial pat on the arm. "Leave it with me, sir, I'll see what can be done."

Gratified, the tourist nodded, mumbled his thanks and led his wife away. As they left the room, the tour guide received a spontaneous round of applause, to which he responded with a slightly self-conscious bow.

The Folk Park is an appealing and authentically accurate reconstruction of nineteenth century Irish village life, with a main street, a post office, shops, a school and a bakery. Being so early in the season, there were few plants to see in the gardens, but the walk was pleasant and we enjoyed looking at the examples of rare-breed pigs, sheep and goats.

As we were soon to become small-scale chicken farmers ourselves, we particularly liked seeing the various breeds that were running wild around the place, free to enter the realistic doctor's office and schoolhouse. The bleak classroom with its hard seats, brown wood desks, inkwells and blackboard, combined with the institutional smell of fear and floor wax, swept me back to the convent school of my childhood. Closing my eyes, I recalled the thick Scottish accents at morning prayers, reading aloud and reciting tables, cabbage boiled grey and stodgy puddings, caned backsides and skinned knees. Suddenly Sister Ignatius was there, pulling my ear until my eyes watered and screaming into my face, *"You're a feckless child, you'll never amount to anything!"* My knees went weak and cold acid filled my stomach.

"Dad? DAD? Are you coming?"

My eyes flew open.

"Yeah. Sure." I shook my head and looked around. It was just an old building with a few tables. Nothing to see and nothing to fear.

Many of the buildings have been moved from other locations and faithfully reconstructed to add to the authentic feel of the park. We took a few minutes to visit the post office – which was identical to the one in our local village – and the confectionary shop where we could indulge ourselves buying sweet delights from the distant past. Fruit bonbons, sherbet saucers, and gobstoppers to name but three. The castle is famous for its raucous medieval banquets and the associated entertainment provided by the local artists. There is also a working pub guaranteed to deliver a hearty welcome and plenty of craic every night. As our time was limited, we chose the pub and enjoyed a pleasant and surprisingly affordable lunch.

"It's been lovely seeing you," Lesley said to Joanne, as we were getting ready to leave.

"Likewise. I'm glad I came. Ireland is truly beautiful, and I love your house."

"Thanks," I said. "I'm glad you like it."

"I'm really pleased for you both. You look so happy and well."

"So far," Lesley said, strangely pessimistic.

"*Mum!*" Joanne warned.

My wife rolled her eyes and grimaced an apology. I wondered if she was suddenly aware of the geographical distance we had created from our daughter.

"You'll come back soon?" I asked.

Joanne nodded. "Perhaps next time I'll bring a friend."

"Becky?" Lesley asked, smiling.

Joanne shook her head. "She'd probably get bored. Perhaps another time."

"There are guided tours of the Guinness factory and museum, if you visit Dublin," I suggested, half-joking.

"Oh well! That'll be fine then." Joanne laughed and checked her watch. "We'd better get moving."

"Promise you'll come back soon?" Lesley asked, holding her hand.

"I will," she smiled. "Next month. I promise."

Although there were many tears at the airport as we waved goodbye to our beloved daughter, our sadness was brief, for we knew she would become a regular visitor, as she and her friends discovered the magical beauty and solitude of rural Ireland.

***

Although our chickens in England were vicious and moody creatures, apt to peck an ankle or nip a finger without provocation, we had enjoyed having them about the place, and nothing beats eating delicious fresh eggs for breakfast. So I had put up only token resistance when, a couple of weeks earlier, Lesley suggested it was time we got a few chickens.

"Are you sure?" I asked.

"Oh yes!" she replied. "I miss having them around."

"You didn't like it when the other lot kept digging up your flowerbeds."

Lesley shrugged. "They'll have to be penned in anyway to keep them safe."

"I suppose you're right," I said. "There'll be lots of foxes and mink up here. They'll need a proper coop."

"It'll need to be stout, to cope with the weather and wind."

"And moveable, otherwise the ground underneath will get trashed," I commented. "You know how chickens like to scrap for worms."

"Good. So that's settled then," Lesley nodded, giving her royal ascent.

"It's cheaper to just buy a few eggs," I said, playing the money card in search of any lingering doubt.

My wife gave me a withering look. "Just get on with it."

I did a little research and came up with a workable design for a secure and movable chicken hutch that we could bump up and down the lawn. This way the chickens could have access to a fresh area of grass each day, as well as protection from predators and the elements. Building the coop had been a simple and enjoyable exercise, making good use of some old lumber and my new tools. Although the result was waterproof and secure, its robust construction only met the 'moveable' element of the specification because I am rather stronger than I look. But it was a close-run thing.

Whereas building the coop was straightforward, acquiring our chickens was surprisingly difficult, particularly for such a rural area. With our Stone Age internet connection, it took me several hours to reach the conclusion that nobody in Clare was advertising chickens online. The business telephone directory had no listings under chickens or poultry farmers, and my enquiries at the local post office produced only a shrug and a blank stare. Just as I was starting to think our chicken coop was doomed to become a quirky door stop, Lesley hit pay dirt. Bursting into the house after a shopping trip, she beamed and told me what she had discovered.

"You need to see the Chicken Lady."

"Excuse me?"

"There's an old woman, called the Chicken Lady," she said. "She visits several markets on Saturdays and sells chickens from the back of a white van."

"How did you hear this?"

"I was at the garage getting petrol, and I saw they had loose eggs for sale in a basket on the counter." She tapped her head with a finger. "So, I thought, '*Eggs equal chickens.*'"

"And visa-versa," I said, risking a stern admonishment. But I needn't have worried, Lesley was too excited.

226

"I asked where they got their chickens, and the garage owner's wife told me about the Chicken Lady." Lesley smiled proudly. "She'll be at Gort market on Saturday morning. You should be there at 9.30 am."

And so I was. But the Chicken Lady wasn't. Miserably, I sat in my car trying to keep warm as I watched the rain streaming down the windscreen. Periodically, I started the engine to run the heater and wipers. I listened to the radio for a while and tried to call Lesley, but there was no signal. After half-an-hour, just as I was considering giving up, a battered white van swept into the carpark. It was small, no larger than my hatchback car, and noticeably lacking in any Chicken Lady signage. It was the first new arrival I had seen for some time, so I took a chance. Climbing out of my car and opening my umbrella against the steadily falling rain, I turned towards the van, only to find it obscured by a crowd of perhaps 30 men.

"Where did they come from?" I thought. *"I was the only person here a moment ago!"*

In other circumstances, I would have suspected they were a group of adoring fans, waiting to meet the latest teenage music sensation, but these were elderly men trying to buy chickens. Like a brazen drug dealer, a tiny, wrinkled woman of indeterminate age, wrapped in a thick coat and a head scarf, was selling chickens to the men. My chickens! How dare they?!

Fearing I was likely to go home empty-handed, I joined the throng. There appeared to be no recognisable queuing system. Rather like a busy British bar, the men crowded in and frantically waved their cash, while the wizened lady randomly chose the next lucky recipient. There was a brisk trade in poultry and ducks, so the crowd soon began to thin, but I was having no luck attracting the Chicken Lady's attention to my waved notes. I resorted to looking harmless and pathetic. It worked!

"What'll it be, love?"

"Three chickens please."

"Table or point?" she asked.

"Excuse me?"

She looked me up and down and smiled benevolently. "First time?"

Feeling (how I imagine) a teenager at a brothel would feel, I admitted I was.

"Do you want chickens for your dinner," she asked slowly, "or do you want point-of-lay?" And she added as an afterthought, "For eggs."

"Oh! Eggs," I babbled. "Definitely eggs."

"Reds or Bantams?"

"Err…"

She smiled and rolled her eyes. "Are you wanting big or little eggs?"

The men were staring at me with obvious curiosity, as if I were a contestant on a game show.

"Big eggs, I suppose," I said, cautiously.

"Right! Three Reds it is." The chicken lady rubbed her hands together. "That'll be €18."

I handed over the money. She tipped her head on one side and made a sad face. "Are you going to put them in your pockets?"

I frowned in confusion.

The man at my side gleefully helped me to understand. "You don't got a box!"

I slapped my forehead. What an idiot I felt. Everyone laughed. They were all enjoying the entertainment. I suspected the tale of the hapless English fool with chickens in his pockets would be doing the rounds of the pubs for some time.

"Can't I put them in the back of the car?"

"Not if you don't want them flying around the car you can't!" someone said.

"Loose chickens 'ave to wear a seatbelt," a second voice added. "It's the law."

"Now lads, give over will ya!" the Chicken Lady snapped, "or I'll send ye all home empty-handed."

There were a few inaudible mumbles of discontent, but the men complied.

She turned her benevolent eyes back to me. "Don't you worry, luv, I've a spare box in the back."

"Thank you," I sighed, genuinely grateful.

She stuffed three chickens into a box, with all the care of someone loading a washing machine, before handing them over to me.

"Thank you," I repeated.

"Any time you want chickens, you come and see me." She smiled and winked.

Devoid of seatbelts, but safe inside their cardboard box, our new chickens happily chatted with me all the way to their new home.

Lesley was excitedly waiting for us.

"How did you get on?" she asked.

"Oh, fine. No problem at all," I said. "They probably thought I was just another farmer."

"Good. Let's get them in the cage."

We were anticipating a mass breakout attempt as soon as the box was opened, but these chickens were calm and happy to be handled. Cautiously, I picked one up and was delighted to discover I could stroke it without receiving the vicious pecks I would have expected from their British counterparts.

"You'd better put them in the top to begin with," Lesley suggested. "So they know where to roost."

I complied, carefully closing the lid.

"They'll soon come down the ladder when they get hungry," she added.

"I was chatting with them in the car," I admitted. "We agreed on their names."

"Really?" Lesley gave me a suspicious look. "What did they decide?"

"Chicken Little, Chicken Nugget and Chicken Drumstick," I said proudly. "If that's okay with you."

"They all look identical. How will you know which is which?"

I smiled and shrugged.

She laughed. "If they're happy, then so am I."

Early the following morning, I watched a sly fox carefully inspecting my handiwork as he circled the chicken coop and tried to work out how to get to his breakfast. To discourage any further visits, I wound up the dogs and encouraged them to *chase the fox!* Inevitably they burst out of the front door, barking and yelping excitedly – and ran off in entirely the wrong direction. The shrewd fox sat by the chicken coop and calmly waited until the dogs were out of sight, before ambling off in the other direction. I was pleased my defences had worked, and we were delighted with our three friendly chickens and the delicious eggs they would soon produce.

Somehow those eggs made our house feel more like a home.

Owning a few chickens brought some welcome routine and responsibility to our otherwise carefree lives. Early each morning, I would let the dogs out, don my wellington boots and trudge across the lawn with my dressing gown flapping in the wind. With a heave and a twist at alternate ends, I would walk the chicken coop across the grass to the nearest undamaged area. Only when it was safely in place, could I replace the feeder and water tray, and untie the rope that held up their little ladder. Almost as the drawbridge was falling, the chickens would climb down to inspect the new ground and search for bugs and worms. Although they appeared to be indistinguishable, we soon learned to identify our hens by their characters.

Nugget was the dominant hen, always first down the ladder, and quick to shoulder her way to the front whenever we brought some kitchen scraps. Little was more laidback. As reluctant as a sleepy teenager, she was always the last to descend the ladder for her morning feed. Sometimes she would choose to sleep in, luxuriating in the warmth of her straw nest, and only moving when I opened the box to check for eggs. Drumstick was the friendliest of the group, and by far my favourite hen. At the slightest provocation, she would squat down, arch her neck, and splay her wings, inviting me to stroke her back. If I obliged, she would shiver in ecstasy before shaking her feathers in mild embarrassment.

Chickens are endlessly curious and quick to rush over whenever they see something of interest. Although Romany remained characteristically aloof, Amber found our new friends to be entertaining. For their part, the chickens seemed unsure if the little dog was a large rat, or a small fox. Chickens Little and Drumstick, remained largely ambivalent towards the beige terrier, but Nugget, being dominant, always felt obliged to watch what Amber was doing – and this soon became a problem.

Each morning, as soon as I had moved the coop, Amber would sprint over to hoover up the previous day's chicken droppings. Despite my admonishments, Amber would savour these stinky black blobs as if they were made from the finest liquorice. Once every trace was gone, it was time for some exercise, which for

Amber involved running anti-clockwise around the coop whilst growling and woofing. The little dog was young enough to keep running for several minutes, causing Nugget to turn in ever decreasing circles to keep a wary eye on this perceived threat. Such rotational gymnastics would test the inner ear of a whirling dervish and it quickly proved too much for a chicken. After a few minutes of turning tight left-handed circles, Nugget would begin to stagger and wobble like a new-born giraffe, before collapsing into an untidy heap. Looking decidedly green, there she would sit, her eyes fixed on a single unmoving spot, until the dizziness and nausea passed. Undaunted, the following morning Nugget would be back on defensive patrol, determined to protect her little flock.

Our chicken coop was a two-story affair, with the nest boxes and sleeping area sitting above a cage. In theory this arrangement gave our charges access to fresh grass and bugs, and sufficient room to exercise. But despite moving the coop to a new position every morning, the lawn was soon scarred by a succession of rectangular mud patches. Furthermore, the chickens spent most of their day pacing up and down and pecking at the wire. Clearly our hens needed more space. Fortunately, they soon came up with a solution.

Whenever I was cleaning out the coop, our inquisitive chickens would climb up the ramp to watch what I was doing. I didn't mind the audience and they generally stayed out of my way. Chicken Little liked to sit at one end of the nesting box, ready to snap up anything remotely edible, Nugget was happy to perch on the apex of the coop, where she had a good view, and Drumstick had taken to climbing up my arm so she could sit like a sailor's parrot on my shoulder. This happy arrangement continued for a couple of weeks, until the day Nugget spotted a distant juicy worm. Without any warning, she launched herself into the air and lurched drunkenly across the lawn to a leafy embankment. Before I could react, Little flew after her leader and Drumstick followed. There was little I could do about this as, in the process of taking flight, my favourite hen had dug her claws into my shoulder and slapped me in the face with her wing.

Concerned a fox was about to jump from a bush and devour our flock, I rushed over to attempt a recovery. However, now the chickens had discovered freedom they had other ideas. At first I tried using verbal directions and some pointing, but this was either ignored or met with a blank stare. With the door to the wire cage open, I tried some corralling techniques involving slow walking and some gentle arm flapping. Each time, the chickens simply walked around me or moved to a different spot where they could scrap for worms uninterrupted. Finally, I resorted to running around and attempting to snatch the chickens with heroic diving rugby tackles, which only attracted the attention of my wife.

"What are you playing at?"

"The chickens got out," I said, brushing some mud from my jeans. "I was trying to get them back in the cage."

"You're not doing very well," she giggled.

"They don't want to go back in," I complained.

Lesley shrugged. "Leave them out. There not doing any harm."

"What about foxes?"

"They're doing a good job of avoiding you," she laughed. "I'm sure they'll keep away from the foxes."

So we left the chickens alone, free to roam and feed. I was concerned about how we would get them back into the coop at the end of the day, but I need not have worried. Towards dusk they wandered back into the cage of their own accord, and climbed up the ladder to their roost. The following morning, we let them out again, but this time Amber decided she would engage in a little chicken chasing of her own.

"Leave them alone!" I warned, but Amber ignored me.

She ran over and began to bark. This time, the chickens did not scatter and squawk as she had anticipated, quite the contrary. They unexpectedly became intrigued by the furry beige rat, and ran over to investigate.

"Now you're in trouble," I warned.

For her part, Amber bravely stood her ground against the three large chickens, right up to the moment she received a painful peck on the nose. Then she turned and ran.

"*Amber!* Come here," I shouted, wiping the tears of laughter from my eyes, but she ignored me and began to run a wide defensive circle around the lawn. Being curious, the chickens decided to follow, and I soon found myself laughing hysterically at the sight of this mixed-breed conga line dancing around our garden.

233

"Amber!" I shouted again, and this time she responded, diving into the safety of my arms just as the chasing pack was about to pounce.

Our little puppy soon learned not to chase the hens, and her constant presence as a chicken poop hoover probably helped to discourage the presence of foxes. From that point on, each day we let the chickens out of the cage so they could scrap and scrape to their hearts' content.

A few days later, Amber got into another predicament, but this one was much more serious.

My wife had gone food shopping in Ennis, leaving me alone at the house with only the dogs and a list of chores to keep me company. When Lesley got home, I was still pale and shaking. Over a cup of tea, I explained what had happened.

"I went outside to drop some vegetable waste into the compost bin and as usual Amber launched herself out of the front door, woofing at the world as if she were a much larger dog."

"Typical," she tutted.

"I shouted for her to be quiet, but she was too busy defending her territory to take any real notice. As we walked back towards the front door together, I noticed a car was approaching along the road below the house. It was going quite fast."

"Oh no!" Lesley's face took on a look of concern.

"The moment she saw the car she sprinted down the driveway. I screamed for her to stop. I even ran forwards for a few paces, but there was no chance I could catch her. There was nothing I could do. She just ran into the road at full speed and collided at right-angles with the front bumper of the car."

Lesley put her hand over her mouth, her eyes were filling with tears. She had guessed what was coming. "Oh, God!"

"Time seemed to slow down," I whispered. "I just stared as Amber slipped past the front wheel and was rolled along the underside of the car. It was like watching a rag doll in a tumble dryer."

"She's dead," Lesley mumbled.

"Don't be silly!" I laughed, putting a comforting hand onto her arm. "She's upstairs asleep on the bed."

"Is she okay?"

234

"She's fine. It was incredible. She rolled out from under the rear bumper and ran back up the driveway and disappeared into the house, barking like a lunatic all the way. After a short search, I found the poor thing hiding under the couch. She was shivering in shock and matted with grease, but otherwise okay."

"You're sure she isn't hurt?" Lesley asked, her voice trembling with concern.

"Don't worry," I replied. "I took her straight to the vet. Katy gave Amber a thorough check over, a good wash and a long cuddle. As a precaution, she gave her an anti-inflammatory injection, which is why she's zonked out on the bed."

"Stupid dog," Lesley said through clenched teeth. "She must have been terrified."

"She's fine. It's me that's in shock."

"Oh, don't be such a baby," my wife complained. She was always the caring one.

Grateful our puppy had survived her brush with death, I moved 'Erect gates and fix fence' to the top of my 'to do' list.

***

As the early spring sunshine warmed our bones and the golfing season got into full swing, my part-time teaching business quickly became a full-time occupation. Although the money was welcome, my long absences and sunburn did not win any favours at home.

"I thought you were going to be home at seven," Lesley snapped as I walked into the kitchen.

"Sorry," I shrugged. "I got a last-minute lesson."

"Well I wish you'd let me know. Your supper is ruined."

"I phoned," I pleaded. "You didn't answer."

"I was probably out in the garden."

"I left a message, and I called your mobile."

"Oh, that thing?" she huffed. "It's switched off."

"Well how am I supposed to..." I gave up.

"You're all sunburnt. Your head looks like a safety match. Did you wear a hat?"

"Most of the day," I replied. "I didn't realise how hot the sun was. It must be because of the lack of pollution."

"It was thick cloud here all day," Lesley complained. "I didn't see the sun once. Just lots of midges."

235

"Oh dear. How odd, we had a lovely day."

"I can see that." She pointed to my head. "You should wear sun cream."

"I will. I just got caught out today."

While Lesley tried to salvage my supper, I had a shower and changed into some fresh clothes. After I'd eaten we chatted some more.

"Isn't it strange how the weather can be so different?" I said.

"Yes. Tom says it's because of the altitude. This being the first high spot since America."

"Good to know." I smiled. "Who's Tom?"

"Ah!" Lesley held up a finger. "Do you remember the dark blue car we kept seeing, the one with the dog running behind?"

I nodded.

"I was walking the dogs this morning and this grey-haired man came by in an ancient tractor and stopped to chat. His name is Tom and he lives at the first farm on the left down the lane. We had a long chat. He's a lovely old boy, very polite and funny. He welcomed us to the area. I was telling him our plans for the house and he seemed very pleased we're here. Apparently, this house has previously been a hot-spot for wild all-night parties and British New Age travellers."

"That fits in with some of the wall art," I said.

"And the old gypsy caravan you saw here that day. Anyway..." she continued, "we're most welcome. Even though we're *blow-ins*."

"What?"

"According to Tom, anyone who isn't local is called a blow-in."

"Anyone?" I asked.

"*Anyone.*" Lesley confirmed. "Tom said any people from overseas, or another county, or even a different village, are all classed as blow-ins."

"Ha! How quaint. How long are we going to be in that class?"

"According to Tom, there's no fixed rule, but 30 to 50 years would be a reasonable assumption."

"Oh dear," I said.

"Don't worry." Lesley held up a calming hand. "He was very nice about it. Tom's a blow-in too. His great-grandmother was from Cork."

"Good to know," I joked. "Did you ask about the dog?"

"Yes!" Lesley laughed. It was nice to see her looking so happy. "The dog's called Patch, it's just a puppy really. It was sitting behind Tom's seat on the tractor."

"Not chasing cars today then?"

She shook her head. "Tom said he's tried everything to stop Patch chasing cars, but nothing short of chaining him up all day works. He told me about this truss he made, an elaborate arrangement of straps to secure a pipe with a line of little bells just below his chest. The idea was, if the dog attempted to chase a car, his knees would bang repeatedly against the bar, causing discomfort and ringing the bells."

"Desperate measures." I smiled and shook my head. "He must love that dog."

"He does," Lesley said. "Anyway, the plan didn't work. Patch just taught himself to run sideways and carried on chasing cars."

"What a silly dog."

Lesley smiled and continued. "Tom said he's given in and accepted the inevitable. So now he drives his car slowly around the various bits of farmland he owns and Patch runs behind. He covers dozens of miles each day."

"Good grief. He must be the fittest dog in Ireland!"

"Also…" Lesley raised her eyebrows, "we had a visitor."

"Someone local?" I asked, intrigued. Apart from our daughter, this would be our first visitor.

"When I got back from walking the dogs, there was an old gent sitting in the kitchen drinking tea."

"*What?*" I exclaimed.

Lesley nodded and grinned. "If I hadn't smelled the smoke from his pipe tobacco, I'd have had a heart attack."

"I bet you would have. Who was it?"

"His name is John Corbett," my wife replied. "He was born in this house and as he was passing, he thought he would pop in to see the old place."

"He'd just let himself in and made a cup of tea?"

She nodded. "He seemed to think it was perfectly normal behaviour. He brought some apples."

"What did he say?" I asked.

"The first thing he said to me was, '*Fierce mild today*,' and, '*Put the kettle on*'. Then he just sat there puffing his pipe and telling me about his life and how different this house was 80 years ago."

"How utterly delightful," I said.

"Yes," Lesley said, quietly. "Yes, it was."

***

Those first meetings with our distant neighbour, Tom, and old Mr Corbett, occurred exactly six months to the day since Lesley and I had decided to begin a new life. Although we still had a long way to go before we would no longer be blow-ins, that day was significant because it was the first time we felt accepted into our new community. Soon we would make friends with many wonderful characters from our local area, and the summer walking season would bring passing strangers from Ireland and far afield. Some would wave and walk on, others stayed for tea and became lifelong friends.

Our home was about to be transformed, but the renovations would take Lesley and me many years to complete, and during that time we would become chicken farmers, rescue several dogs and cats, care for a sick relative, and suffer the joy of triumph and the sadness of tragedy.

But that's all another story. You can read about it in *Fresh Eggs and Dog Beds, Book Two*.

So, what of the move to Ireland – was it worth it?

We relocated to Ireland to get away from the stresses of modern living and to begin a new life, debt-free, without pressure, where the air is clean, the people are friendly and we would have the freedom to do as we please. Like Darwin's finches, we have adapted to our new environment. It is cooler here, so we wear more clothes and enjoy the simple pleasures of sitting by a fire on chilly evenings, and warming our insides with delicious homemade soup.

As I am writing, it is a beautiful and warm early summer day here in County Clare. From the window of my office I can see the hill behind our house is thick with foliage as the trees compete for every ray of sunshine. Early this morning I saw a fox, boldly making his way across the lawn, and last night some deer quietly passed by behind the house, mercifully unnoticed by the dogs.

Today there is barely a breath of wind and I expect the midges will rise later, perhaps to help feed the bats and the hundreds of wild birds that now live within sight of our bird table. Every so often the silence is broken by a passing tractor, as the local farmers race the approaching storms to harvest the sweet meadow grass for winter cattle feed.

Of all the sacrifices we have made, being away from family is by far the greatest. It's always dangerous to play the 'What if' and 'If only' games, and to speculate how things might have worked out differently. We thought through our plan carefully and consulted with our families before coming to a decision, so now we must play the cards life has dealt us. Fortunately, Ireland is a delightful place to holiday, and Glenmadrie makes a good base for anyone visiting the west coast, so we are seldom lonely.

Even though Lesley and I don't have to work every day, we still do. My wife is gradually turning our muddy plot of rocky land into a productive market garden, and I am busy teaching and writing. I sometimes fear we are doomed to repeat the mistakes of the past. Are we judging our worth by the quantity of our possessions and our successes at work, rather than for the quality of our lives, the love of our friends and family, and the simple joy of being together, free to enjoy this spectacular place? I wonder if we are already making the same errors all over again. Is my job what defines me now? If I have a bad day at work, does that make me a bad person? If Lesley has a week off from the grind of tending the garden, should she feel such shame? There is much to do before we can get the balance right.

Despite all the work we will have to do renovating the house and garden, the pain of being away from family, the unrelenting rain, the endless weeks of dull overcast skies and vicious midge bites as soon as the sun emerges, it has all been worth it. We have a beautiful home and a wonderful life with two delightful dogs, clean air to breathe, a little money to spare and the freedom to do as we wish. We really are lucky to be 'living the dream'.

So what of the move to Ireland – was it worth it?

Our answer is yes.

Acknowledgements

Writing a book is very much a team effort and there are many people who I would like to thank:

First of all, to Victoria Teed and the staff at Ant Press, thank you for your vision and belief.

Many, many thanks to Zoe Marr, for your keen eye, honest opinion and exceptional editing.

Lesley, my beautiful intelligent and supportive wife, who gave me the time and space to finish this book, thank you for accompanying me on this search for a better life – and for all the cakes.

Joanne, our daughter, who gave her unflinching support to each of our nutty ideas; she politely pointed out my mistakes and gave me the motivation to continue writing.

Richard Clarke, you are a great friend and an inspiration.

Thanks to our dogs, cats, chickens and ducks, past and present, you make our lives richer and more interesting.

Finally, thanks to the good people of Ireland, who have made us feel welcome and at home in a foreign land.

About the Author

Nick Albert was born and raised in England. After a hectic career as a training consultant and sports coach, Nick and his wife, Lesley, decided it was time to leave the stress of city life behind. In 2004, they made the sudden decision to begin a new life in rural Ireland, a country they had never visited. There they bought a dilapidated farmhouse and, with the aid of a second-hand do-it-yourself manual, began renovations on their new home. When the refurbishments were complete, Nick began writing full-time.

Contact the Author

Facebook https://www.facebook.com/author.nick.albert
Email: nickalbert@outlook.com
Chat with the author and other memoir readers at We Love Memoirs
https://www.facebook.com/groups/welovememoirs/

If you enjoyed *Fresh Eggs and Dog Beds*, you may also enjoy these Ant Press titles:

MEMOIRS

Chickens, Mules and Two Old Fools by Victoria Twead (Wall Street Journal Top 10 bestseller)

Two Old Fools ~ Olé! by Victoria Twead

Two Old Fools on a Camel by Victoria Twead (thrice New York Times bestseller)

Two Old Fools in Spain Again by Victoria Twead

One Young Fool in Dorset (The Prequel) by Victoria Twead

One Young Fool in South Africa (The Prequel) by Joe and Victoria Twead

Midwife - A Calling by Peggy Vincent

Midwife - A Journey by Peggy Vincent

Into Africa with 3 Kids, 13 Crates and a Husband by Ann Patras

More Into Africa with 3 Kids, some Dogs and a Husband by Ann Patras

Fat Dogs and French Estates ~ Part I by Beth Haslam

Fat Dogs and French Estates ~ Part II by Beth Haslam

Fat Dogs and French Estates ~Part III by Beth Haslam

Simon Ships Out: How One Brave, Stray Cat Became a Worldwide Hero by Jacky Donovan

Smoky: How a Tiny Yorkshire Terrier Became a World War II American Army Hero, Therapy Dog and Hollywood Star by Jacky Donovan

Smart as a Whip: A Madcap Journey of Laughter, Love, Disasters and Triumphs by Jacky Donovan

Heartprints of Africa: A Family's Story of Faith, Love, Adventure, and Turmoil by Cinda Adams Brooks

How not to be a Soldier: My Antics in the British Army by Lorna McCann

Moment of Surrender: My Journey Through Prescription Drug Addiction to Hope and Renewal by Pj Laube

Serving is a Pilgrimage by John Basham

One of its Legs are Both the Same by Mike Cavanagh

Horizon Fever by A E Filby

Cane Confessions: The Lighter Side to Mobility by Amy L. Bovaird

From Moulin Rouge to Gaudi's City by EJ Bauer

Completely Cats – Stories with Cattitude by Beth Haslam and Zoe Marr

FICTION

Parched by Andrew C Branham
A is for Abigail by Victoria Twead (Sixpenny Cross 1)
B is for Bella by Victoria Twead (Sixpenny Cross 2)

NON FICTION

How to Write a Bestselling Memoir by Victoria Twead

CHILDREN'S BOOKS

Seacat Simon: The Little Cat Who Became a Big Hero by Jacky Donovan
The Rise of Agnil by Susan Navas (Agnil's World 1)
Agnil and the Wizard's Orb by Susan Navas (Agnil's World 2)
Agnil and the Tree Spirits by Susan Navas (Agnil's World 3)
Agnil and the Centaur's Secret by Susan Navas (Agnil's World 4)
Morgan and the Martians by Victoria Twead

Chat with the author and other memoir authors and readers at
We Love Memoirs:
https://www.facebook.com/groups/welovememoirs/